SPIVEY, Ted Ray. Journey beyond tragedy: a study of myth and modern fiction. University Presses of Florida, 1981 (c1980). 190p index 80-18348. 20.00 ISBN 0-8130-0681-3. CIP
In a series of brief essays, Spivey applies Jungian archetypes, Eliade's insights, and Campbell's voyage of the hero to illustrate that modern literature is moving past the pessimism and tragedy caused by "the disintegrating of institutions of our old culture" and into "epic heroism." After investigating 19th-century movements, he defines the visionary elements of modern literature in three periods—1870 to WW I, the period between the wars, and the contemporary period. Spivey then concludes that the best visions of the greatest modern writers, though usually pessimistic, point to more hopeful visions in the future. He recognizes in George Eliot, Hardy, Hesse, Hemingway, and others, particularly Mann, Joyce and T. S. Eliot, a movement away from tragedy toward wholeness, a quest that does not ignore modern despair but does offer some hope for renewal. The author sees this quest as the source of revitalization in literature—of new myths to carry us past Eliot's "dissociation of sensibility." Useful but not outstanding mythic criticism. Bibliographic notes. Recommended for graduate and undergraduate libraries.

The Journey beyond Tragedy

The Journey beyond Tragedy

A Study of Myth
and Modern Fiction

Ted R. Spivey

A University of Central Florida Book
University Presses of Florida
Orlando 1980

University Presses of Florida is the central agency for scholarly publishing of the State of Florida's university system. Its offices are located at 15 NW 15th Street, Gainesville, FL 32603. Works published by University Presses of Florida are evaluated and selected for publication by a faculty editorial committee of any one of Florida's nine public universities: Florida A&M University (Tallahassee), Florida Atlantic University (Boca Raton), Florida International University (Miami), Florida State University (Tallahassee), University of Central Florida (Orlando), University of·Florida (Gainesville), University of North Florida (Jacksonville), University of South Florida (Tampa), University of West Florida (Pensacola).

The substance of the material in several chapters of this volume first appeared as essays in the following publications: chapter 2, in "George Eliot: Victorian Romantic and Modern Realist," *Studies in the Literary Imagination* 1, no. 2 (1968): 5–23; chapter 3, in "Thomas Hardy's Tragic Hero," *Nineteenth-Century Fiction* 9, no. 3 (1945):179–91, © 1954 by the Regents of the University of California; chapter 7, in "The Reintegration of Modern Man: An Essay on James Joyce and Hermann Hesse," *Studies in the Literary Imagination* 3, no. 2 (1970):49–65; chapter 9, in "Flannery O'Connor's View of God and Man," *Studies in Short Fiction* 1, no. 3 (Spring 1964):200–206; chapter 10, in "Walker Percy and the Archetypes," in Panthea Reid Broughton, *The Art of Walker Percy* (Baton Rouge: Louisiana University Press, 1979).

Permission to use the quotations from the following works has been granted by the publishers: Ernest Hemingway, *For Whom the Bell Tolls* (New York: Charles Scribner's Sons, 1940); William Faulkner, *Go Down Moses* (New York: Random House, 1942), and *Light in August* (New York: Random House, 1946); Romain Gary, *The Roots of Heaven* (New York: Simon & Schuster, 1958), © 1958 by Romain Gary.

Library of Congress Cataloging in Publication Data

Spivey, Ted Ray, 1927–
   Journey beyond tragedy.

   "A University of Central Florida book."
   Includes bibliographical references and index.
   1. Fiction—19th century—History and criticism.
   2. Fiction—20th century—History and criticism.
   I. Title.
   PZ3499.S64   809.3'15   80–18348
   ISBN 0–8130–0681–3

Typography by Graphic Composition
Athens, Ga.

Printed in U.S.A.

Contents

Preface vii

1. Modernism, Postmodernism, and the Uses of Myth 1

2. Modern Realism and the Tragic Vision:
   The Achievement of George Eliot 20

3. Thomas Hardy and the Tragedy of Neoromanticism 41

4. Oscar Wilde and the Tragedy of Symbolism 57

5. Lawrence and Faulkner: The Symbolist Novel
   and the Prophetic Song 72

6. Hemingway's Vision of the Open Road 94

7. The Reintegration of Modern Man:
   The Transforming Visions of James Joyce and
   Hermann Hesse 109

8. Man's Divine Rootedness in the Earth:
   Romain Gary's Major Fiction 126

9. Beyond Diabolism: Flannery O'Connor's
   Religious Existentialism 139

10. Walker Percy and the Archetypes 148

11. The Search for Unity in Modern Times 165

Notes 177

Index 185

*To my father
and the memory of my mother*

Preface

The idea that man might be on a journey in our century that will eventually take him beyond the tragedy of modernism did not occur to me until I had struggled many years with a certain set of ideas related to the pessimism many critics find in modern literature. The pessimism is certainly there, but there are other, more hopeful attitudes too; it seemed to me for a long time that these attitudes were not sufficiently studied or appreciated. I was also aware that the danger of my viewpoint was that I would end up always going back to the views of Van Wyck Brooks and the editors of *Life* magazine, which proclaim that only positive views of life ought to be found in literature. What saved me from the two extremes of optimism or pessimism was a study of myth, ritual, and shamanism. In applying my knowledge of these subjects to a study of modern literature, I discovered that certain modern authors were able to achieve certain effects found in the work of earlier mythmakers. When they were able to accomplish this, something more than a pessimistic view of life resulted; even tragedy, when it is suffused with the mythic vision, is never really pessimistic. But even the best modern artists often lost sight of the mythic vision and fell into sadness and pessimism.

Once deeply involved in the subject, I began attempting to develop a theory concerning the literary history of modernism. To do this I had to examine the relationship between modernism and two earlier periods, the Victorian and the romantic. I found that many modern writers of the late nineteenth century—going as far back as the early Swinburne and Hardy—were opposed to a set of ideas that we today call Victorian. They often believed themselves to be extending the forces of romanticism, though in some ways they reversed certain romantic tendencies in creating a neoromanticism. Victorianism for them seemed to put too much emphasis on literalism, moralism, and systems of knowledge; in short, the Victorians clung to a false stasis and the modern neoromantics wanted a release of energy and movement. Victorians often saw man only in terms of the industrial community, and there was a reaction in favor of extreme individualism, of the imagination, of the exaltation of life over knowledge and morality, and of the quest for a new and good society and a facing of the tragedy of modern man in an industrial civilization.

As I went deeper into modernism, there became apparent the elements of what is called, in the seventies of this century, postmodernism. Now that postmodernism is nearly upon us, we inevitably seek the sources of new artworks which might elucidate the new age. Possibly if we take a long enough view of the period after 1700, when triumph in the West of science and industrialism forced the arts and sciences to take up some of the functions of declining religious institutions, we may well see that postmodernism is a completion of two previous cultural movements—romanticism and modernism—and even a fulfillment of these movements. Although there are as yet only uncertain hints, I have come to believe that many of the best visions of the greatest modern writers point to a new day of hope and that their work, even in a time of pessimism, helps to carry us toward that day.

The investigation of the visionary and mythic elements in modern literature has led me to the belief that there are three periods which make up the modern movement—the period before World War I, going back as far as 1870 (and, in a few cases, to 1855); the period between the wars, beginning shortly before 1914; and the period of what we call contemporary literature, from 1945 through the seventies. To write a book on the subject of these three movements in cultural development is a large task that was better suited for the late nineteenth and early twentieth centuries when learned people were surer of themselves because they had smaller bodies of knowledge to work with. But Hilton Kramer's book *The Age of the Avant-Garde*, concentrating on modern painting, is an example of significant works of the seventies which point the way to another cultural age after modernism. Also, the work of a literary scholar like Ihab Habib Hassan points to elements of a postmodernism already upon us. In the chapters which follow in the present book I have, like Kramer, taken one art form—literature in general and fiction in particular—and examined the development of certain trends from 1870 to 1970; but, unlike Kramer, I have not attempted to write in a period of two or three years a book that covers so much territory. Instead I began with an article written on Thomas Hardy in 1952 and continued with an article written in 1955 on Hemingway that developed some of the ideas of the first article. By then I realized I was working on a book-length manuscript, although each article has been written separately, and all but one has been published; the last was completed in 1976. The total work, written in a period of twenty-four years, deals with the following representative modern authors: George Eliot, Thomas Hardy, Oscar Wilde, Ernest Hemingway, Hermann Hesse, James Joyce, William Faulkner, D. H. Lawrence, Flannery O'Connor, Romain Gary, Walker Percy, T. S. Eliot, and Thomas Mann. As Kramer took the idea of the avant-garde as his own idea of the central concept of modern painting, so I have used the concept of mythic vision as central to the approach of many of the greatest modern fiction writers to the problem of modern man's search for both identity and community.

The term *mythic vision* is necessary because the mere use of stories that are called myths is not enough to lift the work of a writer to the level of either tragedy or epic. The first article I wrote on the subject, an analysis of Hardy's tragedies, establishes the fact that tragedy is actually possible in the industrial age, contrary to the belief of many modern critics. Later I drew from my doctoral dissertation on Hardy and George Eliot the seeds of an essay showing that George Eliot was one with those monumental novelists like Tolstoy and Dostoevski who embodied in their work the struggles of the new creative man of romanticism as well as the sense of suffering and tragic irony pervading even the most creative endeavors of modernism. It was not, however, until I had written the final article that I felt I understood what direction the currents of mythic fiction were taking in the modern period. This article, placed at the end of the study, discusses how three international figures of modernism—Thomas Mann, James Joyce, and T. S. Eliot—present mythic vision in works of both tragic and epic dimensions. The use of the word *epic* will surprise many who study modernism, but in the second phase of the period there are suggestions of epic heroism—mostly hidden—that have led me to entitle this study *The Journey beyond Tragedy.* The mythic visionaries of modernism see man as a hero journeying past the tragedies inherent in the disintegrating institutions of our old culture, but their epic visions do not begin to emerge until the second phase in the years between 1914 and 1945.

Thomas Mann and T. S. Eliot have the distinction of writing important works in all three of the major phases of modernism, as I indicate in my concluding chapter. The second phase is by general agreement the time of the greatest creativity in modern letters. Major works by Eliot, Joyce, Mann, Hesse, Gide, Lawrence, Faulkner, Hemingway, and Yeats show modern man on a quest in search of a vision of wholeness. These works suggest those powers of heroism we traditionally associate with epic literature.

The third phase, lasting from the end of World War II until sometime in the early seventies, reveals a continuation of the quest motif, but visions of epic triumph are few, though not entirely absent. What is more evident in this phase of modern literature, sometimes called contemporary literature, is the sense of powerful destructive forces at work. Many contemporary authors began the third phase with some hope and sank into a despair even blacker than that known by some of the authors of the first phase. Others began their careers with visions of a world dominated by powers of destruction at work eliminating the sensitive, and they remained true to these visions. Still others, however, faced modern despair and depicted nonetheless the continuation of the mythic quest that was characteristic of the greatest earlier modern authors. I have selected three figures who represent this group: Romain Gary, Flannery O'Connor, and Walker Percy.

Authors like Gary, O'Connor, and Percy are undoubtedly bridges to the postmodernist period. It is obviously too early to write a definitive work on a period as complex and long as modernism, when in fact, as I write, the succeeding period of postmodernism is only now coming into existence. Yet we must now begin to attempt to understand modernism as a whole period and to gather those concepts and visions which might be of value in preparing for the next tide of literary creativity. Any new literary period begins with works which are not always recognized for what they are. To search out these works and to encourage other works of the new age are legitimate and necessary functions of literary criticism, particularly at this time in history.

Modernism, Postmodernism, and the Uses of Myth

Everywhere the cultural movement called modernism is waning, even dying, yet still no one is sure what modernism really is. For nearly a century people throughout the world have proudly called themselves modern, and in doing so have felt themselves superior to those holding to views that dominated thought in the middle of the nineteenth century. Their pride has lain in the belief that they could pry into the hidden ugliness of life previously covered by what they considered to be an empty idealism and face that ugliness without fear. The modern temperament is preeminently tough-minded and cerebral, quick to shatter sacred vessels, ever ready to expose Victorianism's denial of the nakedness of modern man. Yet there is also a deep emotionalism that can itself be called modern, which proclaims the essential worth of the modern viewpoint.

The American philosopher Morton White has called the modern period the Age of Analysis. For him, as for many modern thinkers, the prime activity of this century is the clear-headed scrutiny of man and nature and the formulation of concepts about them. However, the same desire to analyze that yields clear arrangements of data also leads explorers to tear their way into hidden

1

chambers of human hearts as well as into physical phenomena in order to release long-repressed powers that, when released, threaten to engulf the contemplating mind. Often these two seemingly opposed tendencies go hand in hand. The careful, analytical social analysis of a Marx can be used to predict the explosion of social powers of revolution and can in fact be one of the chief mechanisms of this release. Freud can apply the careful methods of a mechanistic medical science to the muddled psyche in order to predict a new outburst of sexual passion and to aid that outburst. Darwin's science, likewise, can find its parallel in a philosophical statement by Herbert Spencer, a mind as analytical as any natural scientist's, to produce social Darwinism, which helped to set in movement the fires of Carnegie's forges, the symbol of oil-powered modern capitalism. And what could be more symbolic of the modern age than the science and technology that produced the atomic bomb? Careful analysis and the release of powerful energies within man and nature: sometimes the two are united in one movement, sometimes not, but agility of mind and release of energy are trademarks of modernism. Yet there is also in modernism an emotional and individualistic defiance of attitudes we today call Victorian, a defiance found in the various schools of modern philosophy called existentialist, which Walter Kaufmann says is "not a philosophy but a label for several widely different revolts against traditional philosophy," whose "one essential feature" is "their perfervid individualism."[1]

Defiance, new energies, and careful scrutiny appear at the beginning of modernism in the decade of the eighteen-fifties. In 1856 Flaubert published *Madame Bovary*, revealing an attention to exactness of expression and precision of psychological analysis of sexual passion never before seen in the novel. One year earlier the painter Courbet in a Paris exhibition introduced a new realism he would put to the service of releasing the energies of the downtrodden. In the same decade Baudelaire, the father of much of the best modern poetry, shattered the glittering surface of Paris to reveal in *Flowers of Evil* the deadly forces of perversity. Following his poetic master, Poe, he would foreshadow both a diabolism and a decadence soon to engulf certain areas of Western civilization. Yet by 1870 artistic movements were developing in Paris that revealed new healing and creative powers. Among these were the musical impressionism of Debussy, the poetic impressionism of Mallarmé and his circle, the poetic expressionism of Rimbaud, the new naturalism of Zola, and above all the new impressionistic school of painting, which restored the visionary light and the explosion of color to man's imaginative conception of nature. In Paris from 1850 into our own day the modern arts would find their true capital.

Paris, in fact, is the capital of the spirit of modernism. London, Vienna, Berlin, and New York are its followers and only occasionally its true rivals. It is not what Paris gives you but what it does not take away from you, Gertrude Stein said of the City of Light. Freedom, then, becomes one of the watchwords of the modern spirit, freedom and with it experimentation in life styles, in science, and in the arts. One might even say that we can see the waning of modernism after 1970, as Paris gradually begins to be eclipsed by New York as the capital of Western culture.

Today in New York, and in other great cities of the world following New York's lead, we can see freedom and experimentation as well as analysis and the release of energy carried so far that a longing for order and stability is called forth—a longing, in fact, for the kind of stasis the Victorians sought after the revolutionary fervor of romanticism. Indeed, as the waning process is being completed in the latter decades of this century, we tend to rebel against that element of modernism that emphasizes energy, analysis, and individualism for their own sakes. What one seeks today is a controlling principle. B. F. Skinner's *Beyond Freedom and Dignity* is one sign of this new search for what Skinner frankly calls control. But at the heart of modernism is this same search for a controlling and unifying principle that can be used to stabilize man as he freely plunges into new ways of living and new ways of viewing existence. One controlling principle formulated by poets, painters, philosophers, and other leaders of modern culture is that of comparative mythology. With the aid of stories and legends the artist has in our time often been able to use myth to tie together many of the strands of modernism and to provide a sense of stability often lacking in the work of the period. Our awareness of modern freedoms and the release of modern energies has often made us ignore this attempt to use myth as both a releasing and a controlling and unifying principle.

The importance of the work of Sir James Frazer and other mythologists and anthropologists in the early phases of modernism is well known to students of our age. Studies of the stories and rituals of early peoples have helped to turn the minds of artists to the problem of initiation, of the passage of man from one stage of his existence to another. In a deeper way the study of myth and ritual has led artists and thinkers to contemplate the origins and destiny of man. This study of origins has been, in one sense, a counteraction to the rush to analysis and the explosion of new energies, which often caused modern man to disown his past. Myths are carriers of essential information about the growth of man and help to keep him aware of what he must do to remain human. The separation of millions of people from mythic knowledge has resulted in a growing dehumanization and a corresponding attempt to recover a full humanity. The varied attempts of artists to mythicize their work is an attempt to help restore to man misplaced parts of himself. These attempts do not appear to be as important in our time as the more characteristic tasks of modernism, but it well may be that they are part of a movement that will in our new postmodernist age find fruition: the movement, that is, to anchor humans in their inner essential creative center that many call the true self, a concept certain schools of modern psychology have explored in detail but which other schools, behaviorism in particular, ignore.

Northrop Frye, probably the most influential scholar-critic of our day in the field of literature and myth, presents in works like *Anatomy of Criticism* an acute and subtle analysis of mythology and literature, but he fails to show an understanding of the creative energies that accompany the use of myth. Frye sees modern literature as having fallen under the spell of irony, and he cannot show how we are able to move into a new period because he fails to see the visions of a new age in a portion of the literature of modernism. For all the subtlety of analysis of recent myth and archetypal criticism, Frye's included, there is still the failure of literary criticism to deal with the powers inherent in myth and archetype, and an even greater failure to see this power at work in modern art.

Along with the failure of most myth criticism is the growing influence in the past twenty years of critics who deny that the power of myth can ever be found again in literature or that it ever existed in modern literature. In one of the most influential books of the sixties, *The Machine in the Garden*, Leo Marx says, ". . . the old symbol of reconciliation is obsolete."[2] Possibly failing to understand the implications of this statement, Marx is in effect announcing the death of the archetypal energy of creation summed up in the image called by Jung the mandala. While he does admit that new symbols are necessary, he says that they will appear not in art but in politics: "To change the situation we require new symbols of possibility, and although the creation of those symbols is in some measure the responsibility of artists, it is in greater measure the responsibility of society. The machine's sudden entrance into the garden presents a problem that ultimately belongs not to art but to politics."[3]

Marx is representative of the triumph of the melioristic spirit. We are all meliorists to an extent, but today meliorism, which says that "society" can by hard work and "right thinking" bring about the good life, proclaims itself to be the only possible view. For Marx and many others a combination of the machine and politics will banish the wasteland. For them tragedy and epic are incomprehensible because the mythic hero is incomprehensible. Still, Joseph Campbell reminds us of a knowledge contained in all the mythologies: "It is not society that is to guide and save the creative hero, but precisely the reverse."[4] Campbell has also said often in his public lectures that only three views of life are possible: the melioristic, the negative, and the affirmative. When meliorism is finally triumphant, the wasteland is shortly expected to pass away; but when instead the wasteland grows, then negativism must also flourish. Leslie Fiedler says in an essay on Faulkner's *The Sound and the Fury*: "Here is the ultimate negation, the Hard No pressed as far as it will go."[5] To see in negative terms a great American tragedy like *The Sound and the Fury*, in which the character Dilsey is a living symbol of reconciliation, is to misread literature on the grand scale. The growing negativism of some critics and authors has led to the emergence of a literary style that is in effect a debased form of naturalism; and, what is worse, a criticism has arisen—typified by J. Hillis Miller's analysis of Hardy—that continues to spread the ideas of naturalism in a subtle form.

Fortunately, there are new currents of energy at work in contemporary criticism that already are serving to counteract attempts to force literature to serve such nonliterary purposes as political propaganda and to poison the mind with nihilism. One important new school is that which studies the response of readers to literature as seen in the work of Norman N. Holland and Stanley Fish. Holland in his seminal book, *The Dynamics of Literary Response*, analyzes fantasy literature and points out that fantasy "is not simply a reading parallel to other readings from ideologies, Marxist, Swedenborgian, Christian humanist, or whatever; it is the material from which other such readings are made."[6] Thus in seeing literature from the angle of myth and fantasy one can get below any ideological reading, positive or negative, below any message that seeks to intrude itself on criticism and on literature itself. In his analysis of the reader's reaction to the mythic element in literature, Holland says that with "myth, our conscious awareness (dim or exact) of the myth can provide (if the context permits it) a rationale that lets us gratify an unconscious wish to return to an ancient, timeless, and universal at-oneness with the world."[7] The encounter with mythic materials, no matter where we find them, serves to invoke a return to unity with the world for those who can participate properly in the mythic experience.

Another approach, based in part on Freudian psychology, is the theoretical study of literature contained in Harold Bloom's *The Anxiety of Influence*, possibly the most brilliant and controversial work of criticism of the seventies. Calling most criticism reductionist, he seeks the meaning of a poem in the poetic reaction of one poet to the poetic efforts of another poet working as he must under the "anxiety of influence." The art of criticism, in Bloom's words, "is the art of knowing the hidden roads that go from poem to poem."[8] In redefining both poetry and criticism, Bloom puts his finger on the central issue: "The issue is reduction and how best to avoid it." Schools of criticism "reduce, whether to images, ideas, given things, or phonemes."[9] A criticism that is to take literature fully into account must deal with the work of literature *and* with the powers of creation and destruction related to that work in both the poet and the reader. Only thus will we free ourselves from the influence of what remains of the New Criticism, which once provided some excellent tools of explication but which, Holland tells us, "often seems overtly intellectual, even sterile, certainly far removed from the roots of our pleasure in literature."[10]

Myth and archetypal criticism of the recent past is nearly always reductive, usually reducing the mythic work simply to a statement of the myth on which the work is based. Archetypal criticism simply points to images and calls them archetypes, doing little more than the work of classification. Even Jung, who wrote more to the point about archetypes than anyone else in this century, misleads by often, though not always, calling archetypes images. But, as Joseph K. Davis points out, Jung believed that archetypes appeared "arranged in appropriate images" and that these patterns "are the purposeful, restorative, and empowering agents of human life itself. . . ."[11] Thus the mandala, the most basic archetype according to Jung, is a power represented by many different images, a power that is present in the healing process of the human psyche and that serves to unify the inner life and the outer life of man and man as well as man and cosmos. The kind of myth and archetypal criticism that is needed, I believe, is a new pragmatic criticism that takes into account recent studies of myth and archetype, and also explores the meaning of the ritual and the connection of the shaman to the renewal of the rites of the community, both past and present.

The work of Mircea Eliade on shamanism and ritual has in recent years helped us to see the art of mythic societies in a new light, just as the psychological work of Norman Holland with literature and readers has helped us to see that the mythic level of involvement is still present in modern readers and modern literature. Possibly we should see myths as part of a religio-artistic process in all societies—a process meaningful to all who can become sufficiently involved in its visionary and creative power. This involvement, if properly learned, engages the creative center of the psyche called the true self, which Jung says is symbolized by the various images that represent the archetype of the mandala. Our habit of analysis has become so strong that we believe our human betterment lies in obtaining analytic information from various sources and applying it in some way to achieve desired results. But for art and myth to be known as people have traditionally known them, there must be a participation exactly as one participates in any human ritual. In this participation one encounters knowledge and something more important: the power of the true self, which enables humans to relate to others who have made the same encounter, to relate to that community of those who hold to the common unity springing from relationship with the mythic identity of man.

The great art of modernism has gone far beyond the mere invoking of the mythic materials of the past—though the resurrecting of these materials has been a valuable service in itself. The art of our time has often, at its best, performed the mythic function for millions by providing a ritualistic process for encountering the true self. Modernism as a movement has been declining for the past two decades, and for that reason the functional value of art as mythic ritual has been called into question. Yet if one studies the profound effects of men like Stravinsky, T. S. Eliot, or Picasso upon people of the world in this century, and the even profounder effects of forebears of modernism like Beethoven, Hugo, or Tolstoy, one will see that a sense of human identity and community has resulted from artistic encounter. As the artistic efforts of modernism decline, we tend to forget the task of art in the heyday of this movement. To encounter again the greatness of modern art and to inspire the new art that will appear in the period that we may tentatively call postmodernism, we must recall two mytho-ritualistic concepts of our own art that are redefined by every age. The concepts are, of course, tragedy and myth.

To see literature as a kind of ritual, which itself is based on myth, is not easy for modern man, schooled as he is in antimythic activity. What is called for is a redefinition of myth and literature in terms of tragedy and epic. Tragedy must always be considered in relationship to its opposite, which is epic, or, if one likes, comedy, signifying the joyous conclusion of an action. What tragedy and comedy have in common is the hero, and no definition of either of the two is possible without first examining the hero. The hero is the person endowed with a portion of power for doing good, that is, creative as opposed to destructive energy. The tragic hero, to be a tragic hero at all, as Aristotle points out, must not be a "perfectly good man" but one "whose misfortune is brought about not by vice or depravity, but by some error or frailty."[12] The hero of comedy is the opposite of one whose creative power is brought to nothing by error or frailty; he is rather one who rises above his frailties to accomplish an important task. At least, this is the broadest view of the progress of protagonists in the literary forms known as tragedy and epic. But tragedy from Shakespeare to the present has been far more inward than anything Aristotle and the Greeks knew, until in the modern period inwardness has become everything. To understand tragedy in the modern period, with all its inwardness, one must invoke modern depth psychology and with it the mythic patterns related to the inner development of the hero.

Many critics would maintain that studies of modern literature in terms of heroism, whether tragic or epic, are unnecessary because the anti-hero is at the center of modernism. To think this way is to misread modernism, which has been an age of both great creativity and great destructiveness. When there has been creativity, there has also been heroism, usually of both tragic and epic proportions. When institutions are crumbling and dying, as in our time, the literature of the anti-hero must always emerge. The anti-hero, exact opposite of the hero, is the person of little or no power who is tossed about by events. He is in the modern age the central figure in the endless parade of so-called comedies, which in the classical world were considered a kind of diversion or comic relief after sober minds had encountered the catharsis of tragedy. To view any age from the anti-heroic vantage is to ignore the deepest human aspirations. But in our day many literary critics follow those crowds who ignore not only human inspiration but humans themselves in their search for the creative life. Man becomes in their eyes a machine or an animal, and his only art is the art of "entertainment," or simply the art of stimulation if one is a strict behaviorist.

To study the hero is to study man in his role as creator. The forces of nature and the powers of the mass movement of populations have been so powerfully manifested in the modern age that the role of man as individual creator has often been overlooked. However, a group of thinkers, scientists, and artists in this century who turned to studies of myth and ritual have helped to preserve the concept of the heroic, whether seen in its tragic or its epic aspects. Sir James Frazer led the way with *The Golden Bough* and the Cambridge ritualists followed in such representative books as Lord Raglan's *The Hero*. The latter traces the development of the hero from his journey in search of heroic powers to his return to society as king and finally to his sacrificial death. Scholars at the same time moved into fieldwork with primitive tribes and brought back knowledge of the shaman, the one who withdraws from his tribe, establishes contact with creative powers, and returns to save his people from the wasteland condition into which they have fallen. He saves them by renewing old rituals so that creative power can again be mediated to the whole tribe. All societies, primitive and civilized, bring forth their own shamans to renew themselves. The last great age of shamanism in Western civilization was the period we associate with the movements called the

Renaissance, the Reformation, and the Counter-Reformation. If I have correctly read the prophetic artists of modernism, we are today on the verge of another such age.

The great artists—particularly the great poets—sought those who could give them material for their visions of the creative and destructive powers dwelling within man. They turned to Frazer, but they also turned to Freud because Freud gave them a concept of the psyche based on a knowledge of myth and on scientific analysis. For the modern artist the historical accounts of Frazer were not enough; the accounts of an explorer of the mind like Freud, and later those of his chief disciple, Jung, were needed to bring modern artists to a realization not of myths alone, but of mythic vision. This is because the artist has had to find new symbols or else his work would not last. And the greatest modern artists have reached out for the living symbols of myth in order to find the power to counteract the depressing symbols of the modern wasteland scene.

In one of the important scientific breakthroughs of the age, Jung promulgated a theory of myth, dream, and symbol that would give the artists who would hear his message a springboard into the vast waters of living mythic symbols. Joseph Campbell describes the change in Jung's viewpoint, one that would be radically different from the Freudian vision: "It was this shift of ground from a subjective and personalistic, essentially *biographical* approach to the reading of the symbolism of the psyche, to a larger, culture-historical, *mythological* orientation that then became the characteristic of Jung's psychology."[13] The writing of his *Symbols of Transformation*, begun in 1909, led Jung to see that the dreams of everyone contain the same patterns of symbolism as the world's myths. Campbell thus interprets Jung on this matter that is central to the Jungian position: "Dreams in Jung's view are the natural reaction of the self-regulating psychic system and, as such, point forward to a higher, potential health, not simply backward to past crises."[14] Myth, for Jung, was absolutely necessary for man's growing toward health, or wholeness, which meant achieving the creative energy and knowledge of the true self that accompanies wholeness. Without myth, dream, and vision, man cannot know himself, nor can he relate to the world around him. Campbell makes this point when he quotes Jung's statement upon completing *Symbols of Transformation* in 1912, roughly at the beginning of the second phase of modernism: "'Hardly had I finished the manuscript,' he states, 'when it struck me what it means to live with a myth, and what it means to live without one. Myth, says a Church Father, is "what is believed always everywhere, by everybody"; hence, the man who thinks he can live without myth, or outside it, is an exception. He is like one uprooted, having no true link either with the past, or with the ancestral life which continues within him, or yet with contemporary human society.'" The encounter with one's own lived myth leads the individual, Jung believed, to encounter those basic symbols of his own and everybody's psyche which he called archetypes; and through what he called the "life of the archetypes" one encounters what is deepest in himself and also becomes rooted in his past and in his own contemporary world. Before discussing the archetypes in relationship to modern tragedy and epic, we must consider two contemporary mythologists who in their own ways continue Jung's work and who have the power to inspire artists who seek the mythic vision. They are Joseph Campbell and Mircea Eliade.

Campbell, who might be called the Frazer of this part of the modern period, has systematically examined myth from primitive times to the present; like Jung and others, he proposes, in volume 4 of *The Masks of God*, that the modern artist is the leading discoverer of new myths in our time, pointing to Joyce and Mann as the leaders of this literary journey to find creative myths. In *The Hero with a Thousand Faces* Campbell points to the hero, who is basically the same in all myths, as the center of the mythic life, and his definitions of tragedy and comedy in terms of myth are basic to understanding his theory of the relationship between literature and myth. "Tragedy," he says, "is the shattering of the forms and of an attachment to the forms; comedy the wild and careless, inexhaustible joy of life invincible."[15]

Mircea Eliade, who approaches mythology through shamanistic studies and the history of religion, defines the myth as a story that records the breakthrough of a power that he calls "the sacred." In *Myth and Reality*, a book that sums up many of his characteristic concepts, Eliade says that the "'story' narrated by the myth constitutes a 'knowledge' which is esoteric, not only because it is secret and is handed on during the course of an initiation but also because the 'knowledge' is accompanied by a magico-religious power."[16] Thus Eliade relates the myth to the initiation and thereby demonstrates that the essential function of both is to transmit both knowledge and power. Thus Eliade helps us to see that myth is a power-transmitting device and that without its effective use, there is a decline toward human sterility. It is also a device to overcome powers that threaten human existence.

The modern age, as I have suggested, is a period of the release of enormous powers, some destructive and others creative. Those scholars and artists who use myth creatively in the modern age do so, in most cases, in order to overcome the powers that threaten man's life, that seek to imprison him in a sterile wasteland. They also use myth to stimulate the flow of creative energies within individuals. Great scientific discoveries like those concerning atomic energy and the speed of light have been hailed everywhere; but scholars like Frazer, Jung, Campbell, and Eliade, who have rediscovered the knowledge contained in myth of the creative and destructive powers within man himself, powers expressed through myths and rites, have not yet received their due. This recognition should come in the postmodern period when the creative power of man will be more vividly expressed than it is today, when we are at the beginning of the new period. This expression, in fact, must appear if man is to continue his existence, and certain artists of our time not only forecast this expression but reveal in their work a movement from destruction to a renewed creativity.

No scholar has in such detail examined the transmission of creative power through myth and rite as C. G. Jung, who could draw not only on material from earlier mythologies but also on his clinical analysis of hundreds of patients. Jung's achievement is to see the mytho-ritualistic process of power transmission in terms of the archetypes, which he calls "primordial images" but which are more precisely, as I have suggested, the powers that announce themselves in dream and vision as symbols or images. Where no power appears, there is no archetype, only what today might be called "symbols" or "images." Yet Jung himself sometimes uses *symbol* and *archetype* interchangeably. Of this use of *symbol* as *archetype*, Campbell says, "a sign becomes . . . a symbol when it is read as pointing toward an unknown." Yet the symbol is but the outer form of the hidden power whose presence we know because of the way it affects us, producing not only pleasure in the Freudian sense but also healing and transcendence in the Jungian sense. Through the symbol, Campbell goes on to say, one can achieve "individuation" so that "one might open one's eyes at the center, to see, think, feel and intuit transcendence, and to act out of such knowledge. This . . . is the final good, the Summum Bonum of all his [Jung's] thought and work."[17]

Myth is the pattern of the archetypes, which may be stated thus: (1) a human encounters a wasteland condition, is spurred to go on a journey, or quest, to find the necessary power to bring new life to his people; (2) he encounters helpers in the forms of wise old people and people of the opposite sex, and he also encounters those who thwart and test him, particularly the shadow and the deceptive figures of the opposite sex; (3) he achieves the creative power, encounters his true self, and becomes the hero who triumphs over the destructive energies, returning to his people to renew the rituals of initiation so that the community is bound together creatively by powers transmitted through myth and rite; (4) after a period of rule he dies in a sacrificial manner. The major archetypes include those of the quester, the wasteland, the anima and animus (images of one's sex opposite), the shadow (destructive principle), and finally the hero, or cosmic man. Jung tells us that the chief archetype is the mandala, an image with a center and a periphery. This image represents the essential harmony of the universe and also the hero, or cosmic man, the creative power that is an aspect of the true self. In fact Jung often calls this aspect of the individual the Self.

The quester is taught by helpers to believe in the truth of the mandala, to believe that there is a creative power to be achieved. If he continues his journey with this belief, he will find powers in himself and in the universe that will aid him to overcome those forces that seek to stop his progress. Then he will achieve the powers of harmony and joy that accompany the image of the mandala and that enable him to become a renewer of myth and ritual.

The archetype of the mandala and the image of the hero are thus intimately linked. The hero is not an individual but a power living in everyone, which must be sought; when it is found, the true self is encountered, and the forms are seen as carriers of the one energy that activates man and everything else in the universe. Whoever would understand the flow of creative energy in its overcoming of destructive power must be concerned with the hero, not as an individual but as a principle to be sought and experienced. When the quester returns to his people to share with them his newfound power, he himself becomes a subject of myth. Thus Eliade quotes R. A. Stein concerning the ritual use of epic songs among the Turco-Mongols and the Tibetans: "'The bard recites the epic for several days. They say that in former times the hoofprints of Gesar's horse appeared in the prepared space. Hence the recitation brought the real presence of the hero'."[18] The "real presence" of the hero is the appearance of the hero power to an audience experiencing an archetype.

The rediscovery of archetypal powers is the task of every new age of letters because only with that power can literature be what it must be in order to be literature: language so memorable that those involved with it must continually return to it, language possessing a power to hold large audiences who allow themselves to become involved in it a thousand years or more after it is written. The power of the archetypes gives to literature that vision I have earlier called mythic. The fact that the great fiction of the modern age has a portion of this archetypal power can be seen in the way it continues to grip the imaginations of large numbers of people. Jung, Eliade, and Campbell all have examined myth and archetype and have formulated theories about the way the two work; but artists in general and certain writers in particular in the modern period have continued the tradition of archetypal rediscovery. Eliade says, ". . . it is primarily the artists who represent the genuine creative forces of a civilization or a society. Through their creation the artists anticipate what is to come—sometimes one or two generations later—in other sectors of social and cultural life."[19]

The next great event in literature and the arts, as forecast by James Joyce and others, is the emergence of the triumphant hero who has achieved the powers given to those who overcome the tests that appear on the hero's path. That this event should happen seems inevitable for the continuation of human existence, which the greatest prophetic artists of our period confidently forecast, and there have been signs of the process beginning during modernism. But the study of tragedy also indicates what might be another sign of the movement toward epic.

A study of Greek drama indicates that there is movement from the tragic to the epic mode in that the tragic hero who persists will, even after falling from high position, achieve those shamanistic powers that will enable him to fulfill the role of the mythic hero who delivers his people from the wasteland. For instance, out of the tragedy of Agamemnon and Clytemnestra emerges in the Oresteian trilogy the heroism of Orestes, who encounters the shadow forces called the Eumenides and finally with divine help restores his community, finding his true self and his vocation in the process. In Sophocles' Theban plays, which critics generally believe do not make up a trilogy, Oedipus falls from high position but achieves shamanistic powers in the second play of the group. Antigone, his daughter, achieves both vision and heroic sacrifice in the third play. There are parallel actions, somewhat telescoped, in the careers of Lear and Cordelia in Shakespearean tragedy. The profound influence of Greek tragedy on many artists in this century indicates that a similarity of spiritual events is being felt in our day. Dramas containing Oresteian material by O'Neill, Eliot, and Sartre have had an important effect on this century because they contain some of the old tragic power and because they remind people of the tragic condition of our own day and also of the possibility of overcoming tragedy.

Tragedy has been one of the great literary forms since Shakespeare, yet tragedy seems to be a dying form in this century. Anybody, of course, who is familiar with the form knows that tragic art is far more than that art which deals with unhappy subjects. The novel or play in our century with an unhappy ending does not usually lift us to what has always been thought of as a tragic height, that is, does not provide catharsis. There was far more tragedy in the literature of the nineteenth and early twentieth centuries. The reason, as I have suggested, might be that we are indeed moving into a new period leading toward epic. This movement is obscured greatly by the many artworks of anti-heroism, which serve a purpose but which seem to suggest that they are the only art any longer necessary. One task of literary criticism is to look behind this facade of anti-heroic art and see the beginnings of a new art that will appear in the period of postmodernism. Our thinking about literature and the other arts has been shaped by a spate of criticism that has as its basis a viewpoint basically anti-heroic. I will conclude by examining several viewpoints now predominant, after first making a few points about the hero, both tragic and epic.

The epic hero, as has been suggested, achieves a great power that he uses for the good of his people, eventually giving his own life as a sacrifice in the complete hero myth, which according to Joyce and Campbell is the monomyth, or one story of man. The tragic hero has made some progress on the quest that leads him to creative power, or he has inherited some of the power. The significance of creative power is symbolized by the mandala, the chief archetype. What is symbolized is the creative power of harmony or completeness, a power accepting all because all is contained within it, even the destructive powers which play their part in the universe. The hero, tragic or epic, affirms the mandala, the basic harmony, and it is this affirmation, this sense of reconciliation, that gives the sense of tragic height and artistic pleasure to the tragedy. Thus Hegel says that tragic pleasure springs from reconciliation, and Nietzsche speaks of the affirmation of the will to life. Reconciliation and affirmation accompany the pity and fear (in the sense of awe) suggested by Aristotle as necessary for the catharsis received by the properly receptive audience. The effect on the audience is, as the Greeks knew, that of a religious experience in which the truth contained in the worldwide concept of universal harmony is embodied and apprehended. The end result, in the words of Edith Hamilton, is that "the great soul in pain and death transforms pain and death."[20]

Along with the power of tragedy mediated to the receptive audience there is the teaching of tragedy. Aristotle also uses the word *fear* to mean an awareness that we too might fall from the position we occupy in the world and, even worse, might fall from even that partial relationship to universal harmony that we might possess. It has traditionally been said that a tragic flaw causes the fall of the hero. But this flaw, referred to by Aristotle as error or frailty, is not usually understood as springing from an improper relationship to the spiritual tradition of a society. In short, the tragic hero is shown to be a man who has departed from basic wisdom. Thus, the fool in *King Lear* says that Lear should have become wise before he became old. Othello says of himself that he is one who "loved not wisely but too well." Macbeth is always painfully aware of his betrayal of the wisdom of his native Christianity, and Hamlet searches, tormented, for a lost wisdom deeper than his humanistic education, a wisdom that would enable him to deal with the spirit world.

In archetypal terms, the tragic hero has forgotten or ignored the wisdom embodied in the mandala and as a result has lost his own relationship to universal harmony. This loss has several effects on the hero. He can, like Hamlet, fall into depression, lose the motive for action, and debate with himself the value of suicide; or, like Lear, he can lose all ability to distinguish between good and evil so that he prefers destructive people to creative people; he can become possessed by an archetype, like Othello or Macbeth. Archetypal possession is the result of contemplating an image other than the mandala until one sees that image as the chief good of existence. Obsession with the image of the opposite sex is one of the most common forms of this possession. Caught up in the image of Desdemona, Othello falls from wisdom and becomes an easy prey of the deceptive Iago, who himself is possessed by the archetype of the shadow, as is common to those who live totally for destruction. Macbeth is seized by the image of kingship, not realizing that the king is only a symbol representing in all cultures the achievement of a true heroism.

Yet all tragic heroes return even in their fall to the realization of harmony, and from this realization spring the great speeches of heroes who even in their agony affirm the good of what is happening. Thus Edith Hamilton sums up the value of tragedy as a genre by quoting the Trojan queen in Euripides' *The Trojan Women*: "Yet had God not turned us in his hand and cast to earth our greatness . . . we would have passed away giving nothing to men. They would have found no theme for song in us nor made great poems from our sorrows."[21]

I have discussed at length the hero and his relationship to tragedy and epic in order to establish the fact that tragedy and epic are based firmly on a spiritual tradition, whether it be in Greek society, in Renaissance culture, or even in modern civilization. Greek tragedy illustrates those two statements of Greek wisdom found at Delphi—know thyself, and nothing in excess—but James Joyce's work illustrates both this wisdom and Christian wisdom concerning reason and the conscience. Yet while retaining some belief that there was once an ancient wisdom, we tend to deny that some of this tradition continues even to the present day. Morse Peckham has written a book entitled *Beyond the Tragic Vision* which deals with the theme of art in the nineteenth century and which looks beyond tragedy, but he finds only Nietzsche to be a truly affirmative writer of the period. Still, affirmation of universal harmony is basic to a spiritual tradition, and the present study analyzes eleven authors who in at least some of their works affirm harmony and thus are selected as representative of many others. For Peckham the only representative of what is left of the spiritual tradition of the West is Nietzsche, who at last went mad. "Nietzsche," Peckham says, "found a resolution to the problem of keeping the antinomies, the contraries, the irreconcilable opposites of life, forever apart. Joy wants those opposites."[22] The proof of Peckham's error lies in the fact that the mandala, which is the archetype of the reconciliation of opposites, is found in many literary and artistic works of the nineteenth and twentieth centuries. Where the mandala appears as an archetype, there is creative power, and behind that power lies a spiritual tradition. Creative joy follows the artist's apprehension of the mandala. It is not joy that unites the opposites, as Peckham suggests, but involvement with what Jung calls the transcendent function, or more simply, the center point of the mandala, an involvement taught by all authentic spiritual traditions.

As one great wave of creative energy wanes, it is inevitable that many should deny that the arts have the power to heal men or that there are any valid traditions that teach reconciliation of the opposites. The arts themselves, however, in our time as earlier, point to the fact that creative powers are accompanied by outbursts of destructive energy, and that each age must find new creative energy to push back that energy which accompanies the archetype of the shadow. In postmodernism those who receive the creative power will have rediscovered a spiritual wisdom that is upheld by at least a few in even the worst of ages. In the meantime, as we prepare for the next period, it is necessary to identify those myths and symbols that are necessary for the leap into the next age, just as it is necessary to identify those views that deny the possibility of creativity or fail to understand how energy is renewed.

Many scholars today peer into the next age, but they fail to see the creativity in their own age that will serve as a bridge to the next period. Those who successfully move on through the modern age to accept postmodernism will be the ones who are always discovering and using the visionary and mythic powers of the modern period. Paul Tillich has said that the great quest of our time is that of the search for identity, and Harvey Cox has rejoined that, no, it is really the quest for community. But that individual who has no relationship with his true self—has not encountered his identity, that is—will not relate fully to the common union that is community. He who relates only to an eccentric aspect of his conscious self has little in "common" with anyone else, and where we have collections of individuals who deny the common identity of man we have, in David Riesman's pregnant phrase, a "lonely crowd." Myths, as I have said, are repositories of knowledge that help man find himself, and when properly encountered they provide the means to set free those powers associated with the mandala that unify both the single person and groups of people.

Even in the fragmented modern age we find those who have achieved some measure of unity. The modern age has contained such diverse elements as analysis, the release of energy, and emotional commitment. In the greatest modern authors, such as Eliot, Yeats, Joyce, and Mann, we see all of these different elements represented in various proportions in their several styles of realism, symbolism, expressionism. The critic of literature who would keep up with them must accept this diversity in order to plunge into their works, because it is in their diversity that we see their attempts to unify those different powers in humanity whose disunity is one aspect of the modern tragic age. Where lesser artists set realism against romanticism or moralism against prophecy, they work to unify the sensibility so that we can, in the next age, see unified man come again, the only man we can trust to use the tools of expanding technology. Even the greatest literary artists did not complete the movement leading to unified man, but they did pick up the threads of spiritual development as they inherited them from the earlier romantic and Victorian movements, and they evoked the creative powers of the psyche by renewing language and by pointing man to the road that must lead past our present tragedy to an age of high comedy.

Modern Realism
and the Tragic Vision:
The Achievement of George Eliot

The modern novel and modern realism came into existence in tandem. Some would say that the appearance of Flaubert's *Madame Bovary* in 1856 marked the beginning of the modern tradition of realism in fiction, and others might point to the two great novels of Stendahl (*Le Rouge et le Noir* and *La Chartreuse de Parme*) in 1830 and 1839. By the decade of the 1870s, with the completion of *War and Peace* and the publication of *Anna Karenina* and *Middlemarch* (the first fully modern novel in English), one can say that modern realistic fiction had been established in the literary firmament; but not until the twentieth century would literary critics be fully aware of the difference between the realism that was always present in the development of the novel and the form of realism that is specifically modern. From the first it was suspected that *Madame Bovary* had something sordid about it, or at least dealt with sordid matters, but the readers of Tolstoy and George Eliot in the sixties and seventies did not feel a sharp break with the attitude that has been called the Victorian compromise. William Dean Howells probably spoke for most serious readers in Europe and America when he wrote of George Eliot as a novelist very much like Dickens and Thackeray and of Tolstoy as a Christian socialist and idealist. But the realist for Howells, as he wrote in *Criticism and Fiction*, was a man exalted "not by vain shows and shadows and ideals, but by realities in which alone the truth lives."[1] The Victorians—and Howells remained one all his life—thought that they could encounter both reality and truth, but many moderns came to believe that neither could be grasped during their period of history, though they did believe that life could be analyzed and knowledge amassed. Uncertainty about truth and reality forms a large part of the basis of the modern tragic vision.

By 1920 the Victorian atmosphere had dissipated. No longer would people who took literature seriously speak, as Howells did, of realistic fiction concerning itself with the "more smiling aspects of life."[2] Readers by this time were avid for a modern realism that dealt, in the bold manner of a Flaubert, with the many unsmiling aspects of life. Above all they wanted detailed analysis of the hidden depths of both society and the individual person. It was in this spirit that Virginia Woolf could sharply distinguish George Eliot's masterpiece, *Middlemarch*, from all other fiction of her age as "the magnificent book which with all its imperfections is one of the few English novels for grown-up people."[3] For Woolf, probably the greatest of the twentieth-century feminist critics, George Eliot was the supreme English novelist because she went to the heart of human problems and wrote for newly liberated men and women who could face the tragedy of modern life without flinching. Psychology and the acceptance of the tragedy of modern life were the hallmarks of this newly discovered modern novelist of the nineteenth century. F. R. Leavis, the most influential critic of fiction in Britain after World War II, would echo and extend Woolf's appreciation of George Eliot, showing in his seminal work, *The Great Tradition*, that George Eliot and Henry James engaged in a kind of character analysis in depth that had not been seen in British fiction. George Eliot's analytical abilities have continued to come under scrutiny since Leavis published his pronouncements in 1950. In the sixties Elizabeth Drew could still extol the novelist's "fine mind" and her "deeply tolerant probing of the facts of human behavior, and an expansive grasp of both outer and inner reality."[4] J. Hillis Miller in *The Forms of Victorian Fiction* would link George

Eliot (and several other novelists) with the most basic philosophical and psychological problems of modernism: the themes of the death of God and of man's alienation from his deepest self.

Thus George Eliot, at first rejected by some moderns as a dull Victorian dealing out empty "ideals" and "smiling-realism," has now been enshrined, after lengthy analysis of *Middlemarch*, as a major modern novelist. Her credentials as a modern are based largely on a realistic style that paints the suffering of modern tragedy and probes the depths of the mind. Drew lays down this commonly accepted dictum: "In spite of claims made for Richardson, George Eliot is the first serious psychologist. Her analysis is accurate and searching."[5] In an important work of fictional criticism of the late seventies, *Tragedy in the Victorian Novel*, Jeannette King discusses in detail the relationship between George Eliot's tragic vision and such philosophical and literary problems as the varieties of determinism and the relationship of realism to symbolism.[6] Yet the recent emphasis on the modern virtues of George Eliot has tended to obscure the mythic and visionary background of her work, which at once makes possible her particular kind of tragedy and helps us to define modern tragedy generally. Too rigid an interpretation of George Eliot's realism finally leads the student of modern fiction to ignore her romantic roots as well as elements in her work of a postmodern release from the modern tragic condition. The mythic inheritance of George Eliot must be taken into full account if one is to understand her major achievement.

Even with increasing emphasis on the study of modernism and postmodernism, the prevailing tendency of critics of fiction is still to see George Eliot purely in terms of Victorianism. As I will suggest, the Victorian element in George Eliot's fiction is extremely important, but it is on the modernist elements that her greatest achievement rests. It was George Eliot's Victorianism that was mainly responsible for this century's neglect of her work, and it was her modernism that led Virginia Woolf and other influential critics to restore and even to enhance her reputation. J. Hillis Miller, in so seminal a book as *The Form of Victorian Fiction*, spoke of "George Eliot's version of the notion, so widespread in Victorian fiction, that society is generated and sustained by individual acts of self-denying, self-creating love."[7] This notion may be prevalent in a minor work like *Silas Marner*, in many ways the most Victorian of her works, but it is not the central notion in *Middlemarch*.

In the latter, a few small acts of love are possible, but society is not being sustained by them; rather, society is collapsing because of the absence of a larger vision of unity that can tie individuals together. The absence of this vision is at the heart of both George Eliot's tragic fiction and her modernism.

George Eliot's awareness of the possibility of an underlying vision of unity springs from her awareness of the poetry of Wordsworth and other romantics. In fact, her awareness of what Miller calls "individual acts" of love derives mainly from Wordsworth. Yet, by quoting George Eliot alongside Feuerbach, Miller denies the ontological basis of her work, rooted as that ontology was in romanticism. The course of George Eliot's creative life leads from an early involvement with humanistic rationalists like Feuerbach to an imaginative recreation of the communal life of her childhood in Warwickshire, a recreation accomplished with the aid of Wordsworth. Similarly, Tolstoy turned away from his early rationalistic orientation to find an ontology based on the work of Rousseau and then of Thoreau. Tolstoy and George Eliot have much in common in that they sought an ontology based in romantic philosophy yet never abandoned totally their early rationalistic, humanistic, and science-oriented educations; this fact is probably one of the chief reasons why both authors are realistic and analytical, never abandoning reason, and at the same time are caught up in the emotional currents and visionary activity of nineteenth-century romanticism. To understand this blend of realism and romanticism in Tolstoy, we must study the character Levin in *Anna Karenina*, who is in effect Tolstoy. To know George Eliot's mature fictional and psychological development, it is necessary to study the progress of Dorothea Brooke, the central character of *Middlemarch*.

Dorothea stands for millions of intelligent, well-to-do people who lived in Europe and America during the second half of the nineteenth century. She had inherited a philosophy based on the romantic vision of men like Goethe, Wordsworth, Shelley, Carlyle, and Emerson—a hopeful philosophy that pointed the way toward both personal and social renewal. People like Dorothea, however, found themselves in a world that could not achieve the fulfillment of this romantic philosophy. In fact, the rising tide of materialism and scientism denied the validity of the romantic viewpoint. The reactions to the forces that frustrate the romantic are varied. For Thomas Hardy it is a tragic struggle with human and even superhuman powers of darkness. For the naturalists, who dominate the twentieth-century novel by sheer force of numbers, the romantic protagonist is overcome by forces of heredity and environment that no idealistic philosopher can stand against. For Dorothea Brooke and for other characters in George Eliot's novels, the reaction is a quiet acceptance of the difficulties of the modern world and an affirmation of what little good the individual can do in a world that generally denies his optimistic philosophy. All her life, George Eliot held to her romantic philosophy, but her reaction to those aspects of the modern world that deny romanticism is neither that of a neoromantic like Hardy nor that of a naturalist like Zola. It is the reaction of a realist who is also mythic. This reaction is related to the style and viewpoint of realistic fiction in the modern period; it is in fact inseparable from the style of realism.

Leavis is probably right in saying that Henry James is the novelist most like George Eliot. Both are predominantly psychological realists. In James' *The Portrait of a Lady* the noble acceptance by Isabel Archer of her hard lot in life is paralleled by the same kind of acceptance on the part of Dorothea in *Middlemarch*. Both Isabel and Dorothea come to know the meaning of Harcourt-Reilly's summing up of modern life in *The Cocktail Party*: "The best of a bad job is all any of us make of it— / Except, of course, the saints—."[8] Making the best of a bad job means accepting the quiet, continuing tragedy of a life in which one has found little or no fulfillment of one's idealistic hopes. Works of realistic fiction like *The Portrait of a Lady* and *Middlemarch* are filled with a sense of pain and loss that is peculiarly modern, but they also portray individuals who refuse to accept the total defeat of all their ideals. Some disillusionment is inevitable because of the romantic viewpoint of the protagonists, but there is no sense of the total collapse of the individual that is so often found in naturalistic fiction.

Romantic views in the work of George Eliot are never totally shattered; in fact, they sustain characters in time of great trials. Still, the romantics must inevitably settle for much less than they had expected. Romanticism remained a strong element in the makeup of Victorians, and is still a much greater influence on modern life than many people imagine. The romantic philosophy of Wordsworth and Goethe is what many Victorians, as well as many moderns, embraced instead of Christianity, which was intellectually untenable for many people. After 1800, even the average person, who did not question the assumption of inherited religion, centered his thoughts more and more on ethics instead of worship, which is at the center of religious life in all ages except those of religious decline. The hallmark of Victorianism is its concern with ethics in general and with duty in particular. The history of religion shows that conduct grows out of the worship of an absolute, or, in philosophical terms, ontology precedes ethics. But the Victorian age, influenced as it was by science and rationalism, put great emphasis on the rational choice of ideals of conduct. Victorians, as well as moderns, have often been idealistic without being religious.

The rationalistic ethics of Victorianism, which had grown out of romanticism, had been gradually taken over by the forces of materialism and scientism, which tended to deny the emotional element predominant in romanticism. As a London intellectual, George Eliot had worked at the center of this tradition. Herbert Spencer and Auguste Comte were for a time her intellectual mentors. She followed the most advanced thinking and conduct of high Victorianism, but rationalism and science were not enough for a lady who had grown up in the provinces of England. When George Eliot began writing fiction in the late 1850s, she turned back in spirit to the midlands of England. At the same time she turned again to Wordsworth, the man who more than anyone else had taught her the romantic philosophy. By 1850, the year of his death, Wordsworth had become the prophet of a cult. What he meant to his followers can be seen in Matthew Arnold's "Memorial Verses." In the poem Arnold speaks of "Goethe's sage mind and Byron's force," but it is Wordsworth's "healing power" that Arnold celebrates. Wordsworth, he says, had the ability to make him feel, and this renewal of feeling brought with it a renewal of life. Like Arnold, George Eliot came to believe that man was losing his ability to feel, in the march of scientific progress, and that true spiritual progress lay in a renewal of life, accompanied by renewal of the emotions of love and joy. Both Arnold and George Eliot regarded her literary art as a way of portraying the search for emotional renewal in an age largely antagonistic to this renewal.

George Eliot's affinity for Wordsworth is paralleled by Hardy's affinity for Shelley. Both novelists had lost their childhood Christianity and, after a period of doubt, had turned to the romantics to find a philosophy of the renewal of the emotions. It is the kind of renewal traditionally found in religious worship, a renewal that frees man from indifference and from destructive emotions like hate and fear. George Eliot and Hardy both wanted to see man filled with the emotions of love and joy. They wanted a life akin to that of religious ecstasy. For George Eliot the key word is *enthusiasm*, which, as she uses it, implies a buoyancy of the soul and a throwing open of the windows of perception. For Hardy the great word is *joy*. What they found in the romantics, in addition to philosophy, was a set of myths and a general mythological attitude based on the search of a questing hero for a life of expanded consciousness and deepened emotions. Both George Eliot and Hardy put at the center of their best work a striving hero or heroine who seeks to achieve a higher spiritual state marked by an expansion of love, joy, and vision.

Like so many of the romantics, the heroes and heroines of both authors feel in themselves deep potentialities that call for fulfillment. The question to which they address themselves in their search for fulfillment is: what shall one do to find the true self? The true self experiences love and joy and is united with the processes of nature in their minute as well as in their spectacular manifestations. Hardy and George Eliot both turned back to nature and to the common people of the provinces, as Wordsworth did, to reestablish their organic connections with life. As young people, both had been led, by the dry rationalism of their times, into viewing life abstractly. But from the romantic poets they learned to cleanse the windows of perception so that they could see the commonplace as well as the extraordinary as part of the cosmic process. The vision of a unity underlying man and nature with an accompanying flow of love and joy is the romantic answer to the abstract insights of the rationalist. The romantic vision is not a refutation of the abstract view so much as a statement about a mode of existence that the abstract thinker and the knowledge gatherer tend to ignore. For the romantics, the way to the true self is through the development of the imagination so that one sees the visionary unity and experiences the flow of healing emotions.

The striving characters of George Eliot and Hardy are nonetheless defeated in their attempt to find the true self. They experience moments of unity and joy, but their own faults and the faults of others keep them from knowing for long the experience of the true self. Probably the greatest single vision of modern art is the defeat of man in his attempt to achieve a higher state of spiritual existence. It is this pervading sense of defeat in their fiction that gives the work of Hardy, George Eliot, and many other novelists in the second part of the nineteenth century a tone that today we call modern.

There are different ways of dealing with this defeat. Hardy, like D. H. Lawrence, depicts the passionate affirmation of life in the midst of tragic defeat. Tragedy for George Eliot is what it is for most people in our time—the slow erosion of talents and potentialities, a process most successfully depicted in modern times in the style of realism. The realist has a strong sense of the life of the individual character along with an insight into the interactions of individuals in complex social situations. The realist does not see life primarily in terms of forces, whether they be the forces of heredity and environment with which naturalists deal or the powerful overflow of the psyche that is the central concern of the neo-romantic. A study of the work of the realist is best made by studying the evolution and the interaction of characters in social situations. George Eliot, for instance, is at her strongest in depicting the gradual evolution of character in a society that is set against the spiritual strivings of the romantic idealist.

George Eliot's major characters fall into three groups: those who never know a spiritual call to higher life and who devote themselves to hindering the development of characters who do; those who have known the call but renounce it entirely; and those who, though defeated, never give up their idealism and continue to struggle to make the best of a bad job. Part of George Eliot's greatness is shown in the interaction of her major characters with minor provincial characters. Minor provincial characters in her work, like the rustics of Thomas Hardy, maintain an organic connection with the provincial setting without ever having known the romantic vision and its call to a higher life. They serve as a kind of chorus which comments both on the actions of those characters called to serve the vision and on the actions of mankind generally. George Eliot's provincial characters seem timeless and are chiefly what endeared her to those Victorians who longed to escape from the march of science and industrial progress. Her major characters illustrate her own concern with the romantic vision and its defeat in the modern world.

Three characters in George Eliot's fiction who best represent that idealistic character who makes the best of a bad job are Maggie Tulliver in *The Mill on the Floss*, Romola in *Romola*, and Dorothea Brooke in *Middlemarch*. All three are basically the same person and represent in the deepest sense the life of George Eliot. All three seek to serve the romantic vision, which sometimes seems almost undefinable. They feel that there is for them some higher life of love and duty, but they find little or no help from their societies in their search for this higher life of spiritual duty and renewal.

Maggie, for instance, is distinguished for her "wide hopeless yearning for that something, whatever it was, that was the greatest and best on this earth."[9] For Maggie the old-fashioned religion of her childhood is not enough. That religion for Maggie is summed up in her vicar: "The vicar of their pleasant rural parish was not a controversialist, but a good hand at whist, and one who had a joke always ready for a blooming female parishioner" (p. 597). But in the day of hardship, Victorian religion fails: " . . . it is then that despair threatens; it is then that the peremptory hunger of the soul is felt, and eye and ear are strained after some unlearned secret of our existence, which shall give to endurance the nature of satisfaction" (p. 599). The rustics still have some inherited knowledge of the secret of the true self, but the striving heroines of George Eliot live in a middle-class, commercial society that denies the hunger of the soul.

When George Eliot writes about rustics and craftsmen, she can portray successfully the renewal of life through the vision of unity provided by religion and through the release of love that springs in the heart of the rustic who is still close to nature. *Silas Marner*, the story of a linen-weaver who is purified and renewed by his love for a child, is a Wordsworthian ballad in prose. It does not appeal greatly to us today because it has in it little of the defeat and suffering that serious modern readers like. George Eliot's first important novel, *Adam Bede*, also deals with the good effects of lower-class religion on the lives of rustics. In this novel the spiritual leader is Dinah Morris, a lady minister of the Gospel. She has some of that power of love and joy and an understanding of the true self that the yearning heroines search for, but neither Maggie, Romola, nor Dorothea can turn to provincial religion. They must press forward in search of new ideals and visions, inspired as they are by the prophets of their own time.

George Eliot modeled Dinah Morris on an aunt, Elizabeth Evans, who was a Methodist preacher. But she never believed that women could lead the mainstream of society to a higher spiritual life. Gordon Haight, in the preface to *George Eliot and John Chapman*, says that Nat Bray's description of her as one who "was not fitted to stand alone" is the key to understanding her life.[10] In other words, George Eliot expected a man to lead the way, especially in matters of the spirit and intellect—ironic in view of the fact that she towered above many of the male literary figures of her time. The striving heroine in her books wants the leadership of a man who will show her how to make her own meaningful contribution to the growth of the spiritual life.

Although the striving heroine never finds the man she seeks, she nevertheless does not fall into despair. Maggie, for instance, turns back to her family, and to her brother in particular, to reaffirm the values of kinship. After losing faith in Renaissance Florence in general and in Savonarola in particular, Romola turns to self-sacrificing service to others. Dorothea marries Will Ladislaw and takes her place among the intelligentsia of her day, much in the manner of George Eliot making her peace with the world in the company of George Henry Lewes.

The George Eliot heroine turns to the small duty at hand, but she always knows this duty can never satisfy the yearning of her soul for a life of spiritual heroism. Prophets like Goethe, Wordsworth, Shelley, Carlyle, and Emerson had announced the coming of new spiritual heroes who would lead man to a higher life; but although the vision of the new man had arrived, the man himself had not. Those who would be his followers had sought and not found him, and they were left to make the best of the bad society they lived in.

In *The Mill on the Floss*, *Romola*, and *Middlemarch*, George Eliot depicts the search for a true spiritual leadership. Maggie Tulliver is released from the confines of her narrow provincial religion by Philip Wakem and Stephen Guest, but neither man can provide her with the vision that leads to the renewed life of joy and love. They have culture but not vision. For one grounded in the romantic philosophy, vision is necessary for the new life. In *Romola* and *Middlemarch* George Eliot depicts the confrontation of her romantic heroines with leaders of their time. *Romola* is set in Renaissance Italy and the heroine takes as her spiritual leader a man who she thinks has uttered the prophecy of a new day in Italy. In *Middlemarch*, which is set in Victorian England, Dorothea marries a man who has given up his active role as clergyman to write the book that will explain the true meaning of religion. But the Renaissance prophet and the Victorian sage are both failures. Savonarola, whose career had begun with great hopes, ends in the novel by identifying his own ego with the will of God. Casaubon, the clergyman who takes as his task the stating of the underlying vision of all myth and religion, becomes lost in pedantic detail. Both men are failures because of their enormous egoism.

Wordsworth believed that egoism blocked the vision of unity and the flow of love that accompanied it. The romantics provided in their poetry a new vision to sustain man, but none was able to translate this vision into social action. The reason was that most men were self-centered. The vision of the poets was not enough; what was needed also was the translation of vision into philosophy to feed the conscious mind, so that the egoism as well as the underlying unity that makes for love and joy could be understood for what they were.

In *Middlemarch* Dorothea comes to see that the first step in building a new and coherent social order is to find again the lost wisdom that will enable man to live by vision and love instead of by egoism. In the prelude to *Middlemarch*, George Eliot compares Dorothea and Saint Theresa. She says of the Spanish saint: "Theresa's passionate, ideal nature demanded an epic life: what were many volumed romances of chivalry and the social conquests of a brilliant girl to her."[11] Theresa had found her way of life "in the reform of a religious order" (p. xv). But George Eliot, referring to Dorothea, notes that "these later-born Theresas were helped by no coherent social faith and order which could perform the function of knowledge for the ardently willing soul" (p. xv). Without a coherent social order, Dorothea must find again that knowledge that will help her to develop her "passionate, ideal nature." For this reason she marries Mr. Casaubon, a clergyman and scholar whose life task will, if successful, provide a new philosophical basis for a unified society. Dorothea sees the opportunity of lending her own vision and energy to a man who will be exploring the very basis of religion—the failure of which, in the nineteenth century, had, as George Eliot and so many others believed, left the way open for the gradual disintegration of society.

Mr. Casaubon sets out to write a study of the underlying meaning of myth, which he calls his *Key to All Mythologies*. But being an egoist, he has no insight into the real meaning of the facts he gathers. He is a pedant who gets lost in his data because he lacks the Wordsworthian prescription for true insight, which is summed up in the following lines from *Tintern Abbey*: "While with an eye made quiet by the power / Of harmony and the deep power of joy / We see into the life of things." Dorothea, on the other hand, grasps the essential nature of the task of the scholar-visionary who must "see into the life of things" if he is to find the mythic wisdom necessary for man's triumph over despair. Dorothea had expected to aid her husband in his great work; instead, she finds herself rudely rejected. It is only as Casaubon is dying that he reaches out for her help. His task hopelessly confused, he believes that Dorothea will carry on his work after he dies, not for the sake of a new philosophical vision, but as a monument to his ego. But Dorothea sees his work for what it is, a failure: "It was not wonderful that, in spite of her small instruction, her judgment in this matter was truer than his: for she looked with unbiased comparison and healthy sense at probabilities on which he had risked all his egoism" (p. 512).

Mr. Casaubon hopes to control Dorothea's life and to force her to be a slave to his egoism long after his death. Good sense and clear insight do not desert Dorothea, however, and in time she marries a man very much like George Eliot's own mate, George Henry Lewes, a good man who pursues knowledge but who lacks deep vision. He is, George Eliot seems to be saying, the best man of the day but not a prophet or a seer. Thus Dorothea makes the best of a bad job, but she does not delude herself concerning her own suffering.

At the end of *Middlemarch* the author speaks for all the Dorotheas of modernity by saying that the people of her day are "preparing the lives of many Dorotheas, some of which may present a far sadder sacrifice than that of the Dorothea whose story we know" (p. 896). Even though Dorothea is given by life no epic task that her soul yearns for, she still performs the "little, nameless, unremembered, acts / Of kindness and of love" that Wordsworth speaks of in *Tintern Abbey*. Dorothea pours out her life in good deeds to others: "Her finely-touched spirit had still its fine issues, though they were not widely visible," the author tells us (p. 896).

Suffering has taught Dorothea the meaning of service to others through small acts of kindness, but her powerful soul knows that these acts are no substitute for the epic task. Though she never lives out the romantic vision in all its power and greatness, she does live out a portion of the Wordsworthian idealism in her deeds of "kindness and of love."

George Eliot seems to say that the life of Dorothea is the best of a bad job because there is no readily available knowledge and wisdom that can teach people how to develop their souls. Happiness is possible for rustic and provincial characters who feel no calling to seek a higher life, but for one like Dorothea all of her life is a kind of hidden tragedy as she watches the slow decline of her early dreams, though she does know small moments of joy because of her good deeds. The cause of her tragedy is to be found primarily in the egoism of those who should be the real leaders of society, not in forces of heredity or environment, as in naturalistic fiction—though it is true that the pettiness of the provinces does contribute to the destruction of Lydgate and to the frustration of Dorothea. Casaubon never knows a call to higher life but instead clings to the worship of his image of himself as a great author. Trapped by his narcissism, he betrays his life role of helping to provide leadership for man's spirit. He is paralleled in *Middlemarch* by Bulstrode, the religious humbug who stands for all the egoists who helped to give Victorian religion a bad name everywhere. Like Savonarola in *Romola*, Casaubon and Bulstrode seem like true spiritual leaders to many of the people of their day who do not know them well, but in fact they live only for their egos. Thus they delude and mislead most of the people of their time and make it impossible for people of true worth, like Dorothea, to find the help and encouragement they need to achieve the full development of their soul's demand.

The greatest bitterness of spirit is felt by those characters in George Eliot's work who have felt the call to development of soul, but who totally renounce the vision by following the false leadership of the egoists. Such a character in *Middlemarch* is Tertius Lydgate, who begins his career with a passion to help mankind. He is a doctor who hopes by scientific research to show man how to live in full and lasting health. Unlike Dorothea, he falls victim to the ideals of one who has followed the leaders of society in egoism and in the lust for power and money that accompanies this egoism. He allows himself to be dominated by the woman he marries, and becomes "what is called a successful man" (p. 892). His tragedy is that of the slow unraveling of a life, the unnoticed decline of a talented man devoured by a vampire. And Lydgate is intelligent enough to observe and understand his fate: "He once called her [his wife Rosamond] his basil plant; and when she asked for an explanation, said that basil was a plant which had flourished wonderfully in a murdered man's brains" (p. 893).

Lydgate dies at fifty, never having accomplished anything he set out to do. Nevertheless, he is envied by all his acquaintances because of his charming wife and his many paying patients. His life is ruined because, unlike Dorothea, he does not choose to live out that part of his idealism that can still function in an egocentric society. He loses everything because he does not choose to make the best of a bad job. His intelligence will not allow him to share the lust for money and power that governs his self-centered wife; yet because he turns his back on all of his old dreams of service to humanity, he finds himself destroyed by his wife's corrupt philosophy.

In a society dominated by egoists like Bulstrode and Casaubon, women like Rosamond are easily led astray because they have never heard any call to a better life. Not only are religion, philosophy, art, and science contaminated by egoism and the lust for power, but the home itself becomes a school for self-centeredness, destroying those who believe that the dominant way of life in a bad society is the only way of life there is. The lives of people like Dorothea—as well as the lives of rustics and provincials still untouched by the will to power—prove that a better life is still possible. However, in such a society idealists like Dorothea can only perform small acts of goodness, because when they try to enlarge their endeavors, particularly in the fields of scholarship and religion, they are blocked by the Bulstrodes and Casaubons. What is needed, George Eliot is continually saying, is a leadership that will show people how to live together in harmony, love, and joy.

Nineteenth-century prophets like Carlyle proclaimed the need for a new heroism to lead man out of the modern materialistic jungle, but their visions were hollow because they were based on a desire for such heroism and not on any known reality of such heroism. In two of her novels—*Felix Holt* and *Daniel Deronda*—George Eliot created characters who lead others to a higher life.

Both characters are failures because George Eliot never knew such people. *Felix Holt* is about a young man who sets out to achieve political reform and a Dorothea-like heroine to whom he gives both law and love. *Daniel Deronda*, George Eliot's last book, presents a hero who leads a band of spiritual seekers out of the old decaying society of nineteenth-century England to a new land. Daniel Deronda discovers that he is a Jew and, in order to help erect a modern Jewish state, becomes a Zionist. As a character Deronda is an even greater failure than Holt. The need for heroism is strongly felt in George Eliot's fiction, but there is in her work little depth of insight into the nature of the great man who would unify and spiritualize modern society.

By the time she came to write her last novel, George Eliot's deepest insight was into the nature of evil. F. R. Leavis has noted that *Daniel Deronda* is really two books. The Daniel Deronda section he considers almost worthless, but the section he calls *Gwendolen Harleth* he considers one of the great works of English fiction: " . . . Henry James wouldn't have written *The Portrait of a Lady* if he hadn't read *Gwendolen Harleth* (as I shall call the good part of *Daniel Deronda*), and of the pair of closely comparable works, George Eliot's has not only the distinction of having come first; it is decidedly the greater."[12] Grandcourt, who lures Gwendolen to her ruin, is easily the greatest villain in George Eliot's work. As an egoistic aristocrat, he sums up the author's view of the corruption of the ruling classes of nineteenth-century England. Like Lydgate in *Middlemarch* and Isabel in James' *The Portrait of a Lady*, Gwendolen is trapped by the inability to understand the reality of evil that lurks beneath a glittering surface. Unlike Isabel, who chooses to do what good she can, Gwendolen is overcome by the destructive element.

In her last work George Eliot shows the kind of psychological understanding of evil we see in Browning, Hawthorne, and James. Yet she must be seen in the totality of her work as one who stands, like so many great figures of the nineteenth century, with one foot in the old romantic idealism and the other in modern critical realism, which presents a decaying society and the tragedy that accompanies it. Her belief in the good that can still be done in modern society comes out of her romantic background. She never gave up her romantic idealism, although as a major novelist she must be called a realist. More than anyone else in our time, F. R. Leavis has put George Eliot in the tradition in which she belongs by showing her relationship to James and Tolstoy. He has said that she "is not as transcendently great as Tolstoy, but she *is* great, and great in the same way."[13] He has analyzed the quality of her work by demonstrating her psychological study of character and by pointing to her moral earnestness. Finally, he has summed up her best work by saying that it has "a Tolstoyan depth and reality."[14] Although George Eliot today does not have the wide following of either Tolstoy or James, I think in time a more careful consideration of her greatness will lead readers to see that she is both broader and deeper than these two. Furthermore, study of her work will yield an understanding of the complex relationships of romanticism with both modern realism and neoromanticism.

George Eliot's romanticism was, as I have tried to show, essentially Wordsworthian. An essential harmony existed, she believed, between man and his fellow man and between man and nature. An individual could deny this harmony and fall thereby into egoism, or he could, through a wise passiveness, accept it and live in joy and love. There were people in the nineteenth century who took this philosophy seriously enough to try to live it, but George Eliot and her heroines found that it was hard to live in a state of wise passiveness for long without the help of leaders who would demonstrate in their lives and utterances the meaning of unity, love, and joy.

George Eliot, early in her career, joined that branch of humanitarianism represented by the Utilitarians and became an assistant editor of the *Westminster Review*. She found, however, that though humanitarianism could help to lift the workers of England to a position of some social dignity, it could not create the emotional flow of acceptance that would unite rich and poor. Workers were still separated in their hearts from the middle class as much as provincials were from the new urbanites. George Eliot also found that her intellectual labors had dried up her own emotional flow, and, like Matthew Arnold and John Stuart Mill, she turned to Wordsworth to find the "healing power" that would restore the soul. Too great a concern with knowledge, she found, could create an emotional blight. Yet she also saw that modern science, like the romantic idealism she believed in, was based firmly on a sense of underlying unity. Nowhere does she state her own belief in unity better than in *The Mill on the Floss*: " . . . and we need not shrink from this comparison of small things with great; for does not science tell us that its highest striving is after the ascertainment of a unity which shall bind the smallest things with the greatest? ... there is nothing petty to the mind that has a large vision of relations, and to which every single object suggests a vast sum of conditions" (p. 596). This large vision of relations is often found in her work and it is accompanied by an emotional flow that binds man to man and man to nature.

In spite of the romantic vision of harmony and joy found in her work, the pervading tone of George Eliot's major fiction is tragic, because it deals primarily with the failure of the vision in a society dominated by egoists. What is particularly modern in her work is its honesty and clarity as well as its sense of the pain of modern life. Also modern is the author's psychological and sociological analysis, which is at once deep and subtle. George Eliot's particular approach to tragedy places her in one of two important schools of modern fiction. Both schools deal with the frustration of romantic idealism in a society that denies that idealism, but one school shows characters affirming life with powerful emotional reactions and the other depicts affirmation in small acts. One shows great collapse and the other the gradual, almost unseen decline of man's deeper emotional powers in a society that will not give the idealist scope for working out his vision.

We are still uncertain today what to call these schools of modern fiction; the terms often attached to them are at best ambiguous. It is generally agreed that George Eliot is a realist. Many critics have maintained that realism is a word that applies only to literary method; but technique in the hands of a master has behind it a certain tone, which means the author has an emotional attitude and a world view. The realism of George Eliot is clear-sighted, often humorous, always moralistic. It accepts the humble in life as well as the great. It depicts the slow development of character in social situations and shows the possibility of individual freedom. Even for those who accomplish something in life, there is a sense of tragic failure, summed up in Dorothea Brooke's words: "There is no sorrow I have thought more about than that— to love what is great, and try to reach it, and yet to fail" (p. 820). What Leavis calls the great tradition is mainly a realistic tradition. Realism includes, along with George Eliot, some of the great modern novelists: Stendhal, Flaubert, Tolstoy, Turgenev, James, Mann.

The other school is equally important. Because it emphasizes strong emotions it has been called neoromanticism. Great names in this school of fiction are Emily Brontë, Hardy, Melville, Dostoevski, Lawrence, and Faulkner. It is this tradition that E. M. Forster has in mind in *Aspects of the Novel* when he singles out Brontë, Melville, Dostoevski, and Lawrence for special praise. He sees in their work a deep lyrical power missing in the work of another novelist he examines, who does not have this lyrical flow. That author is George Eliot. But I see no reason in preferring one school to the other. Both contain great names, and in fact the great figures in both schools—and George Eliot is certainly one of these figures—have some of the qualities of both realism and neoromanticism. But in each of them one viewpoint tends to prevail, and it is this prevailing trend that must serve as a basis for studying the two schools of fiction.

What the realists and neoromantics accomplished might best be understood when their work is seen in relationship to that of a third school, peopled by many of the second-rate writers of our time: naturalism. All three schools use certain realistic techniques, such as the careful recording of ordinary details. Writers in the three schools often have philosophies that are in part romantic. But the philosophy that dominates naturalism denies individual freedom by claiming that man is controlled by his heredity and environment. In contrast, the writers of the other two schools show that even in tragedy man can choose the good instead of the bad, thus maintaining a sense of his own individuality while at the same time affirming the powers of the cosmos that work both for harmony and love and for destruction and chaos.

Wherever the possibility of freedom of choice is denied, as it is in the work of the naturalists, then literature suffers. The greatness of a realist like George Eliot lies, in part, in the fact that she affirms the freedom of the individual caught in a tragic society, and that she writes with a clarified viewpoint that helps the individual to maintain a sense of his own identity. Naturalism encourages the individual to accept without hope the forces that destroy him, to accept, that is, the death of his humanity. The Viennese psychiatrist Viktor E. Frankl, in his account of life in a concentration camp, sums up the difference between the two viewpoints when he says that with a clear view of man's freedom it is possible to "make a decision, a decision which determined whether you would or would not submit to those powers which threatened to rob you of your very self, your inner freedom. . . ."[15] Frankl shows how some prisoners made personal decisions to remain human and how others succumbed to the routine of the concentration camp and were turned into something inhuman. He notes that one of the values cultivated by those who chose to remain human is clarity of mind. To illustrate, he quotes Spinoza: "Emotion, which is suffering, ceases to be suffering as soon as we form a clear and precise picture of it."[16]

A book like *Middlemarch* represents the triumph of clarity, humor, and individual free choice over the forces of chaos, egoism, and slavery, because it shows how a few people can live in freedom and sanity in a society dominated by egomaniacs. The fiction of the two great schools of modern realism and neoromanticism contains an awareness of both the unity underlying all experience and the freedom of choice of the individual. Both ideas are important in the philosophies of romanticism, and both are developed by the great novelists of the West.

Finally, one may ask about the vision of the romantics concerning the coming of men who will lead humanity beyond the tragedy of modern life to a unified society that will help idealists to live out their visions of joy and harmony. Was George Eliot's own vision of new spiritual leadership a delusion? I think not. The poets of the romantic revival were prophets of a new day of unity and joy. Like everyone else in their time they could not live out their own idealism and were forced to make the best of a bad job. But they, and those like George Eliot who adopted their viewpoints, adumbrate and help to prepare for a time when men will live once again in unity and joy. They preserve a fragment of the vision of unity and they show what happens to those who lose all sense of unity. A few of the greatest writers—like Tolstoy and Dostoevski—show characters pushing on toward a personal fulfillment containing enlarged and renewed vision. In the work of these two great Russian novelists, and of novelists like them in this century, there is a strong forecast of the possibilities of epic heroism.

When *Middlemarch* was being written in the late nineteenth century, there were only a few signs of the coming of new spiritual leadership; but since World War I many writers have pointed toward the coming of the wise man, the seer, the shaman, the saint. In *The Cocktail Party*, T. S. Eliot defines the task of the good man of the old, dying society of the modern world as that of making the best of a bad job, but in Celia he depicts a character who sets out on the journey that will lead to sainthood. Modern poets like Eliot say that society can only be unified by the person who has first achieved an inner unity and then teaches others how to find this unity.

A study of the visionary and mythic progress of man indicates that the loss and recovery of unity and the healing emotions are recurring facts of man's existence. Not only have many poets and novelists in our time caught a glimpse of the coming of new sages, but scholars and scientists have also played a role in this process of recovering the image of the spiritual leader. In the twentieth century, students of myth, religion, and psychology—people like C. G. Jung, Mircea Eliade, and Joseph Campbell—have worked out in scholarly detail the patterns of social decay and renewal as they are affected by the disappearance of that kind of visionary leader for which George Eliot's Dorothea Brooke so desperately longs. But for Dorothea and her creator this work had not come, and the study of myth remained in the hands of men like Mr. Casaubon, who sought the inner meaning of the world's mythologies and religions but lacked the vision to see the meaning of the saint who stands at the center of myth and religion.

I have said that at the heart of George Eliot's fictional tragedy is the absence of a sustaining vision of unity that will serve as the basis of true community, though the author was aware through her study of Wordsworth and other poets that such a vision was possible for man. Tragedy for Dorothea Brooke is also based on an inability to discover either a master or what the author calls in the prelude to *Middlemarch* a "coherent social faith and order which could perform the function of knowledge for the ardently willing soul." These "later-born Theresas" must suffer tragedy because they cannot find the epic role they are meant to fill. George Eliot is clear enough concerning this need for the epic life in her reference to her human standard of heroism, St. Theresa of Avila, who demanded and found an epic life in the religious life of the day. And even though George Eliot knows that tragedy is the lot of people like St. Theresa in our day, she is aware of the possibility of new epics at some later time. The achievement of George Eliot in creating a modern tragedy about a "later-born" Theresa is sometimes marred by the author's own self-pity; had she known that tragedy is a literary form as worthy as epic, she might have achieved a greater literary objectivity. Had she known that the ful-fillment of a tragic destiny in certain periods of history is neces-sary to prepare the way for epic accomplishments in other periods, she might have maintained a greater artistic calm. Yet her achievement is so great as it is that, given her involvement in a newly emerging modern period, one can hardly ask for more.

Thomas Hardy
and the Tragedy of Neoromanticism

Both George Eliot and Thomas Hardy were Victorian intellectuals who pondered and often accepted the skepticism and meliorism of the second half of the nineteenth century, but as artists they turned to the poets of the romantic revival and to a contemplation of their native heaths to inspire them to create the first novels in English that were fully modern. George Eliot mastered the style of psychological realism and, as Leavis and others have so carefully shown, served as inspirer of Henry James and others who would seek to maintain a balanced view of society while exploring the inner depths of certain complex characters. Hardy began as a realist in *Desperate Remedies* in the early seventies because realism was the only fictional style he knew at that time. He had been in the sixties an unknown poet who, with Swinburne and others, felt himself to be part of a new romantic revolt, in effect a neoromanticism that would surface in the nineties and would defy the rationalism and skepticism of earlier decades. Hardy would find himself as a novelist when he tapped these neoromantic currents, and his novels would have a far different quality than those of George Eliot. Both would be essentially tragic—but the tragic effects of psychological realism are not the same as those of neoromanticism.

41

George Eliot turned to the mythic vision of Wordsworth's poetry to free herself from the fragmented thinking of skepticism that she had encountered as a professional intellectual, but she retained in her style the techniques of realism, particularly irony and use of surface detail, to protect herself from the excessive emotionalism often found in romanticism, both the pure emotionalism of earlier romanticism and the debased romanticism found in the sentimental chapters of some of the novels of Dickens, Thackeray, and lesser writers. Indeed, so did Hardy, whose use of irony is famous and whose use of detail, particularly in his country scenes, is widely admired. But when Hardy came to write his major novels—*The Return of the Native, The Mayor of Casterbridge, Tess of the D'Urbervilles, Jude the Obscure*—he evolved a style that can only be called romantic—suffused with emotion, filled with defiance of a corrupt society, bathed in an atmosphere heavy with symbolism—a style that projects, as J. O. Bailey spent much of his scholarly life demonstrating, an environment filled with extrasensory and preternatural events. The major feature of Hardy's fictional romanticism is his presentation of characters with strong emotions who enact a kind of tragedy that must be called romantic, or, more precisely, neoromantic, since Hardy was at the beginning of a new and modern wave of romanticism.

Possibly because modernism is such a difficult quality to analyze, and probably because we still think of ourselves as being modern even while we are moving into a new, postmodern period, there is still much misunderstanding about the concepts of neoromanticism, as well as about modern tragedy. There is no better author than Hardy in modern literature to provide insights into these two problems, because Hardy consciously worked with concepts of tragedy, both ancient and modern, to construct what he considered to be tragedies concerning people of our time. Also, he was influenced both by the romantic poets and by contemporary poets like Swinburne who thought of themselves as the beginning of a new wave of romantic revolt. Ironically, as a poet, Hardy's style is mainly realistic and shows the influence of Browning, but it contains, largely suppressed beneath an ironic and realistic surface, some of the old romantic fire of revolt and outrage that Hardy reserved for his major novels. The two problems, as I will seek to show, are vitally linked because the basis of Hardy's tragedy is not so much the Aristotelian concepts that he knew so well as it is the struggle of romantic individuals who get their power to suffer tragically from Hardy's own romanticism. It is, I believe, Hardy's blatant romanticism that makes his best novels seem more like authentic tragedies to readers in our time than the works of realists like George Eliot, James, or Tolstoy. In fact, the revival of Hardy's fiction all over the world that began after 1958, particularly in Japan, is one of the most interesting phenomena of literary appreciation in this century, and the rapid growth of interest in Hardy is a sign that Hardy's blend of neoromanticism and tragedy says much to people of our period.

Not until the 1970s was there a sustained effort by some critics to consider Hardy's tragedies on their merit. The general trend of literary criticism for many years had been to deny Hardy any validity as a writer of tragedies. Much of the attack was based on the idea that philosophical concepts like that of the Immanent Will, which Hardy sometimes used as a metaphor, reduced the individuality of Hardy's tragic heroes to impotence. Concentrating on philosophy, critics have usually ignored powerful currents of romantic feeling that propel Hardy's protagonists to their tragic doom. Thus the venerable historian of the English novel, Ernest Baker, wrote in the thirties that Hardy's heroes suffer not defeat "but paralysis of the will."[1] Samuel C. Chew in *A Literary History of England* sums up a standard critical view of the forties: "Critics have deplored the sacrifice of tragic grandeur which this concept [the Immanent Will] requires, for since human protagonists are reduce to automata so that even in their struggles against destiny they are merely pulled to and fro by the 'halyards' of the Will, there is no room for that eternal conflict which is the essence of tragedy."[2] Even Albert J. Guerard, who brought to his studies of Hardy new psychological perceptions of inner struggle, maintains that Jude is not a tragic hero, "if only because he is a modern."[3] But the most devastating blow ever delivered against Hardy as a tragic novelist was dealt by Arthur Mizener, who charged that there is no tragic tension in *Jude the Obscure* because Hardy was unable to place the source of his idealism "outside of time."[4] In his well-known article in the *Southern Review* Mizener in effect says that Hardy's philosophy of meliorism makes it impossible for him to be tragic and that meliorism is the basis of Hardy's fictional vision. Thirty years later a perceptive critic like J. Hillis Miller would place the theory of the Immanent Will at the center of

Hardy's vision: "The Immanent Will is the unconsciousness of nature and of all Hardy's characters. It is his own unconsciousness too. The Will is the secret motive force behind everything which happens. . . ."[5] Thus the tragic nature of Hardy's characters is once again denied because their individuality is seen as being submerged in some larger, all-controlling will.

Mizener's view of Hardy, in many ways echoed by Guerard with psychoanalytic variations, is that of modern secular liberalism, which makes humanitarianism the central fact of Hardy's novels. Miller's view of Hardy, on the other hand, would turn him into a naturalist by showing his characters to be chained to an immanent process in which they lose the native force of action. With this kind of critical analysis still having an effect on the appreciation of Hardy, it is necessary to stress the centrality of the romantic vision in Hardy's work and to affirm that romanticism is primarily an outlook that emphasizes above all others the revolt, the outrage, the emotional release of the individual. With this in mind, one would have to say that the dominant philosophical outlook in Hardy must be called existential, a philosophical term not known to Hardy and one hardly ever properly understood today. For definition of the term we can turn to a noted Nietzsche scholar, Walter Kaufmann, who says that existentialism "is not a philosophy but a label for several widely different revolts against traditional philosophy," and that "one essential feature shared by all these men [writers and philosophers under discussion] is their perfervid individualism."[6] Perfervid individualism is what romanticism and neoromanticism are all about.

In the work of Jeannette King and Michael Millgate, published in the seventies, we get a more complex view of Hardy's tragedies, though King makes it clear that what is still needed are new concepts of tragedy for modern literature. In dealing with a character like Eustacia, she points out that the character's "world offers no opportunity for the grand life-style and noble super-human actions she associates with tragic heroines."[7] Millgate is even more pronounced about the importance of the individual at the center of Hardyean tragedy, though very few could accept his belief that Henchard is comparable in grandeur to Lear or Ahab: "Yet Hardy nonetheless compels us to recognize in Henchard a man of almost superhuman grandeur, of great if uncontrollable passions, a tragic hero whom it is not ludicrous to compare with Captain

Ahab, or even with King Lear."[8] Thus, criticism of Hardy in the seventies begins to draw the reader back to Hardy's own view of himself as artist and creator of character—a view of romantic defiance of both social and cosmic ills and an awareness of the psychic wounds of individuals. If there is an essential center for most serious modern literature, it has to be the complex and interesting individual. Aristotle may have thought plot was the most important part of tragedy—and King points out that Hardy went along with this idea—but it is the individual character who causes the serious reader, nourished as he is on characters like Lear, Hamlet, and Ahab, to become involved in modern tragedies. And, as I will point out, it is the romanticism of Hardy that gives his characters the kind of force that reminds us of Shakespearean and even of Greek tragedy. What the modern reader is concerned with is not so much an author's use of a theory of tragedy, or the use of a particular philosophy (which might cause Hardy to write that great misleading phrase "President of the Immortals"), but rather the tragic effects produced by the portrayal of powerful characters.

For there to be that particular esthetic pleasure that millions have gained from involvement in tragic art, there must be an affirmation of the glory of man. F. L. Lucas, in considering the tragedies of John Webster, makes this clear: "The Muse of Tragedy indeed is of her nature infidel at heart. . . . It is not the glory of God that she declares, but the glory of man in his doomed defiance of his destiny and the bounds it has set to his mortal endeavour, whether it be Prometheus on Caucasus, or Capaneus on the wall of seven gated Thebes, or Faust in his study, or Macbeth on the wall of Dunsinane."[9]

As Lucas suggests, the great tragic effects of pity and fear, the Aristotelian catharsis, are bound up with this "doomed defiance" of a great man, regardless of what philosophy the author holds. We feel pity for the doomed hero, but there is a kind of terror or awe, or fear, as Aristotle puts it, present in his downfall. Edith Hamilton in *The Greek Way to Western Civilization* states: "Only individuals can suffer and only individuals have a place in tragedy. The personages of the Greek drama show first and foremost what suffering is in a great soul, and therefore they move us to pity and awe."[10] Although tragedy may deal with ethical and philosophical problems, it is not philosophical speculation in a work of literature that produces the effects of pity and fear. Hardy handles moral problems, but like all writers with a tragic view of the world he is not primarily a problem novelist. He had, as Abercrombie says, a profound "tragic apprehension of the world."[11] In his great novels Hardy saw man beaten down by forces within and without himself, and sought to record man's eternal struggle with fate. This is also what the Greeks and Shakespeare did.

It is true that Hardy, at least in *Jude*, seems to alternate between a philosophy of grim pessimism that sees man as the victim of ruthless forces and a metaphysics that will allow for the possible development of man and society into something better in the future. It is possible to accept either or both of these philosophies and arrive at a view of man that is not tragic. Naturalists, like Dreiser, see small, struggling individuals crushed by imponderable forces. On the other hand, writers who are consistently melioristic expect man to set the world right sometime in the near future. Despite being, philosophically, something of a meliorist and also a pessimistic naturalist, Hardy the author was essentially neither. He was a tragic poet who could never see man as little or insignificant. The tragic poet never loses sight of the fact that there is something in the nature of things that is working for man's overthrow. If he has a metaphysical turn of mind he may, like Hardy, seek to erect a system to explain man's fate; and he may, again like Hardy, wonder what, if anything, can be done to alleviate man's tragic lot. A bent for metaphysics and social philosophy does not change the essential nature of the tragic poet. The final test of his greatness lies in his creation of great tragic heroes.

For this reason I would like to examine Hardy's view of "the glory of man in his doomed defiance of his destiny." Instead of bringing a formal definition of tragedy to bear on Hardy's work, let us see what tragic effects Hardy achieves. Let us find out exactly what kind of tragedy Hardy did write. We at least can point to individual works and say that here are to be found the tragic effects of pity and awe. Above all, we must look squarely at the protagonist to determine if he is indeed a tragic hero, for without the tragic hero there can be no tragedy.

Some tragedies are unquestionably greater than others, and it is impossible to discuss tragedy without calling forth the names of Shakespeare and the three great Greeks. There are certainly differences between Shakespeare's and Hardy's tragic heroes. Shakespeare's heroes with their rich intellect and imagination reveal at great dramatic moments in the plays the breadth and depth of

man's tragic existence. Their own self-realization and their realization of man's tragic nature give them a kind of universality that
Hardy's heroes do not always have. Both Greek and Shakespearean
heroes have a loftiness and a grand style that Hardy at his best
cannot equal. There is certainly neither an Oedipus nor a Lear in
Hardy. The question remains: just how tragic are Hardy's heroes,
and what do Hardy's tragic effects consist of?

Hamilton refutes the old notion that a tragic hero has to be of
exalted social rank: "Tragedy's one essential is a soul that can feel
greatly. Given such a one and any catastrophe may be tragic."[12]
She points out that the "great soul in pain and in death transforms
pain and death."[13] If Hardy created anything, he created souls capable of great feeling, souls capable of exaltation. When Tess cries,
"I thought, Angel, that you loved me—me, my very self! If it is I
you do love, O, how can it be that you look and speak so?," we
realize that we are confronted with a certain nobility of passion.[14]
A defeated Henchard using every trick he knows to keep the love
of Elizabeth-Jane is not easily forgotten. Because of the very
strength of their passions Hardy's characters demand our sympathy, and we experience a feeling that someone of great worth has
been lost when we see them destroyed. The glory of man cannot
be fully realized except at the sight of the fall of a great soul. Paradoxically, real tragedy reaffirms life. It is the passionate defiance
of fate by Jude, Sue, Henchard, and the other great protagonists
that makes their downfall more than merely pathetic. A character
who goes to his doom without fully facing the forces of evil that
work to bring about his downfall may be pathetic but cannot be
tragic. The tragic hero cries out defiantly against the fact that the
forces arrayed against him must finally bring about his downfall.
It is a complex attitude—this acceptance and defiance. It demands
not only a passionate spirit but also an imaginative intellect that
realizes the enormity of the forces of evil. There is the fierce defiance of Macbeth's "Blow wind! Come Wrack!" and his sad acceptance of the inevitable: "They have tied me to a stake." There is
Macbeth's sad realization that "all our yesterdays have lighted
fools / The way to dusty death."

Concerning the type of acceptance that is not acquiescence or
resignation but rather is tragic defiance, Hamilton says:

To endure because there is no other way out is an attitude
that has no commerce with tragedy. Acceptance is the temper

of mind that says, "Thy will be done" in the sense of "Lo, I come to do thy will." It is active, not passive. . . . It accepts life, seeing clearly that thus it must be and not otherwise. . . . Men are helpless so far as their fate is concerned, but they can ally themselves with the good, and in suffering and dying, die and suffer nobly.[15]

I suggest that Hardy's greatest heroes have this attitude of acceptance and defiance. Although Tess finally accepts her fate calmly, she also rages against the forces of evil that have worked for her downfall, as, for example, her denunciation of Alec Stoke-D'Urberville indicates:

"And then my dear, dear husband came home to me . . . and I did not know it! . . . And you had used your cruel persuasion upon me . . . you did not stop using it—no—you did not stop! . . . And he is dying—he looks as if he is dying! . . . And my sin will kill him and not kill me!! O, you have torn my life all to pieces . . . made me a victim, a caged wretch! . . . My own true husband will never, never—O Heaven—I can't bear this!—I cannot!" (pp. 486–87)

Henchard cries out in defiance at Elizabeth-Jane: "What do you say?—*Mr.* Henchard? Don't, don't scourge me!"[16] With his final realization that he has forfeited her love, he also accepts with "proud superiority": "I'll never trouble 'ee again, Elizabeth-Jane—no, not to my dying day! Good-night. Good-bye!" (p. 423). His will reveals an attitude of both defiance and acceptance. In it is a deep realization of some ingrained evil both in himself and in the scheme of things. The defiance of a protagonist who fails to realize the full extent of evil pitted against him is meaningless. Sue in *Jude the Obscure* at times reveals a prophetic insight into the evil that brings calamity upon her and her loved ones. Note her moving speech made after the death of her children:

"We went about loving each other too much—indulging ourselves to utter selfishness with each other! We said—do you remember?—that we would make a virtue of joy. I said it was Nature's intention, Nature's law and *raison d'être*, that we should be joyful in what instincts she afforded us—instincts which civilization had taken upon itself to thwart. What dreadful things I said! And now Fate has given us this stab in the back for being such fools as to take Nature at her word!"[17]

The ill fortune that befalls a tragic hero is the result not only of forces working against him from without but of forces within him that hasten him toward his downfall. Aristotle tells us that the tragic hero is not preeminently virtuous but must make some error of judgment.[18] Hardy's great heroes—Tess, Sue, Jude, Henchard, Clym, and Eustacia—are all driven by forces within them that act as tragic flaws. The exact nature of the flaws of Hardy's heroes is usually left undefined. They come to grief through the blind force of passion or through a lack of sufficient knowledge of the world around them or through some tormenting impulse. Jude has a weakness for women and drink. Henchard is driven by compulsions that turn awry his best plans. Even Tess, who always seems much more sinned against than sinning, finally turns again to Alec, an action that is certainly an error of judgment. With all his ideals, Clym is the dupe of his own passions. His failure to go to his mother to be reconciled helps bring about her death. He can only stare in amazement at his own mistakes. After his mother's death he tells Thomasin, "You laboured to win her round; I did nothing. I, who was going to teach people the higher secrets of happiness, did not know how to keep out of that gross misery which the most untaught are wise enough to avoid."[19] Along with their realization of the evil of the world, Hardy's characters usually come around to realizing their own fatal flaws. There is a passionate realization of a dark force within, as when Henchard cries, "Why should I still be subject to these visitations of the devil when I try so hard to keep him away?" (p. 397).

I have suggested that Hardy's tragic heroes have a passionate defiance and a final acceptance, both of which spring from a realization of, and a certain amount of insight into, the nature of the forces that bring tragedy. The forces of destruction come from within and without. Tragic awe and terror result from seeing a passionate but noble person defy and finally accept the forces of destruction. At the same time, pity follows the realization by the reader of the waste of an awesome person. Despite their flaws, we sympathize with Hardy's characters. Their passion and their ability to suffer help to reveal their great worth. The characters finally prove themselves to be far nobler than the forces that destroy them. But what are the sources of their deep passion? What makes them so memorable? To understand Hardy's tragic heroes, one must realize that they are romantic heroes worthy to be ranked with the most remarkable heroes of the great romantic tradition of the nineteenth century. They are heroes whose desires are never fulfilled, but whose spirits, in the best traditions of tragedy, are never crushed.

The nineteenth century had many romantic heroes. They were often figures of great daring. Byron's Manfred defies the spirits who come for him by boasting of power achieved by his own strength. Shelley's Prometheus and Goethe's Faust labor for mankind, while Melville's Ahab sets sail looking for the secret of existence. Other heroes strive to achieve higher states of personal existence. Emily Brontë's two great romantic heroes, Heathcliff and Cathy, strive to be united. Hardy's Jude and Sue strive in much the same way. In the case of both couples the two lovers are separated and are driven by an inner compulsion to become one. Phillotson's description of Jude and Sue as being "one person split in two" reminds us of Cathy's fervent "Nelly, I am Heathcliff."[20] Those heroes who were seeking greater personal development were often doing so through some kind of union with another person. Interestingly, this union often had little or nothing to do with sex: Cathy is almost sexless and so are Angel, Sue, and Tess. It is a kind of spiritual union with another of like soul. Another good example of this is Sue's affair before she met Jude.

The romantics were always seeking wide varieties of experience and personal development, but as the century wore on more and more of them turned away from the outside world. Edgar Allan Poe created Al Aaraaf as a place where the soul could realize those intense moments that it only glimpsed in the drab everyday world. By the end of the century this self-exploration to achieve new spiritual experience was being carried on by many of the greatest literary artists of France and England. Holbrook Jackson describes the new romanticism of the decadents:

> It is a demand for wider ranges, newer emotional and spiritual territories, fresh woods and pastures new for the soul. If you will, it is a form of imperialism of the spirit, ambitious, arrogant, aggressive, waving the flag of human power over an ever wider and wider territory. And it is interesting to recol-

lect that decadent art periods have often coincided with such waves of imperial patriotism as passed over the British Empire and various European countries during the Eighteen Nineties.[21]

If the reader thinks this has little to do with Hardy, let him reread Sue's letter to Phillotson in *Jude*: "I know you mean my good. But I don't want to be respectable. To produce 'Human development in its richest diversity' (to quote Humboldt) is to my mind far above respectability. No doubt my tastes are low—in your view—hopelessly low!" (p. 272). I am not suggesting that Hardy has a great deal in common with the decadents, but there are striking similarities, especially in the character of Sue. Actually Hardy was deeply influenced by earlier romantics like Shelley, but the perversity and the thirsting for forbidden fruit of the decadents can also be detected in some of Hardy's characters.

Readers of Hardy will recognize Jude, Sue, and Eustacia Vye as romantic heroes of the Cathy-Heathcliff stamp. Probably the most fully developed romantic hero in Hardy is Eustacia. For her love is to be a great means of fulfillment. "Her greatest desire is to be loved to madness . . . " (p. 81). She is a living embodiment of passion. At a first reading Tess and Henchard might seem to have little in common with such romantic heroes as Eustacia and Jude. But both are very much in the tradition. It is through the love of Angel that Tess hopes to find fulfillment. Her deep passions are not aroused until she is frustrated. She does not pant for love and ecstasy like Sue and Eustacia, but her strongest drives are directed toward this higher state of union with Angel. In Angel's presence she is capable of exaltation: "Tess was conscious of neither time nor space. The exaltation which she had described as being producible at will by gazing at a star, came now without any determination of hers . . . " (p. 158). Even before she met Angel, Tess was ripe for love: "The irresistible, universal, automatic tendency to find enjoyment, which pervades all life, from the meanest to the highest, had at length mastered her, no longer counteracted by external pressures" (p. 134).

The search for romantic joy, the by-product of a heightened spiritual state, is found in many nineteenth-century romantic poets and especially in Shelley. Hardy's heroes are only continuing the tradition. Sue Bridehead, a sort of latter-day Shelley, proclaims the new reign of joy: "I feel that we have returned to Greek joyousness, and have blinded ourselves to sickness and sorrow, and have forgotten what twenty-five centuries have taught the race since their time . . . " (p. 362). For Shelley, Swinburne, and many others joy was associated with classical paganism. As several critics have noted, there is in Hardy's work a longing for the paradisiacal state—a state which Hardy's heroes can never reside in for very long at a time.

Henchard as a romantic hero is somewhat more complex than the others. As *The Mayor of Casterbridge* opens, he seems to belong to that branch of heroes who mold the outside world with their wills. The iron will is Henchard's trademark. As the book progresses, however, he seeks affection—a continued closeness to his beloved Elizabeth-Jane: "Shorn one by one of all other interests, his life seemed centering on the personality of the stepdaughter whose presence but recently he could not endure" (p. 373). Being near Elizabeth-Jane uplifts the battered man's spirit. She is nearly as necessary to him as Sue is to Jude. Jude is at once driven by the desire for union with Sue and by the need for greater intellectual development. Seen in this light, *Jude the Obscure* is much more than just the "history of a worthy man's education," as Mizener calls it.[22] It is a story of a man reaching for—and grasping momentarily—a higher spiritual and intellectual sphere. Clym Yeobright is another hero who has more than one drive. In his desire to better the lot of his fellows we see some of the old Promethean fire, but in his passionate love for Eustacia we find the quest for joy and ecstasy—the heightened spiritual state.

The point of this discussion of the romantic hero in Hardy should be obvious by now. Tragedy for Hardy is the defeat of the romantic hero's desire to reach a higher spiritual state. The drives of Hardy's characters to achieve states of love and ecstasy are powerful enough to make his chief characters among the most passionate in English literature. Put Thackeray's or George Eliot's or nearly anybody else's characters beside them and their real intensity will become evident. In the early part of the century, with the first wave of romanticism, the great heroes often triumphed. Faust and Prometheus are two great examples of romantic triumph. By mid-century, romantic heroes were finding it harder to gain the object of desire. But for all their suffering, two mid-century heroes, Cathy and Heathcliff, are able to overcome death by a kind of supernatural triumph. This solution is not possible for Hardy's heroes. The nature of things in Hardy's universe is set against triumph. They are defeated by chance without and their own passions within. In *Prometheus Unbound* Shelley envisioned the creation of the paradisiacal state on earth. This vision is impossible for Hardy. The bird of joy has fallen. In Hardy's poem, "Shelley's Skylark," the bird lies afield

> In Earth's oblivious eyeless trust
> That moved a poet to prophecies—
> A Pinch of unseen, unguarded dust.[23]

Failure to reach higher states of personal development is the fate of Hardy's great heroes; but, it must be emphasized again, their spirits are never crushed. A protagonist such as Tess may finally accept defeat, but her great personality is not broken. Power is the mark of the romantic hero—power and the need for more power in order to attain some far-off, ever receding goal. The power they have and the power they seek give them a heroic stature; they thus have the necessary loftiness to make their fate truly tragic.

It is only after understanding the nature of the romantic hero that one can answer Mizener's attack on *Jude the Obscure* as a book centered in the philosophy of meliorism. The tragedy of Jude and Sue turns on the defeat of their desire for a higher state of personal development. Jude seeks both prophetic power and intellectual development as well as the ecstasy of union with Sue. After his defeat he acknowledges that he and Sue have lived fifty years too soon; already there is a possibility, he says, that poor students will be helped. This, I take it, is what Mizener would call idealism that is placed in the future instead of "outside of time." Actually, the world as Hardy knew it could never allow heroes like Jude and Sue to fulfill themselves. Simply giving scholarships to poor students might help Jude to become a young prophet, but it could never bring Sue and Jude into that heightened state of ecstasy their spirits long for. There is also something basically wrong in their own natures. Jude cries out that "human nature can't help being itself" (p. 431), and Sue replies by saying that it must learn self-mastery. Her words become a mockery because there is something within herself that drives her to self-torture. Jude sees this and cries out against it: "That a woman-poet, a woman-seer, a woman whose soul shone like a diamond—whom all the wise of the world would have been proud of, if they could have known you—should degrade herself like this! I am glad I had nothing to do with Divinity—damn glad—if it's going to ruin you in this way!" (p. 429). After reading a passage like this, one realizes that the romantic protagonists in Jude are up against more than corrigible evils in society. A malignant fate in the form of chance without and their own irrational, ungovernable impulses within (their tragic flaws) brings about their downfall when they seek the paradisiacal state—a state that exists only in some kind of eternity.

Mizener is disturbed about the effect that Hardy's meliorism has on his tragedy. There is certainly a kind of meliorism in Hardy that believes to a certain extent in a better order of life in the future. The romantics were many-sided. In their desire for spiritual advancement, they worked for the overthrow of social barriers which they believed stood in the way. Shelley envisioned a utopia in which man was free to fulfill himself. Hardy had a touch of this utopian spirit. But the world that Clym and Jude longed for was something entirely different from the everyday world with outstanding abuses corrected. It would have had to be the paradisiacal state where all striving is stilled and joy reigns forever; it would certainly have had to be a place "outside of time."

Hardy was not all of a piece in his world outlook. He was capable of both a tragic apprehension of this world and a belief that the world might, in some cases, be made better for men. Possibly Hardy's utopianism detracts from the power of his tragedies. Regardless of this, Hardy's vision in his great novels is fundamentally tragic. To concern oneself too much with his meliorism or with his supposed lack of ethical significance is to take the risk not only of losing sight of his tragic effects but also of missing his contribution to our deeper understanding of man. Like Dostoevski and Poe, Hardy explored the depths of man's soul and found dark forces there that helped to drive him to destruction in spite of his surface desires for worldly happiness. It is particularly in the torn and divided souls of Jude, Sue, and Henchard that we see these forces at work—forces that finally act as fatal flaws to bring about the downfall of otherwise worthy individuals. They seek undefined goals of ecstasy and power and, unable to achieve them, turn on themselves. The thwarted ego of the romantic is finally driven by forces both within and without to destruction.

Some critics may hold that it is impossible for romantic heroes to be tragic. Such a view seems to limit unnecessarily the field from which tragic heroes can be drawn. Certainly the sympathetic reader must feel a certain amount of awe and pity while watching the downfall of characters so powerful as Clym, Henchard, Tess, Sue, and Jude.

There is in Hardy's later work a vision of the continuing development of man in this life, and it is this sense that links him with the continuance of a neoromantic tradition and with the concept of the journey beyond tragedy. Literary historians like Holbrook Jackson and Ernest Baker have tended to limit the romanticism of the nineties to one decade. Baker even says that the major romanticism of Wordsworth, Keats, and Shelley, which found expression in the novels of the Brontë sisters and Meredith, had its "backwash in the period described by some as 'the Romantic Nineties.'"[24] The nineties period no doubt marked the end of something, but it was also the beginning in Britain of a new and darker romanticism, a movement exploring the depths of neurosis and even psychosis, and evoking the powerful forces of an unconscious mind that earlier romantics hardly knew existed. One proof of this fact is that Hardy's influence on twentieth-century British literature has been enormous; the early D. H. Lawrence grew largely out of Hardy. And though, as I have said, Hardy has little in common with the so-called decadents, *Jude the Obscure* was considered as perverse when it appeared in the nineties as Wilde's *The Picture of Dorian Gray*. Hardy's later fiction, whose power would not be fully felt until the twentieth century, was clearly something new on the horizon. But in spite of the shock in this work of something new and modern in literature, there is also a renewal of the old romantic defiance of the individual who protests what Jude calls "an old civilization" which cramps "the instinctive and uncontrolled sense of justice and right" (p. 440).

Romanticism has always pointed to the coming of a time when man would be liberated not in some imaginary paradise removed from earth but on earth itself—thus Blake's Jerusalem, to be built "In England's green and pleasant Land." Even Jude in all his despair at the end of his life looks forward to a time, even fifty years hence, when his ideas will bear fruit: "Our ideas were fifty years too soon to be any good to us" (p. 492). Romanticism's problem has been its inability to provide what in our day we call role models. The English romantics that inspired modern authors like

Hardy and George Eliot all began with power and came to an end either of their creative powers or of their lives before they reached middle age. Those people the moderns were forced to turn to as teachers after they had passed through the influence of the youthful romantics are pictured by both Hardy and George Eliot as misleaders and corrupters. Mr. Casaubon misleads Dorothea Brooke and then leaves her high and dry, but Angel Clare and the Oxford clerks also leave Tess and Jude in a state of romantic rebellion against the forces of society that shaped their leaders' minds. Nowhere does Harold Bloom's theory of the anxiety of influence work better than in explaining pupil-teacher relationsips in Hardy and George Eliot. The influence of pedantic and worn-out social and religious conventions that control the minds of social leaders becomes an anxiety that leaves Dorothea in a state of psychic pain and drives Tess, Sue, and Jude to despair and death. The tragedy of modern writers often turns on the inability to find those leaders who can provide the necessary knowledge to overcome the anxiety and psychic turmoil that become their tragic flaws, an anxiety based on their inability to tear themselves free from the deadly influences of used-up concepts.

   In Hardy's later fiction we can see the neoromantic's attempts to push beyond the tragedy of people who are living with used-up ideas and conventions and are unable to find new intellectual and spiritual leaders. The storm that greeted *Tess* and *Jude* in the nineties caused Hardy to give up his quest in fiction and to turn to his poetry, where as late as 1917 he recorded the efforts of his own journey beyond the tragedy of his life in the poem "For Life I Had Never Cared Greatly." It remained for his chief follower, D. H. Lawrence, to carry on the journey beyond personal tragedy.

Oscar Wilde
and the Tragedy of Symbolism

Neoromanticism after 1890 takes several forms, but they all have certain aspects in common: defiance of Victorian morality, exploration of previously forbidden aspects of life, concern with the decay and rebirth of language, use of myth, and prophetic vision. Literary historians in recent years have pointed to deep underlying connections between all the different aspects of modern romanticism, which, though modern, is also an extending and deepening of the currents of the earlier romantic movement. In her study of the symbolist movement in the nineties, done from the viewpoint of comparative literature, Anna Balakian has written: "If at a certain point in the development of the movement critics were justified in separating 'symbolist' from 'decadent', everything points to the fact that in the last ten years of the century the two become so intertwined that without the 'decadent' spirit there would be little left to distinguish symbolism from Romanticism."[1] This statement indicates the underlying unity between symbolism and other currents of the neoromantic movement.

Decadence (which in Balakian's view consists of a withdrawal from life, a contemplation of self, and a concern with death) is indeed the chief way in which the artistic movement called sym-

bolism, which is also connected with the impressionistic style, differs from a more robust current of modern romanticism, in which
strong emotions and symbols from a fecund nature are evident.
Although the two currents often run together (even in such robust
neoromantics as D. H. Lawrence), symbolism with its decadence
and its morbidity is different in important ways from the literature of strong emotion—even as Wordsworth's romanticism, concerned with nature and emotion, differed from Coleridge's, which
emphasized the supernatural and problems of guilt and psychic
suffering. Indeed, symbolism differs mainly from other forms of
neoromanticism in its handling of myth and in its use of the supernatural, and in its turning from strong emotion to seek a fine-
ness of tone often expressed in obscurity and complexity. It is well
known that the poets of the nineties were influenced by the French
symbolists, but it is not so clear that the first symbolist novel in
English was written by Oscar Wilde under the strong influence of
Huysmans. Symbolist novels are, as William York Tindall says,
"the outstanding literary development of our time," distinguished
by the fact that "the burden is carried not by narrative or dis-
course as tradition demands but by image, pattern, and rhythm,
devices once peculiar to poetry or music."[2]

Whenever critics have taken Oscar Wilde's work seriously, it is
usually with apology and denigration. Yet to omit his name from
the history of modern British literature or even the history of modern fiction is to leave a gap in either. The growing interest in Harold Bloom's theory of poetry, developed in *The Anxiety of Influence*,
should help to bring about a resurgence of interest in Wilde, because few men of letters ever suffered more from the anxiety of
influence than Wilde. That anxiety was not only because of Victorian moralists like Arnold that Wilde sought to replace but also
because of those closer to him—Pater, Huysmans, and Baudelaire—whose work he thought he was making known to a large
public. In fact, the two major symbolist tragedies that Wilde
wrote—*Salomé* and *The Picture of Dorian Gray*—both spring from
an anxiety toward both schools of letters. And if, as Bloom says,
criticism "is the art of knowing the hidden roads that go from
poem to poem,"[3] then we must study how Wilde took up Pater's
dictum of a life burning as a flame burns and suffered it until he
found his own and Dorian Gray's tragedy, and then we must go on
to follow Wilde's tragedy into the poetry of André Gide, James

Joyce, T. S. Eliot, and a throng of lesser symbolist poets and novelists. Having appropriately (for Bloom's theory) misread Pater's
Renaissance, published in that pivotal period of the early seventies, Wilde plunged into a search for as large and strange a variety
of sensations as he could find and then recorded his findings in his
two tragedies.

The anxiety of enjoying more sensations than had been possible in most earlier ages led Wilde to depict in *The Picture of Dorian Gray* a literal attempt at superhuman transcendence. In short,
Wilde made Dorian Gray's tragic flaw basically the same as that of
Shakespeare's Macbeth. Macbeth listens to the plan of his wife,
who has assumed leadership over him, and then accepts his wife's
instructions to follow the guidance of agents of a world other than
the human. Dorian follows the advice of a sinister aristocrat with
vaguely Mephistophelian traits and uses a preternatural talisman
to obtain the occult ability to hide his soul in a picture. The result
of the tragedy for both Macbeth and Gray is that they lose their
souls. The difference is that Macbeth simply follows the advice of
an ambitious wife, whereas Gray is guided by an initiatory figure
who promises to show by means of his knowledge the gateway to
the good life but whose advice leads to death. He is not any different essentially from Mr. Casaubon or Angel Clare: he is the Victorian who seems to know all but whose knowledge is deadly. Gray
sees too late that it is a knowledge that denies the reality of the
soul and man's need to develop the soul or lose it. Gray's tempter
begins by enunciating the Pater doctrine of art for art's sake and
the need to enjoy as many sensations as possible, and ends by de-
ceiving Gray about the soul and its need for development. Too late
the protagonist realizes that he is living out a tragic myth of the
loss of the human soul.

Wilde was one of the master mythmakers of modern literature, but his place as one of the founders of the modern movement
in literature continues to be denied. Is it because of a fear, inherited from the nineties, of Wilde as a homosexual who stood alone
before Victorian Philistines? Even the young Gide confessed his
fear of Wilde in those last days before 1900, when the broken literary leader took up his exile in Paris. Only partly, one may answer. Bloom's idea that we create our own precursors applies to
Wilde, and Bloom himself begins *The Anxiety of Influence* with the
usual denigrating reference, saying that Wilde "knew he had failed

as a poet because he lacked strength to overcome his anxiety of influence."[4] Bloom then goes on to quote Wilde's own denial of his chief master, Pater, as if to justify denying Wilde's leadership in the movement in modern literature that Bloom most admires. Everyone knows that symbolism began in France, but who will admit that Wilde is the chief precursor of the movement in English, that in fact the work of Yeats, Shaw, Joyce, Auden, Huxley, Forster, Eliot, and even Lawrence, James, and Conrad, in part derives from his prodigious and interrupted efforts? In fact, much of the criticism of those who think like the symbolist poets, Bloom included, derives in greater part from Wilde's extension of Pater's criticism than they can ever admit.

What Wilde contributed to British fiction has particularly been buried. Who could admit that attributes of many fantasy novels of modern English, many novels dealing in the occult and supernatural, and many of those employing myth and fairy tales are traceable to Wilde? Who would ever think of linking the fiction of Wilde with that of C. S. Lewis or Charles Williams? The influence, nearly always denied, is there. Bloom says that poets must create their precursors to escape the anxiety of influence because of their fear that their precursors have left nothing for them to do. It might very well be that they also must deny a side of their precursors that they cannot deal with at the time they themselves are setting to work. Wilde himself could not face the fact that though Pater recommended that others burn with a hard, gem-like flame, Pater himself remained aloof from the world. Max Beerbohm noted long ago that there were critics like Arnold who recommended that others do exactly as they had done and other critics like Pater who recommended that others do exactly the opposite of what they had done. I believe that what those who followed in Wilde's path most hid from themselves was the fact that modern man, to escape certain mythic knowledge he must embody if he is to remain fully human, flees into knowledge and art, covers his nakedness with systems of knowledge and objects of art in order to escape that art and that knowledge that it is his destiny to encounter on his own journey. Joyce partly and Yeats totally—both in part disciples of Wilde—admitted this in effect as they approached their final years. It was what Wilde had already confessed in his two greatest works in the symbolist style, *Salomé* and *The Picture of Dorian Gray*.

In the following analysis of Wilde's *Dorian Gray* the emphasis on the role of knowledge in the career of the protagonist may seem strange when one considers also the role of art and sensation in the philosophy of the corrupting Lord Harry, but the emphasis on "knowing" is exactly what the symbolists, who themselves paradoxically were deeply involved in knowledge, wanted to escape. Dorothea's rejection of the pedantic knowledge of Mr. Casaubon is parallel to Wilde's rejection of "knowledge" as a way of life. For the symbolists, the Victorian realists with their heavy moralizing and their knowledge systems were the precursors to be overthrown. The way of attack was through the mythic image and the music of style, pointing to a reality beyond the dead facts of a Victorian science, which was sometimes the source of moralizing demands on the new breed of artist. This new kind of artist proclaimed himself in the work of Baudelaire, Swinburne, Pater, and Mallarmé, who never expounded a knowledge system but always suggested and symbolized a way of life too mysterious to sum up in a single vision. In the full development of symbolist literature, we see the triumph of the living individual moving toward higher states of consciousness as opposed to the individual who stops and makes himself and his art and knowledge the center of personal and social aggrandizement. The Victorian thirst for knowledge was for the symbolists of modernism a cause and a sign of their destructive will to power over human souls. Out of the symbolist reaction would come new philosophical formulations, like Bergson's *Creative Evolution* and Heidegger's *Being and Time*, in which the power of life is elevated over the power of intellect, which can either help life or, if misapplied, hinder it.

Wilde presents his vision of evil in terms of a tempter and one who is tempted—that is, Lord Henry Wotton and Dorian Gray. The brilliant and corrupt Wotton, in fact, plays the role of the devil. Wilde limits his use of the supernatural to the device of the picture which assumes Dorian's sins, but there are occasional hints that Lord Harry is more than mortal. He remains an urbane gentleman of the period, but his Christian name is traditionally associated with the devil; and in one important way he is like the biblical devil: he persuades Dorian to eat the fruit of the tree of knowledge. Lord Harry also resembles Goethe's Mephistopheles, who offers Faust a kind of knowledge that can come only through intense experience. Having tired of the inert lore of books, Faust is ready to try Mephistopheles' magic, which enables him to know a kind of heightened experience. When he is awakened with the desire to know, Dorian accepts the magic of perpetual youth and beauty from a source Wilde never makes known. Dorian's wish is mysteriously granted, but a connection between Lord Harry's remarks in the temptation scene and the granting of Dorian's desire is easy enough for the reader to make. With the help of magic, Dorian Gray is able to set out on a life of intense experience. But to what purpose? This question is of utmost importance for understanding the anxiety of Wilde's Victorian influence.

In the temptation scene in chapter 2 there is a great deal about both the desire for knowledge of life—or curiosity, as Wilde called it—and the direct experience of life. Two significant interpretations of the book see Dorian's damnation as being due to his experiences. The obvious interpretation is that Dorian is finally damned because of such conventional sins as cruelty, lechery, and, particularly, pride. The other interpretation, which readily occurs to those who know something about the cult of estheticism, is that Wilde, by damning Dorian, also damns the ideas of Walter Pater. This view, for instance, is found in Baugh's *A Literary History of England. The Picture of Dorian Gray* can indeed be taken as a handbook of Pater's philosophy because Dorian does burn with a hard, gem-like flame; above all, he believes, in Pater's words, "in getting as many pulsations as possible in a given time."[5]

While accepting both these interpretations as partly valid, I would like to propose a third interpretation, which I believe necessary to the understanding of Wilde's vision of evil.[6] Instead of placing the major emphasis on experience or the life of sensation, I suggest that the root cause of Dorian's damnation, as well as the source of Harry's evil, is an insatiable curiosity, a never-ending desire for knowledge that is essentially Victorian in its tendency to control the individual's life. It is curiosity above all else that is behind the ironclad egocentricity of Dorian and Harry. There are three key words whose meanings must be explored in order to understand this egocentricity. They are *experience, art,* and *curiosity,* and curiosity is the most important. The kind of knowledge that Lord Harry teaches Dorian to be curious about can be had only through the experience of intense sensations; thus, experience and also art, as we shall see, become only means to an end. Wilde's emphasis on curiosity thus makes the novel more than just a reflection of Pater's ideas, or, for that matter, more than just a damning of them.

Both *curiosity* and *experience* are important words in chapter 2, when Dorian is first tempted to wish for everlasting youth. The important thing is that Lord Harry helps to satiate Dorian's curiosity about life. We see Dorian thinking: "Suddenly there had to come someone across his life who seemed to have disclosed to him life's mystery."[7] Dorian's fall begins in the awakening of curiosity. A short time later he tells Harry just how he was affected at their first meeting:

> "You filled me with a wild desire to know everything about life. For days after I met you, something seemed to throb in my veins. As I lounged in the Park, or strolled down Piccadilly, I used to look at every one who passed me, and wonder, with a mad curiosity, what sort of lives they led. Some of them fascinated me. Others filled me with terror. There was an exquisite poison in the air. I had a passion for sensations." (pp. 90–91)

Thus, without any transition between the ideas of curiosity and experience, or without showing that he realizes what the connection between the two is, Dorian announces that the desire for sensations is what naturally follows from the desire for knowledge. The ideas of curiosity and experience are often juxtaposed throughout the book, and the relationship of the two is sometimes puzzling, as it is on first glance in the passage above. To get a better idea of their relationship we must examine Lord Harry's own life, because, as the representative of total damnation, his state is presumably what Dorian is gradually moving toward.

In chapter 2 Lord Harry has a good bit to say about experience: "The aim of life is self-development. To realise one's nature perfectly—that is what each of us is here for" (p. 38). Along with his injunction to yield always to temptation he makes a curious statement: "It is in the brain, and the brain only, that the great sins of the world take place" (p. 39). This is the pattern of Lord Harry's philosophy throughout the book—no matter how much he honors the senses, it is always the brain that he comes back to. Actually Lord Harry recommends one set of pleasurable experiences for Dorian—the pleasures of sensation—and finds another for himself—the pleasures of the intellect. Dorian is told to go out and live the full life, to search for beauty, to yield to all temptations, to help bring about the new hedonism. Lord Harry himself, of course, does none of these things. His chief activity is manipulating the life of his disciple, Dorian, in order to satisfy better his curiosity concerning this rare youth. Harry is driven by an insatiable desire to know about the inner workings of human beings. He often speaks of theories and of analysis and he thinks of himself as a scientist, an analyst, and an experimenter. One of several passages that show the true analytical spirit and also suggest the motivating force of the newly damned Dorian is the following: "It was clear to him that the experimental method was the only method by which one could arrive at any scientific analysis of the passions; and certainly Dorian Gray was a subject made to his hand, and seemed to promise rich and fruitful results. His sudden mad love for Sibyl Vane was a psychological phenomenon of no small interest. There was no doubt that curiosity had much to do with it, curiosity and the desire for new experiences; yet it was not a simple but rather a very complex passion" (p. 110). Thus Wilde drives home his point that curiosity is the one trait that above all others characterizes Lord Harry and incidentally now characterizes Dorian, who has become a Victorian scientist of the passions.

Along with curiosity and experience in Wilde's book goes another important idea: art. For Wilde, art is that which is shaped and molded. Experience itself must be molded and shaped so that it can be studied, and in Lord Harry's case it is mainly the experience of Dorian that is artfully arranged. As Lord Harry thinks, "There was nothing that one could not do with him. He could be made a Titan or a toy" (p. 70). Obviously the magical preservation of Dorian's youth and beauty is the chief example in the book of the application of art to life. Works of art have their proper place in the life of sensation, but the esthetic movement was chiefly concerned with making one's life a work of art. It was enough for Lord Harry, however, to help shape Dorian's life and then observe and analyze it in order to satisfy his own curiosity. The connection between art and analysis is seen when he explains at the end of the book, "If a man treats life artistically, his brain is his heart" (p. 388). Wilde's devil then is a kind of artist-intellectual, with particular emphasis on the intellectual. And he is an experimental scientist.

Because he is human, Dorian can never be totally damned,

although throughout the book he is gradually becoming more like Lord Harry. He still has a soul and can never know the tempter's aloofness. With Harry's evil philosophy as his guide, Dorian sets out on the life of artfully shaped experience. He ends his career dominating and controlling the lives of others. That Dorian is driven by curiosity, that seed of damnation, is evident as soon as he meets the actress Sibyl Vane. When Sibyl falls so much in love with Dorian that she loses all desire and ability to act on the stage, Dorian is shocked. He cries: "You used to stir my imagination. Now you don't even stir my curiosity. You simply produce no effect" (p. 160). He desires to artfully shape her life, just as Harry has indirectly molded his own. Unless she can be shaped and is a shaper of the artificial life of the stage herself—that is, unless she lives artificially instead of naturally—she is of no use to Dorian.

After he has ruined Sibyl's life, Dorian systematically sets out to shape his own experience so that he can satisfy his curiosity about life: "For there would be [he thinks] a real pleasure in watching it. He would be able to follow his mind into its secret places" (p. 195). After Sibyl's death, Dorian explains to Basil Hallward the connection between the sensations gained from art and the nature of curiosity: "I love beautiful things that one can touch and handle. Old brocades, green bronzes, lacquer-work, carved ivories, exquisite surroundings, luxury, pomp, there is much to be got from all these. But the artistic temperament that they create, or at any rate reveal, is still more to me. To become the spectator of one's own life, as Harry says, is to escape the suffering of life" (pp. 202–3). Dorian receives an esthetic thrill from *objets d'art*, but his main purpose in studying them is curiosity, which enables him to escape that activity all humans have in common: suffering. He then adds one of those seemingly unconnected sentences so often found in both his and Lord Harry's conversations. The point of the statement seems to be that he will not only study the artistic temperament of others but above all will observe his own life, turning poseur and playing many roles in order to do so:

> . . . and in his search for sensations that would be at once new and delightful, and possess that element of strangeness that is so essential to romance, he would often adopt certain modes of thought that he knew to be really alien to his nature, abandon himself to their subtle influences, and then,

having, as it were, caught their colour and satisfied his *intellectual curiosity*, leave them with that curious indifference that is not incompatible with a real ardour of temperament. (p. 241; italics added)

Curiosity becomes the driving force of his life, and to satisfy it he must continue to play roles. Dorian's restless life leads him to two things he did not foresee at the time of his temptation: the desire to shape the lives of others—he becomes notorious as a corrupter of young men—and, finally, after normal sensations have worn thin, a search for perverse ones. He feels pursued by a sense of sin, which leads him to kill that voice of conventional morality, Basil Hallward; to turn to opium and other vices in order to forget his own sin; and, of course, finally to hate himself so much that he drives the knife into his own soul, which he had left behind him in the hidden picture.

If Wilde had sought to write only the tragedy of a man who follows occult influences to his doom, he would have stopped with his story of Dorian and Lord Harry. A study of the structure of the book, however, will reveal a pattern of concepts that are opposed to the corrupting philosophy of Lord Harry. It must always be kept in mind that, though *The Picture of Dorian Gray* is best remembered for its witty, paradoxical dialogue, it is as much a philosophical novel as the later works of George Eliot and Thomas Hardy; and, even more, it is a novel of ideas that anticipates the satirical works of Aldous Huxley and Evelyn Waugh. Therefore, even though the two characters Wilde uses to create a counter-concept are essentially wooden—like most modern authors, Wilde found it difficult to create good characters—a view is presented in the novel's structure that reveals at once Wilde's attitude toward his two chief characters and his antipathy toward a constricting Victorianism.

The way of life that Wilde opposes to Lord Harry's deadly philosophy of experience artfully shaped to satisfy an obsessive curiosity is summed up in several key words. The most obvious is *love*. Another one is *reality*, and another is the *natural*, or *nature*, as opposed to the artificial or that which is artfully shaped. The word that might be opposed to love is *egoism*, which, as we have seen, accompanies both curiosity and the desire to shape and control the lives of others. As one learns to shape his own life and the lives of others in order to satisfy the curiosity of the brain, then, like Lord Harry, one comes to worship his own image as a man of both power and what had come to be called "culture."

In studying the book's structure, we soon become aware that it has five sections. The first one is devoted mainly to two things: an elaboration of Lord Harry's philosophy of evil, which is opposed only by the conventional morality of Basil Hallward, and the temptation of Dorian. Once Dorian has eaten of the fruit of Harry's knowledge, the stage is set for section two, which introduces Sibyl Vane, who more than anyone else in the book is the embodiment of Wilde's ideal of love and nature and reality. She makes several statements that are important for an understanding of Wilde's views of the good. One is that art is but a reflection of life. When she loves, she tells Dorian, she is a bad artist. As we have seen, Dorian the shaper, the artist of love, rejects her love because it makes her a second-rate artist. In doing so he rejects reality, for, as Sibyl tells him, he has caused her to love and thus has taught her the nature of reality: "You taught me [she says] what reality really is" (p. 159). Thus, Wilde equates love and reality. But Dorian cannot understand either, for he sees Sibyl's death as an artifact of experience; as he puts it, "It has been a marvelous experience" (p. 191). When Dorian reflects upon the death of Sibyl, he thinks of his life and wonders if it is too late for a change, but—again the key word—curiosity and his own life have made it impossible for him to turn back: "Tears came to his eyes as he remembered her childlike look, and winsome fanciful ways, and shy tremulous grace. He brushed them away hastily, and looked again at the picture. He felt that the time had really come for making his choice. Or had his choice already been made? Yes, life had decided that for him—life, and his own infinite curiosity about life" (p. 194). He ends by telling Basil that he regards Sibyl's death as one of the "romantic tragedies of the age" (p. 201). Her life is now, he thinks, not a thing of nature but an object of art.

In section three Dorian sets out to shape his life artfully to satisfy his compelling curiosity. Wilde fails to give a very clear picture of the process. Instead, with a shoddiness that helps to keep the novel from being a profound work of art, he merely tells the reader that Dorian took up many ways of life in order that he might observe his own sensations. A new note, however, is struck in the fourth section. Dorian becomes both pursuer and pursued.

It is not enough that he must shape his own life; like Lord Harry he must shape the lives of others. Again the book fails to show the full effects of his evil influences on others. Instead, it is only hinted at, except in the case of Alan Campbell, the scientist whom he forces to destroy Basil Hallward's corpse; and even the brief attempt to dramatize Dorian's influence on Campbell succeeds only in being melodramatic.

Dorian not only pursues others, he also pursues and destroys the voice of his conscience, embodied in Basil Hallward. Basil too is an artist, but not an artist of life; instead he is dedicated to making *objets d'art*. Although he does not know firsthand the nature of love and reality as Sibyl did, he does prefer the ideal of reality, for he tells Dorian and Harry that "Love is a more wonderful thing than Art" (p. 156). By the end of the fourth section Dorian also realizes this: "'I wish I could love,' cried Dorian Gray, with a deep note of pathos in his voice. 'But I seem to have lost the passion, and forgotten the desire. I am too much concentrated on myself. My own personality has become a burden to me'" (p. 371). Curiosity and art have led to the inevitable and complete egoism, which is only another word for damnation.

Another person who represents the principle of reality is Sibyl Vane's brother, who joins Dorian's conscience as one of his pursuers. James Vane is, significantly, a sailor, and thus he is in constant association with the source of life, from which Dorian in all his artificiality has removed himself. James is the primitive man who has never known the temptations of curiosity or the need for artifice. But it is artifice that destroys this man of the unshaped, everlasting sea. As he is about to take his revenge on the young-old dandy, Dorian asks him if so young a man could have wronged his sister fourteen years ago. Not knowing about the devil's artifice that has preserved Dorian's youth, James Vane loses his victim and eventually his own life in his pursuit of the damned and aged youth. Dorian is to meet his own doom alone.

At the beginning of the fifth section, almost at the end of his career, Dorian finds a girl like Sibyl Vane and now realizes that, because she can love, she embodies the principle of reality: "She knew nothing, but she had everything that he had lost" (p. 397). The suggestion here is plain: knowledge and egoism are on one side and love and reality are on the other. In this book only the simple, the "natural," the unknowing can possess love. When he finds that sparing the girl from his possessive will only adds the stain of hypocrisy to the picture, all of his self-hatred comes to the fore and he stabs the picture which contains the record of his sins. By killing his soul, which resides in the picture, he kills himself. Significantly enough, Dorian thinks of the picture as "this monstrous soul-life" (p. 404), a term which suggests that the soul contains the principle of life, that essence which is the opposite of artificiality.

Before Dorian destroys himself, Wilde brings back Lord Harry for a final statement to sum up, as it were, his philosophy. Nowhere does Wilde choose to call the devil by his true name, nor does he suggest that he is having him come for Dorian's soul, but it is significant that Lord Harry carefully points out just what Dorian has gained by eating the forbidden fruit: "Nothing has been hidden from you" he tells Dorian. "Life has been your art" (pp. 392–93). Thus the devil has upheld his end of the bargain. Dorian has been given what he asked for, and his soul is the price he pays. Lord Harry blasphemes against the soul-life by relating an anecdote about a street preacher: "I thought of telling the prophet that Art had a soul, but that man had not" (pp. 389–90). Dorian by now knows better, and his answer is passionate: "Don't, Harry. The soul is a terrible reality. It can be bought, and sold, and bartered away. It can be poisoned, or made perfect" (p. 390). Harry, who is soulless, can only reply that the soul is an illusion. Man, Wilde seems to be saying, can never escape the knowledge of his soul no matter how far he leaves it behind him in whatever quest he may undertake. No matter in what dark room he may hide it, man must always return to encounter its power.

The tragedy of Dorian Gray, as I have suggested, is the same as that of Macbeth, or even of Othello, two characters whose souls are gradually poisoned until their destructiveness forces them to face the fact that they have been deluded about their advisors, whose knowledge they have used to destroy life. Dorian is so deluded that he does not even know, until the end of his life, that he has been living out a tragedy. Instead, he considers the death of Sibyl to be tragic, telling Lord Harry that her death is one of the "romantic tragedies of the age." Actually she is one of the innocents of literature, destroyed as she is by the tragic character whose flaw has allowed him to fall under the influence of evil. Sibyl and her brother parallel Gretchen and her brother in Goethe's *Faust*, and also Desdemona and Banquo in *Othello* and *Macbeth*. Ironically, it is the knowledge of what tragedy really is that is missing in Dorian's life. Dorian's idea of tragedy grows out of the concept of art given him by Lord Harry, who says that art is a product of the brain and the shaping will; according to this view, Sibyl is the central figure of tragedy created by Dorian. But Sibyl, an artist herself, tells Dorian that art must be a reflection of life. Without knowing it, she is an Aristotelian in her proclamation of the theory of the imitation of nature. To be an artist, one must encounter both nature and what she also calls reality, one aspect of which is love. She has done this, but her tempter, Dorian, has been in flight both from nature and from such realities as love because he increasingly has withdrawn into his own brain, which in his theory is the source of art. Sibyl's theory of art leads her into a deepening quest into both nature and reality, but Dorian's quest leads him into the contemplation of his own conscious mind and ego so that he becomes more like Harry all the time, a manipulator of people, an arranger of "tragedies" in which the innocent are destroyed and their deaths called' romantic tragedy. Art in this sense serves the deceptive purposes of the curiosity-seeking mind and the manipulating will.

If, as Harold Bloom says, criticism is "the art of knowing the hidden roads that go from poem to poem," then we must, in order to see Wilde in context, be aware of his reaction both to his immediate, modern precursors and to his Victorian precursors. Anxiety resulted from his reaction to both groups. All of Wilde's works are an attempt to throw off the anxiety all modern people feel in relationship to their Victorian precursors. The Victorian precursor, as created by the modern mind to free itself from anxiety, hid a manipulating, egocentric personality behind an empty morality and a supposed love and cultivation of art and science. Victorians, in the modern mind, based their vaunted morality on systems of knowledge that were pedantic and that denied the essence of life. Thus Lord Harry is not really so different from Mr. Casaubon or Angel Clare, except that he seems to be consciously in league with the devil. If he has a prototype in Victorian literature, it would be the monsters of the Renaissance created by Browning, which are in fact only masks for Victorian monsterdom. Yet Lord Harry has about him something of Walter Pater, of one who has left behind morality, which is represented in the book by the ineffectual Basil Hallward. At the same time Lord Harry's estheticism, under the cover of Pater's ideas about putting living before knowing, is really only a front for his obsessive curiosity and his insane desire to manipulate people as if they were laboratory specimens. At heart Dorian's corrupter is a Victorian scientist of the sort we find in Hawthorne, one who placed life under his own microscope in the name of some ideal. He is then the great Victorian deceiver, one of the most important characters in all of modern fiction, whose creation was one of modern man's attempts to free himself from the anxiety of Victorian influence.

How Wilde dealt with the anxiety of his modern precursors is a more difficult question, one that cannot be dealt with at length here. Suffice it to say that the two chief precursors of Dorian Gray were Pater and Huysmans. The former gave Wilde a philosophy that marked a break with Victorianism, and the latter gave him the new symbolist novel. The anxiety they gave him sprang from their vision of a new life, a vision so strong that it left nothing more for Wilde to accomplish. Thus the conscious and unconscious influence of Huysmans' *A Rebours* is felt throughout *Dorian Gray*. Wilde's answer was to create in his novel a tragedy, much as a greater poet, Goethe, created a tragedy he called *Faust* in answer to the storm and stress of early romanticism. Pater had said that one should get "as many pulsations as possible in a given time," and Huysmans had presented a picture, in the words of Balakian, of a neurasthenic, "engaged in an excessively morbid cult of the personal Ego, lost in dreams and hallucinations."[8] Wilde combines the life-styles suggested by his two modern precursors and then bases his tragedy on the need of modern man for a leader and on his inevitable proclivity to fall under the influence of a Victorian pseudo-leader dressed in the clothes of the new modern philosophy. The novel offers a hope for the future in that there still live people like Sibyl and her brother who have not denied the power of the soul or man's total relationship to the cosmos, but these people are innocents doomed also to deception because they have no vision that will make creativity possible in the new age. Yet in the affirmation of the reality of the soul, Dorian himself points the way for those who will in time discover how to fly out of the labyrinth created by Victorian monsters. The death agony of Dorian, minor though it might be in the world's art, is nevertheless a voice sounding a challenge to the major symbolist writers to come—to Joyce, Mann, Lawrence, Hesse.

Lawrence and Faulkner:
The Symbolist Novel
and the Prophetic Song

In 1908 Ezra Pound went to Great Britain to find an established poet he could instruct in the new symbolist vision, which had not yet become fully established in poetry written in English. He went to Swinburne, fittingly enough, because it was Swinburne more than anyone else who breathed the new breath of romanticism into English poetry. Pound found Swinburne too senile to work with, and he chose then to go to that poet who would eventually bring together in his life and work the chief strains of neoromanticism, both those of symbolism and those of strong emotion and prophetic power with an exaltation of both nature and the mythic community. That poet was, of course, William Butler Yeats.

Five years later there appeared in England the first major symbolist novel that would combine symbolist techniques with the power of romantic emotion. Published the year before World War I began, Lawrence's *Sons and Lovers* announced (along with Stravinsky's *Rite of Spring*, which appeared the same year) the beginning of another period of modernism. Lawrence went on to write even greater novels, completing the task begun by George Eliot in *Daniel Deronda*: he showed at once the tragedy of modern man and the moving of other modern human beings beyond this tragedy. He did so with the power of what one of his chief fictional disciples, E. M. Forster, called the prophetic song. In *Aspects of the Novel*, Forster, himself one of the great symbolist novelists of the age, exalted four novelists—Emily Brontë, Melville, Dostoevski, and Lawrence—as writers who wrote with the power of the prophetic song and ranked above the realists and traditionalists. The prophetic novelist, Forster wrote, "proposes to sing, and the strangeness of song arising in the halls of fiction is bound to give us a shock."[1] Forster announced that these writers had, in effect, accomplished what some of the poets of the French symbolist tradition, Mallarmé in particular, had decreed to be a necessary work of the new literature: to bring to poetry a power of vision that would reveal to man his past, present, and future and would lead to the renewal of language. These prophetic and language-renewing roles were stated by T. S. Eliot, one of the three greatest symbolist poets in English—Yeats and Stevens being the other two—at the end of *Little Gidding*:

> Since our concern was speech and speech impelled us
> To purify the dialect of the tribe
> And urge the mind to aftersight and foresight.[2]

Two novelists more than any others in this century have achieved the power of the prophetic song. They are Lawrence and Faulkner, and the two, though not much connected in the usual literary ways, should be seen as creative brothers. Both used many of the techniques of symbolist fiction while at the same time retaining a vision of nature and the mythic community; both moved into the realm of mythmaking beyond tragedy, although tragedy hangs over much of their work. Tragedy in their hands is presented in a style that is filled with the rhythms of great poetry. E. K. Brown, in the excellent *Rhythm in the Novel*, analyzes the ways in which Lawrence, for instance, achieves through style the rhythmic effects found in *Sons and Lovers* to accomplish "an interactive relationship" between theme and style.[3] Thomas H. McCabe has even more acutely analyzed Lawrence's prose rhythms, concluding that "D. H. Lawrence saw the meaning of life in its rhythm; the endlessly changing to-and-fro relationship between man and woman; life's recurring cycle of birth, growth, and fading into death."[4]

Both Lawrence and Faulkner have been regarded by many people as sages, Faulkner having often been called the sage of Yoknapatawpha County. Lawrence has been such a popular spokesman on sex and love that we have a whole group of people in the twentieth century who are known as Laurentians. Actually, neither was a prophet or sage in the old sense of these words. As men, they had many failings, and these failings have been reported. They were primarily men of letters. Although they were not prophets in the old sense, a prophetic voice sings throughout the work of both novelists. Lawrence was a novelist, an essayist, a dramatist, and a poet. Faulkner wrote a few poems, but he spent most of his life writing fiction. He was a storyteller.

The two novelists are both similar and different in many ways. Their similarities are these: they study the decline of the provinces and in particular the decline of people living in the country and in towns; they deal with the collapse of the man-woman relationship and with the collapse of society generally; they portray the evil effects of mechanization and of urban life generally; and they write well about simple people and the life of myth and religion among those who still live close to the earth.

Their differences are rather striking. Faulkner stayed close to the land; although he traveled a great deal and lived in cities like New York and Hollywood, his work is primarily and at its best about life in Mississippi. In contrast, Lawrence had a split career. Before 1920 he lived chiefly in England, but after that he became a world traveler. He is in fact one of the great travel writers of English literature.

Faulkner also differs from Lawrence in that his fiction expresses few ideas, although, as Panthea Broughton has pointed out in her study of abstractions in Faulkner's work, "Faulkner himself makes no pretense of dismissing ideas, nor does he aim merely at delineating facts."[5] Several critics, among them Thomas McHaney, have pointed out ways in which Faulkner was influenced by the concepts of Sir James Frazer and the philosophy of Bergson and Schopenhauer. Lawrence, however, was very definitely an intellectual who dealt with a good many different ideas and who put knowledge and ideas to good use in his essays and novels. Lawrence was, in fact, interested in all types of literature, far more than Faulkner, who was chiefly a novelist and short-story writer. Lawrence associated freely with intellectuals like Bertrand Russell, the foremost philosopher in England in the twentieth century. He studied psychology, mythology, archaeology, anthropology, and various other subjects; in fact, Horace Gregory says in a revised edition of *D. H. Lawrence: Pilgrim of the Apocalypse*, referring to the early edition, "I did not realize then, as I know now, the enduring brilliance of Lawrence's intellect."[6] Lawrence was in part self-educated, but his grasp of knowledge is often visionary. And what most noticeably links Faulkner and Lawrence as writers is their use of myth.

They are both mythic in that they portray in their writing the search or quest of man for a new and better way of life. As mythic novelists, they both are deeply aware of the modern wasteland. Their pictures of this wasteland are among the best of the twentieth century. They also give us glimpses of a new life as it is worked out by a few of their characters, and they show us people still carrying on the old mythic way of life close to the land. They are profoundly aware of the modern corruption of the mythical and the religious traditions of man, and they indicate a new quest in our time for spiritual, mental, and emotional renewal. Above all, they both prophetically proclaim the coming of a new way of life, and they write with a style, when they are at their most prophetic, that has all the lyric power Forster credits to Lawrence.

Lawrence has been thought of by many as being chiefly a writer about sex; he was indeed deeply aware of the sexual problems of modern man. He considered these problems to be symptomatic of the modern wasteland, as, for that matter, did Eliot in *The Waste Land*. Lawrence puts the major emphasis in his portrayal of the wasteland on man's corrupted will rather than on acts of sexual violence. Lawrence asks how modern man went wrong and why he has sexual problems. His answer, summed up quite simply, has to do with the desire of man to control by his conscious will the activities of other people.

This control by the will is primarily what the novel *Sons and Lovers* is about. It deals with the tyranny of a woman over her family. This tyranny is the essential element of Freud's Oedipus complex. Tyranny results from the control of other people by the conscious will. Paul Morel, the hero of the novel, is controlled emotionally by his mother. His father has withdrawn from the control of Mrs. Morel by becoming an alcoholic and has been put out of the family by his wife. We see the same kind of female tyranny in *The Rainbow*, Lawrence's novel about Will and Anna Brangwen. Gradually Anna gets full control of the family by reducing her husband to the level of one of her children. She also controls her children by not allowing them to grow up; however, Ursula, the chief character in this novel, manages to break away from the tyranny of her mother.

Lawrence's fiction often deals with people breaking away from the tyranny of other people's wills. Lawrence is at his best in writing about family relationships between men and women. He also writes well about large-scale social relationships in which people are controlled by the conscious wills of those placed over them. The character who best represents this social control is Gerald Crich in *Women in Love*. Gerald is one of those modern men of action who control other men's lives and who force people to fit into a mechanical tyranny. He is a coal-mine owner, and he manipulates the lives of the miners and forces them to live like robots. This manipulation of people by the conscious will, however, destroys Gerald as it destroys most of the people who come close to him. In *Women in Love* we see Gerald viewed through the eyes of a woman who has escaped his domination and can at last see its true meaning:

> . . . the Geralds of this world. So manly by day, yet all the while, such a crying of infants in the night. Let them turn into mechanisms, let them. Let them become instruments, pure machines, pure wills, that work like clock-work, in perpetual repetition. Let them be this, let them be taken up entirely in their work, let them be perfect parts of a great machine, having a slumber of constant repetition. Let Gerald manage his firm. There he would be satisfied, as satisfied as a wheelbarrow that goes backwards and forwards along a plank all day—she had seen it.[7]

The modern mechanization of life, Lawrence tells us, is caused by the desire by a few men of power for control over others. And women imitate these men of great control. They too want to control other people in their own spheres of activity. A good example of this is found in *Sons and Lovers*. Paul Morel is trying to escape from his mother, but he finds himself entangled with Miriam, a woman very much like his mother. Miriam thinks thus of Paul:

"Her bitterness came surging up. Her sacrifice, then, was useless. He lay there aloof, careless about her. Suddenly she saw again his lack of religion, his restless instability. He would destroy himself like a perverse child. Well then, he would!"[8]

Miriam desires to control Paul's life, but he will not be controlled. Although he does lack religion, and he is unstable and destructive, by the end of the book Paul does begin to get away from the emotional and psychic control of the wills of two powerful women who try to enslave him. At the end of *Sons and Lovers*, Paul's dead mother still calls out to him:

> "Mother!" he whimpered—"mother!"
> She was the only thing that held him up, himself, amid all this. And she was gone, intermingled herself. He wanted her to touch him, have him alongside with her.
> But no, he would not give in. Turning sharply, he walked toward the city's gold phosphorescence. His fists were shut, his mouth set fast. He would not take that direction, to the darkness, to follow her. He walked toward the faintly humming, glowing town, quickly. (p. 491)

In the case of Paul Morel, the young man escapes from the provinces to the city. Later he will find that the city does not contain an answer to his problems. He will come to see that what he needs is a new way of life, a spiritual regeneration that will give him a wholeness and a fullness of personality. In one sense, Ursula, in *The Rainbow*, the second of Lawrence's great novels, is a continuation of Paul Morel. (There are three novels that should be read in sequence—*Sons and Lovers*, *The Rainbow*, and *Women in Love*.) In *The Rainbow*, Lawrence shows us a heroine set against the provincial background achieving a kind of spiritual regeneration that is symbolized by a rainbow. The rainbow is his great symbol of unity and wholeness after a storm. The storm is a psychic storm caused by the struggle to escape from possessive wills that seek to control Ursula's life:

> And again, to her feverish brain, came the vivid reality of acorns in February lying on the floor of a wood with their shells burst and discarded and the kernel issued naked to put itself forth. She was the naked, clear kernel thrusting forth the clear, powerful shoot, and the world was a bygone winter,

discarded, her mother and father and Anton, and college and all her friends, all cast off like a year that has gone by, whilst the kernel was free and naked and striving to take new root, to create a new knowledge of Eternity in the flux of Time.[9]

What man is moving toward in Lawrence's novels is a new knowledge of eternity in the flux of time, which is to say, a new mythical and religious statement of the nature of time and eternity. The failure of religion is the most obvious failure in the world of Lawrence's novels, as it is in the world of Faulkner's novels. When religion fails, the will of man becomes dominating and destructive. Love dies and sex becomes painful. But when man sets out on a new journey of spiritual quest, there is a gradual rebirth, in fact a series of rebirths. Lawrence records in his fiction his own spiritual rebirths as they occurred during the time of his personal quest. Another statement about this rebirth is made by Ursula in the last paragraph of *The Rainbow*:

> And the rainbow stood on the earth. She knew that the sordid people who crept hard-scaled and separate on the face of the world's corruption were living still, that the rainbow was arched in their blood and would quiver to life in their spirit, that they would cast off their horny covering of disintegration, that new, clean, naked bodies would issue to a new germination, to a new growth, rising to the light and the wind and the clean rain of heaven. She saw in the rainbow the earth's new architecture, the old, brittle corruption of houses and factories swept away, the world built up in a living fabric of Truth, fitting to the over-arching heaven. (p. 467)

That, I submit, is prophetic prose at its best in the twentieth century. Lawrence says that a new birth is inevitable and that man, if he recognizes it, can accept this new birth and allow the spirit to work through him. Lawrence, more and more, became interested in symbols of new birth, one great symbol being the acorn. Another is the phoenix, Lawrence's own personal symbol of the death by fire of an old life and the rebirth of a new bird out of the ashes of the old life—the bird of spirit, which would be the basis of a new society. After *Women in Love* Lawrence ceases to be a novelist in the old sense of the word, as he himself once said. He sees that for him the prophetic function is more important than his function as novelist. His best statements after 1920, then, are statements in an essay form. He continued to write novels, as well as essays, poems, and travel books; but he speaks at his best, even in his later novels, as an essayist. Among the later novels are *Aaron's Rod, Kangaroo,* and *Lady Chatterley's Lover,* all good in their way. However, Lawrence's prophetic voice is, by the time he wrote them, so loud that it drowns out plot and characterization.

At the end of *Women in Love,* Lawrence shows us his two leading characters together, Birkin and Ursula. *Women in Love* shows us many corrupt people in the modern wasteland, but it shows us good people, too, and among these are Birkin and Ursula. They are two people who have a good marriage with a satisfactory sexual relationship. Yet the journey of life does not stop when one has achieved a satisfactory marriage. Birkin must fulfill a prophetic function in life. He must search for a new society. His wife seems to hold him back. She thinks that marital love alone is enough and she asks him:

> "Aren't I enough for you?"
> "No," he said. "You are enough for me as far as a woman is concerned. You are all women to me. But I wanted a man friend, as eternal as you and I are eternal."
> "Why aren't I enough?" she asked. "You are enough for me. I don't want anybody else but you, why isn't it the same with you?"
> "Having you, I can live all my life without anybody else, any other sheer intimacy. But to make it complete, really happy, I wanted eternal union with a man too: another kind of love," he said.
> "I don't believe it," she said. "It's an obstinacy, a theory, a perversity."
> "Well—" he said.
> "You can't have two kinds of love. Why should you!"
> "It seems as if I can't," he said. "Yet I wanted it."
> "You can't have it, because it's false, impossible," she said.
> "I don't believe that," he answered. (p. 548)

The last line of the novel, "I don't believe that," becomes the basis for Lawrence's search for the good society, which for him was a religious society. He once said that the most basic frustration he had was the frustration of his societal instinct. I don't believe Lawrence felt that his sexual instinct was particularly frustrated. He had solved for himself the sexual problem, as most people have not in the twentieth century. But Lawrence knew that man cannot take love and put it in a vacuum. Love is something that belongs in a social context, and so Lawrence, after writing *Women in Love*, set out on a journey around the world. It took him to Italy, and to Ceylon, and to Australia, and finally to New Mexico, and old Mexico. Lawrence said that the place he liked the most was New Mexico, and his wife moved there after his death and finally carried his ashes there to be placed in a little chapel in Taos, New Mexico. Lawrence, however, went back to the old world to die. In the south of France he met his end, feeling that he was a failure. His prophetic song failed him when his life ceased to be a quest to go beyond the tragedy of modern personal relationships.

Lawrence did not really find what he was looking for, but he did discover that there is no truly religious, mythical society still in existence. He found that there are a few individuals who continue the old ways, but that these ways are gradually being destroyed by the forces of modern society. He found that man must set out again on his own to find a new relationship between time and eternity.

Lawrence came to believe, as he says in *Kangaroo*, that man cannot exist purely on love. Human love and human trust are always perilous because they break down. The greater the love, the greater the trust, and then the greater the peril and disaster, because to place absolute trust in another human being is in itself a disaster. Each human being is a ship that must sail its own course, even if it go in company with another ship. Two people must not lean on each other. Everybody must be on his own journey, even though people go together. What then is needed in society? Above all, there is needed a true relationship with the cosmic energy, which Lawrence calls, using the old term, simply God. The center of all life is God, who is the source of all passion. Once accept God and human passion takes its right rhythm. But human love without God always kills the thing it loves. Man and woman today are killing each other with possessive love.

When there is no submission to a higher cosmic force that works through the universe, there is the will, or desire, to possess love, and people long to possess one another. Thus, people seek to control other people, whether it be their mates or their children.

The source of the form of tyranny that we call the Oedipus complex, as well as the tyranny found in modern industry and modern life generally, is the desire of people for love in order that they may escape from their isolation. Still, man cannot escape from his isolation, Lawrence keeps telling us, unless he can go down before the one God. In *Kangaroo*, Lawrence says, "Yet the human heart must have an absolute. . . . With no deep God who is source of all passion and life to hold them separate and yet sustained in accord, the loving comrades would smash one another, and smash all love, all feeling as well."[10]

Here we have the paradox of the separateness of man, which must be preserved along with the unity of man. They can only be preserved in man's relationship to the God power as well as to other individuals. If man lives a totally separate life, he goes mad with the pain of isolation. If he lives a totally unified life, without any sense of separateness, he is caught up in a destructive, merging relationship. He must live the paradox of unity and separateness, and this comes only through true religious experience. Lawrence in *Kangaroo* also says: "Any more love is a hopeless thing till we have found again, each of us for himself, the great dark God who alone will sustain us in loving one another. Till then, best not play with more fire" (p. 221).

The basis of the pain of the modern wasteland is lovelessness. This is what Eliot says in *The Waste Land*, and this what Joyce says in *Ulysses*. Without love, man suffers painfully and gradually withers and dies. The pain of isolation causes people to seek once again the new relationship with the cosmic energy. Thus begins a renewed quest, a beginning again on the one great spiritual journey of man to higher forms of life.

Lawrence did not find what he was looking for in Australia or in America. He found fragments of the old mythical way of life among the Indians of New Mexico and old Mexico. Lawrence and Faulkner both have made striking contributions to the development of an understanding of modern relationships between red man, white man, and black man. Both have a deep sense of the dark soil of human communal relationships that allows them to treat sympathetically the souls of people of races other than their own.

Lawrence in *The Plumed Serpent* wrote one of the great stories about Mexico and about Indian life. The book is a failure as a

novel. The good writing in it is travel writing and prophetic statement in essay form. There is a woman in the novel who sees, as
Lawrence did, the fragments of mythic life among the Indians of
New Mexico and old Mexico. What she finds is an underlying unity
of the blood and an acceptance of people as people. She feels something in Mexico of this old world before the Flood. Lawrence re-
calls the lost continent of Atlantis, part of which was in America;
then he records Kate's feeling of the basic equality of the blood:

> *Blood is one blood. We are all of one bloodstream.* Some-
> thing aboriginal and tribal, and almost worse than death to
> the white individual. Out of the dark eyes and the powerful
> spines of these people, all the time the unknown assertion:
> *The blood is one blood.* It was a strange, overbearing insis-
> tence, a claim of blood-unison.
>   Kate was of a proud old family. She had been brought up
> with the English-Germanic idea of the *intrinsic* superiority of
> the hereditary aristocrat. Her blood was different from the
> common blood, another, finer fluid.
>   But in Mexico, none of this.[11]

    Kate finds that at last she can achieve a kind of rest and peace
from always trying to prove her superiority to ordinary people.
She has been caught in the old aristocratic trap of feeling better
than most other people. Then in Mexico she senses a kind of unity.
Lawrence found the old Mexican blood rotting away because of
the disappearance of the mythic life. He found the same horror
there that he had experienced in other places. But he captured in
his novel a sense of an earlier way of life that still had in it some of
the old mythic unity that he himself had felt as a young man and
as a child in rural England. Lawrence believed that people really
were basically equal in the blood, that is to say, in their souls. I
think the word *blood* for Lawrence is simply a symbol of the unconscious mind. He felt that white men, particularly white aris-
tocrats, had set themselves above other people. To maintain this
feeling of superiority requires ceaseless activity, a mad restless-
ness, which nonwhite people find so strange in Europeans and
Americans. But Kate in Mexico finds a kind of peace: "The strange,
heavy, *positive* passivity. For the first time in her life she felt absolutely at rest. And talk, and thought, had become trivial, superfi-
cial to her: as the ripples on the surface of the lake are as nothing,

to the creatures that live away below in the unwavering deeps" (p. 462).

By the time he wrote *The Plumed Serpent*, Lawrence felt that he had been caught up too much in ideas. One does not find quite the same anti-intellectualism in Faulkner because Faulkner never had all that much to do with the intellect in the first place. Lawrence probably had had an overdose of British intellectualism; too much head and too little instincts, he was always exclaiming in his prophetic prose. Thus he can say in one of his prophetic essays, entitled "Books":

Once all men in the world lost their courage and their newness, the world would come to an end. The old Jews said the same: unless in the world there was at least one Jew passionately praying, the race was lost.

So we begin to see where we are. It's no good leaving everything to fate. Man is an adventurer, and he must never give up the adventure. The venture is the venture: fate is the circumstance around the adventurer. The adventurer at the quick of the venture is the living germ inside the chaos of circumstance. But for the living germ of Noah in his Ark, chaos would have redescended on the world in the waters of the flood. But chaos *couldn't* redescend, because Noah was afloat with all the animals.

The same with the Christians when Rome fell. In their little fortified monasteries they defended themselves against howling invasions, being too poor to excite much covetousness. When wolves and bears prowled through the streets of Lyons, and a wild boar was grunting and turning up the pavement of Augustus's temple, the Christian bishops also roved intently and determinedly, like poor forerunners, along the ruined streets, seeking a congregation. It was the great adventure, and they did not give it up.

But Noah, of course, is always in an unpopular minority. So, of course, were the Christians, when Rome began to fall. The Christians now are in a hopelessly popular majority, so it is their turn to fall.

I know the greatness of Christianity; it is a past greatness. I know that, but for those early Christians, we should never have emerged from the chaos and hopeless disaster of the Dark Ages. If I had lived in the year 400, pray God, I should have been a true and passionate Christian. The adventurer.

But now I live in 1924, and the Christian venture is done. The adventure is gone out of Christianity. We must start on a new venture towards God.[12]

The chief idea in Lawrence, then, is the mythic quest, the journey toward God. He sums this up finally in what I think is his greatest work of nonfiction, *Studies in Classic American Literature*. The last chapter is on Whitman. He disapproves of Whitman's attempt to merge with other people. What he believes in, he says, is sympathy and staying on the open road and not trying to tell the soul what to do. He believes that the man who tries to force his soul to do something destroys his soul. The will must not be predominant; man must submit himself to his own soul, to the guidance of his soul. He says at the end of the book:

> It is not I who guide my soul to heaven. It is I who am guided by my own soul along the open road, where all men tread. Therefore I accept her deep motions of love, or hate, or compassion, or dislike, or indifference. And I must go where she takes me. For my feet and my lips and my body are my soul. It is I who must submit to her.
> This is Whitman's message of American democracy.[13]

Lawrence was a great believer in democracy, as defined by Walt Whitman. He was a great believer in the quality of unconscious minds. He felt that the old European aristocratic way of life was dead, that the new mechanical, industrial way of life which was taking its place would soon destroy itself, that it was in fact destroying the land. When it destroyed the land, it would then collapse. After that, a few people who would continue the venture, like Noah and the early Christians, would reclaim the world and a new society would then come into being.

Now this is a sweeping vision. But Lawrence continued to seek new revelation all of his life. He did not have one single, final vision. Therefore, we don't have to take all he says as his final word on anything. Toward the end of his life he was thinking about Christ and the Old and New Testaments. His last book, *Apocalypse*, an interpretation of the great revelation of Saint John at the end of the New Testament, brings him to a consideration of the cosmic power underlying all life. In no other essay does his prophetic song ring so true.

Lawrence was interested in symbols and their power to call forth the cosmic energy in man's soul. He wrote *The Man Who Died*, a reinterpretation of the life of Christ, and, of course, he wrote *Lady Chatterley's Lover*. He wrote many things, even at the end of his life, even as he was dying. He had many personal failings, but he had a great creative power and he was not a dogmatist. He did not stop with one idea or one vision. He kept traveling, kept moving. He was not moving toward sex or the good society for their own sake. I think he was moving toward what he called in *The Plumed Serpent* "the strange star between the sky and the waters of the first Cosmos: this is man's divinity" (p. 458). A realization of man's divinity would then restore man's sexual and love relationships.

William Faulkner is in many ways unlike Lawrence. Faulkner is a writer who, I think, was influenced by Joseph Conrad more than by anybody else. He was also the greatest experimenter the novel has seen in the twentieth century, greater even than James Joyce. He was a very great novelist, and Europeans, more subtle than we, noticed this first. Since 1950 he has received widespread acclaim in America, yet his work is still not understood as a part of the larger international tradition of the symbolist novel.

Faulkner is, first of all, a great creator of modern wasteland scenes. Some people consider his best novel to be *Sanctuary*. I do not. Still, *Sanctuary* is a fine portrayal of modern life set in northern Mississippi and in the city of Memphis, Tennessee. It is a novel about the corruption of the modern woman and about gangsters, about rape, and about prostitutes. It is a very difficult novel, yet it has scenes of great beauty. Many Europeans consider it a masterpiece, but surely Faulkner's masterpiece is *Absalom, Absalom!*, in which he creates a saga about nineteenth-century America, particularly southern America. Faulkner is most like Lawrence in recording that the modern European white man, since 1800, has sought to impose his will on other people and has sought to set himself above all other races. This has been the cause of his spiritual and moral decline in the twentieth century. It also represents a sexual and a social decline. This decline, as it appears in the old South, is dealt with in *Absalom, Absalom!*

One of Faulkner's great characters, Quentin Compson, seeks the meaning of the southern past in *Absalom, Absalom!* He is a

student at Harvard, telling a friend from Canada what life in the
South is like. He must go back over the past of many people, particularly the past of a man named Thomas Sutpen, who set himself up as a southern aristocrat by his strong will, and who brought
destruction upon himself and upon many people. Thomas Sutpen
stands, then, for the southern aristocrat and also for the aristocratic spirit of the European white man all over the world.

Thomas Sutpen begins as a poor boy, as did William Faulkner's grandfather, who was a similar southern aristocrat. In Virginia, the boy Sutpen comes up to the great white mansion of a
southern aristocrat, and a Negro servant tells him to go to the back
door. He cannot stand to be humiliated. Driven by anger and
shame, he goes to the West Indies. He gets money. He deals in
slaves. Finally, with money and power and people to do his bid-
ding, he comes to Mississippi; he seizes land and creates what he
hopes will be a great southern aristocratic dynasty. But his many
sins doom all his frenzied efforts. The final collapse of his evil dynasty does not come until early in the twentieth century, when
Quentin Compson is on hand to view that collapse. Faulkner calls
Thomas Sutpen "Beelzebub." Like Lawrence describing Gerald
Crich, the mine owner, Faulkner sees Sutpen as an evil man because he wills himself to take over other people's lives and property, and because he tries to use other people for his own selfish
purposes:

That this Faustus, this demon, this Beelzebub fled hiding
from some momentary flashy glare of his Creditor's outraged
face exasperated beyond all endurance, hiding, scuttling into
respectability like a jackal into a rockpile, so that she thought
at first, until she realized that he was not hiding, did not
want to hide, was merely engaged in one final frenzy of evil
and harm-doing before the Creditor overtook him next time
for good and all—this Faustus who appeared suddenly one
Sunday with two pistols and twenty subsidiary demons and
skulldugged a hundred miles of land out of a poor ignorant
Indian and built the biggest house on it you ever saw and
went away with six wagons and came back with the crystal
tapestries and the Wedgwood chairs to furnish it and nobody
knew if he had robbed another steamboat or had just dug up
a little more of the old loot, who hid horns and tail beneath
human raiment and a beaver hat and chose (bought her, out-

swapped his father-in-law, wasn't it) a wife after three years to scrutinize, weigh and compare, not from one of the local ducal houses but from the lesser baronage whose principality was so far decayed that there would be no risk of his wife bringing him for dowry delusions of grandeur. . . . [14]

What will happen as a result of this rape of the land by southern planters? On the physical level come soil erosion and the failure of crops. The failure of nature is a typical by-product in the world's mythology of the wasteland that tyrants create. There is also the erosion of the soul, which leads to the death of the family. At last, Quentin must witness the burning of Sutpen's great house, long after the death of the tyrant. One of Sutpen's children still lurks about the house. As the house burns, Quentin can also hear the cry of Jim Bond, a Negro heir, who is an idiot.

The last of the Sutpens is an idiot Negro. Quentin's roommate, after hearing the story, then tells what he thinks will happen:

> "And so do you know what I think?" Now he did expect an answer, and now he got one:
> "No," Quentin said.
> "Do you want to know what I think?"
> "No," Quentin said.
> "Then I'll tell you. I think that in time the Jim Bonds are going to conquer the western hemisphere. Of course it won't quite be in our time and of course as they spread toward the poles they will bleach out again like the rabbits and the birds do, so they won't show up so sharp against the snow. But it will still be Jim Bond; and so in a few thousand years, I who regard you will also have sprung from the loins of African kings. Now I want you to tell me just one thing more. Why do you hate the South?"
> "I don't hate it," Quentin said, quickly, at once, immediately; "I don't hate it," he said. *I don't hate* it he thought, panting in the cold air, the iron New England dark; *I don't. I don't! I don't hate it! I don't hate it!* (p. 378)

But of course he does hate it. He is caught up in a love-hate relationship with the land that, like his own soul, has been violated by possessive men. We have to go back to an earlier book, *The Sound and the Fury*, written a few years before *Absalom, Absalom!* to see what happens to Quentin and his family. Quentin is a mem-

ber of an old family, the Compsons of Jefferson, Mississippi. His
sister Caddy, symbol of the violated woman, finally becomes the
mistress of a Nazi staff officer in 1942.

Yet in *The Sound and the Fury*, and in other works of Faulkner
as well, strangulation in the modern wasteland is not the final
statement. Like Lawrence, Faulkner writes about spiritual regeneration. They both write about the modern wasteland, but they
also write about man getting free of modern corruption; not all
men but some.

I have selected three characters who rise above modern corruption. One is Dilsey in *The Sound and the Fury*, the old Negro
servant of the Compson family. She watches the Compsons dying
and going mad all around her, but in the midst of all she preserves
her Christian piety. She remains loyal to her faith, and so she can
love those who mistreat her. She is entrusted with the care of one
of the sons in the Compson family, Benjy, who is an idiot. The first
part of *The Sound and the Fury* is Benjy's part, in which he describes the world as he sees it through his idiot eyes. Dilsey, in part
three of the book, looks after Benjy. She takes him to her church,
because the white people won't let Benjy go to their church. Proud
white people don't want to be reminded of their idiots. So Dilsey
takes him to the Negro church, and as they walk to the church one
of her daughters complains:

> "I wish you wouldn't keep on bringin him to church,
> mammy," Frony said. "Folks talkin."
> "Whut folks?" Dilsey said.
> "I hears em," Frony said.
> "And I knows whut kind of folks," Dilsey said, "Trash
> white folks. Dat's who it is. Thinks he aint good enough fer
> white church, but nigger church aint good enough fer him."
> "Dey talks, jes de same," Frony said.
> "Den you send um to me," Dilsey said. "Tell um de good
> Lawd dont keer whether he smart er not. Dont nobody but
> white trash keer dat."[15]

She takes Benjy to the service, and there occurs one of the
great events in Faulkner. It is a religious ceremony of spiritual regeneration, one in which the preacher invokes the power and glory
of God, and Faulkner must have truly captured the essence of this
kind of Negro rite. It is the sort of ceremony generally looked down

upon by white southerners. The ritual process is one of the preacher involving his congregation in a mystical participation in his vision of the power and glory of God. Faulkner has done something few modern writers have achieved: he has rendered a religious experience in literary symbols. Lawrence tried this and failed in *The Plumed Serpent*, possibly because he never saw an effective religious ceremony.

The Reverend Shegog is a traveling evangelist, who physically is unimpressive. Dilsey reminds those who are doubtful about him that she has seen the Lord use stranger tools than the Reverend Shegog. The preacher lives up to the highest expectations by invoking the spirit. As people leave the church, they know they have participated in a mystical regeneration of the spirit. They have had a vision of man's destiny:

> "He sho a preacher, mon! He didn't look like much at first, but hush!"
> "He seed de power en de glory."
> "Yes, suh. He seed hit. Face to face he seed hit."
> Dilsey made no sound, her face did not quiver as the tears took their sunken and devious courses, walking with her head up, making no effort to dry them away even.
> "Whyn't you quit dat, mammy?" Frony said. "Wid all dese people lookin. We be passin white folks soon."
> "I've seed de first en de last," Dilsey said. "Never you mind me."
> "First en last whut?" Frony said.
> "Never you mind," Dilsey said. "I seed de beginnin, en now I sees de endin." (p. 313)

Dilsey is talking about the end of the old aristocratic way of life, set up by Compsons and Sutpens, which stood in the way of the realization of democracy and brotherhood. After the church service, she goes back to take up her lowly duties with the other servants in the house of the Compsons. The first person she meets is mother Compson, the typical madwoman of the aristocratic world, who constantly persecutes her. Dilsey represents the only voice of sanity and humanity in the decadent world of the Compsons. Because of her faith and love, she can convert the pain of her life into the gold thread of spiritual regeneration.

Another Faulkner character who achieves regeneration is

Hightower in *Light in August*, a member of the white aristocracy whose grandfather fought in the Civil War. Hightower is a preacher, but one who has betrayed his calling, betrayed his ministry, because he found the church to be corrupt. He has also betrayed his wife, who then went mad. But he eventually finds a kind of spiritual rebirth.

Hightower becomes the friend of a man of the people, an artisan named Byron Bunch. The two of them manage together to forge a new life based on the mythic religious tradition, while all around them the people in the town of Jefferson are going mad in what is probably the greatest lynch scene in American fiction. With a new vision of life, Hightower can begin to understand how his life has gone wrong in the past. For one thing, he has sought to escape the pain of life in the church:

> He thought that he could say that, at first. He believed that they would comprehend. He went there, chose that as his vocation, with that as his purpose. But he believed in more than that. He had believed in the church too, in all that it ramified and evoked. He believed with a calm joy that if ever there was shelter, it would be the Church; that if ever truth could walk naked and without shame or fear, it would be in the seminary. When he believed that he had heard the call it seemed to him that he could see his future, his life intact and on all sides complete and inviolable, like a classic and serene vase. . . .[16]

The seminary and the church turn out not to be places of escape, nor are they places of truth. Finally, though, Hightower sees where he has failed, and he sees also the failure of the church:

> It seems to him that he has seen it all the while: that that which is destroying the Church is not the outward groping of those within it nor the inward groping of those without, but the professionals who control it and who have removed the bells from its steeples. He seems to see them, endless, without order, empty, symbolical, bleak, sky-pointed not with ecstasy or passion but in adjuration, threat, and doom. He seems to see the churches of the world like a rampart, like one of those barricades of the middleages planted with dead and sharpened stakes, against truth and against that peace in which to sin and be forgiven which is the life of man. (pp. 426–27)

At last he comes to find a forgiveness within himself, and he sees that he is not alone in the world. He sees that he has been the instrument of his own destruction, but he sees too that he is also an instrument of something higher than himself: "Then, if this is so, if I am the instrument of her despair and death, then I am in turn instrument of someone outside myself" (p. 430).

So he knows at last that the spirit can work through him and that he need no longer be a part of a corrupt organization which has already discarded him anyway, that he can now search for his true self and thereby be reborn. He had used the church to run away, but he now turns to face life on a renewed quest.

Ike McCaslin is yet another character in Faulkner's fiction who breaks free of the old corruption in order to search for the good life on his own. McCaslin has found a way of life through a man named Sam Fathers, who initiated him into a hunting rite that made possible a sense of union between man and nature:

> Old Sam Fathers was alive then, born in slavery, son of a Negro slave and a Chickasaw chief, who had taught him how to shoot, not only when to shoot but when not to; such a November dawn as tomorrow would be and the old man led him straight to the great cypress and he had known the buck would pass exactly there because there was something running in Sam Fathers' veins which ran in the veins of the buck too, and they stood there against the tremendous trunk, the old man of seventy and the boy of twelve, and there was nothing save the dawn until suddenly the buck was there, smoke-colored out of nothing, magnificent with speed: and Sam Fathers said, "Now. Shoot quick and shoot slow:" and the gun levelled rapidly without haste and crashed and he walked to the buck lying still intact and still in the shape of that magnificent speed and bled it with Sam's knife and Sam dipped his hands into the hot blood and marked his face forever while he stood trying not to tremble, humbly and with pride too though the boy of twelve had been unable to phrase it then: *I slew you; my bearing must not shame your quitting life. My conduct forever onward must become your death*; marking him for that and for more than that: that day and himself and McCaslin juxtaposed not against the wilderness but against the tamed land, the old wrong and shame itself, in repudiation and denial at least of the land and the wrong and shame even if he couldn't cure the wrong and eradicate the shame. . . .[17]

McCaslin has been taught a ritual by one who is both Indian and Negro, one who still knows something of the old mythical life, of the union of the blood. Therefore, the blood of Sam Fathers is somehow connected with the blood of the deer Ike shoots. He also sees that the Delta, the richest farmland in America, has been ruined by people who tried to use it for their own selfish benefit. He cannot do anything about it, but he will somehow try to survive and live a good life though the old land is dying. And he thinks: "No wonder the ruined woods I used to know don't cry for retribution. The people who have destroyed it will accomplish its revenge."

McCaslin sees, as Dilsey does, the end of a way of life, but he feels that somehow the blood of people like Sam Fathers will live on, that goodness can be achieved even in the midst of the ruin of the land.

In spite of their differences, Lawrence and Faulkner both have a sense of the blood unity of man, of the essential unity of Negro and white man, of Jew and Gentile, of aristocrat and peasant. There is also a sense of a new life, a new birth of man springing up amidst the old life which is dying rapidly in the twentieth century. The two novelists portray the evil of the wasteland, of men forgetting who they are and trying to will their destinies and control their lives and the lives of other people. They also portray the good that is in people who retain some of the old faith and the good in those who seek to find new faith. There is in both Lawrence and Faulkner a great awareness of the American destiny, a sense of democracy at its best, which sees that people can be different and yet united. They are both nonconformists in that they believe people ought to be themselves, but they also believe people ought to work together.

There is a reaching back in both authors to the basic sources of man's wisdom. Faulkner late in his career wrote a fable that is a modern telling of the Christ story, set in World War I; Lawrence wrote an interpretation of the life of Christ and the last book of the New Testament. We can see the deep influence of both the Old and the New Testaments on both of them, especially the Old Testament on Faulkner and the New Testament on Lawrence. Above all, we can see a great awareness of the power and the glory of man's life, even in the twentieth century; this power and glory shine through their prophetic songs.

Even in their visions of man's evil, there is an awareness of the greatness of man. The mother of Paul Morel in *Sons and Lovers* does many bad things, and yet Lawrence presents her as a very great person. Faulkner can portray the ugly side of the South without ever losing his feeling for the greatness of the South. Both have a sense of man's tragic destiny and of man's common suffering. Both, at their best, are deeply prophetic in their proclamation of the possibility of finding new life even in the midst of tragedy.

The prophetic voices of Lawrence and Faulkner say that man will overcome the modern wasteland and will move on to a higher development in the future. Humans do not have to settle for selfishness and cruelty, those by-products and causes of tyranny; those who do settle for cruelty only perish from the land to make way for those who seek new life. The prophetic writer not only points to a new age but reflects, in his way of writing, the power and glory that come to those who move in the direction of an epic age, leaving behind past tragedy. The power and glory reflected in the prophetic writer's style is but a hint of greatness to come. Yet great prophetic writers have a way of unsettling people who deny or have learned to live with the tragedy of an age. Probably no novelist has ever unsettled more people than Lawrence and Faulkner. They well may have ended their life's work in the "sweat and agony of the human spirit," to use Faulkner's words, with the sentence the Spanish philosopher Miguel de Unamuno used to end his *Tragic Sense of Life*: "And may God deny you peace, but give you glory."[18]

Hemingway's Vision
of the Open Road

By the 1920s, symbolist fiction had established itself as an international mode of expression for many of the advanced writers of
modernism. By this time, one of modernism's chief aims was
clearly that of purifying the dialect of the tribe. No writer of the
twenties sums up the international complexion and the linguistic
aims of symbolism better than Ernest Hemingway. Joseph Conrad
with his rich impressionistic style and his sense of a tragic abyss
always threatening man's efforts, and D. H. Lawrence with his
powerful symbolism and prose rhythms, had established a new
novel in English that went far beyond traditional English realism
and the naturalism that was beginning to dominate much of
American writing. Hemingway schooled himself in Conrad's techniques and moral attitudes, and he studied the post-impressionist
paintings of France. In Paris he accepted instruction from Pound,
Stein, and Joyce. The result was a refining and simplifying of the
rich, luxuriant style of earlier symbolist fiction.

Hemingway did such a good job of simplification that many
readers, and even some critics, took his style to be "realistic" or
even "naturalistic." A close analysis of it, however, reveals an impressionism and use of symbols of an extremely subtle nature. In

94

fact, Hemingway did more than any other prose writer, more than Pater, Conrad, or Lawrence, to establish as a part of modern literature a prose style that is poetic. Hemingway himself said that his job, as he saw it, was to "strip language clean, to lay it bare down to the bone."[1] This cleansing process was accompanied by a poetic use of symbol, diction, and rhythm that would fulfill, for a time at least, the symbolist hope for a purified language.

Hemingway's style is infinitely more subtle than even careful readers generally realize. In fact, I think that if there is anyone in the twenties he should be compared with, it is not Joyce nor Faulkner, both greater writers, nor Fitzgerald, a lesser writer. He should rather be compared with a fiction writer he had almost nothing in common with personally, but whose life and work in some ways paralleled his own at the deepest psychic level. That writer is Virginia Woolf. In her two best novels, *Mrs. Dalloway* and *To the Lighthouse*, Woolf made a masterful contribution to the art of symbolist fiction. Both books have a refinement of style and a subtlety possibly found elsewhere only in Hemingway, of all the writers of the twenties. The two have in common a vision that makes possible this style. The vision is based on a balanced view both of tragedy and of the happiness attendant upon every step of a journey that must be taken if one is to overcome tragedy. Both create characters who are seized by the great sense of nothingness found everywhere in modern life and are being carried off into death, and right beside them they place characters who, openly facing death, defy nothingness and move at least a few steps beyond the tragedy everywhere surrounding them. In *The Sun Also Rises* and *To the Lighthouse* Hemingway and Woolf have created characters who, in spite of handicaps, can both create and love, who accept the tragedy of their times and not only make the best of a bad situation but also make steps toward creative joy and love.

The movement into an open-ended future, in which the quester denies the great nothingness, leads to moments of love, the greatest fact of human existence for Woolf and Hemingway. The existentialism of Sartre and Camus has made moderns, because of journalistic exposure, acutely aware of the concept of nothingness. It must be remembered, however, that the French existentialists are, in philosophical terms at least, minor offshoots of Martin Heidegger, who posits not the dichotomy of being and nothingness, as does Sartre, but the interaction of being and time.

Time is tragic, but being is the eternal element best represented in ordinary life as love and joy for writers like Woolf and Hemingway.[2] It is partly because of the influence of critics and thinkers like Sartre that so many people are more aware of the concept of the great nada, as Hemingway deals with it in the famous short story "A Clean, Well-Lighted Place," than they are with the fact of love in Hemingway. Indeed, this story and other Hemingway writings about states of nothingness inspired Sartre and Camus in the development of their own philosophical concepts.

Robert Penn Warren in a well-known early essay on Hemingway established the connection between love and nada in Hemingway. He writes: ". . . the initiates of the cult of love are those who are aware of nada, but their effort, as members of the cult, is to find a meaning to put in place of the nada."[3] Warren goes on to link Hemingway's cult of love with violence and with fidelity to a code and to the discipline that the code demands. Thus, for Warren, violence "represents a sinking into nature" and also "represents a conquest of nature, and of nada in man."[4] Except possibly Malcolm Cowley's writing on initiation rituals in Hemingway, no article has had such an influence on Hemingway critics as Warren's. In fact, it might be said that Cowley and Warren helped to establish Hemingway as a part of the kind of modernism they themselves stood for, which is related to the use of myth and ritual to overcome tragedy or, at least, to make it bearable. Frank Kermode and other recent critics have explored the role of love in Forster, Woolf, and others in the Bloomsbury Circle, but the mistaken idea that Hemingway was the leading writer of the lost generation still weighs most of the criticism in favor of the wasteland view of the American writer. In spite of the earlier efforts of Cowley and Warren and the later efforts of Carlos Baker, Hemingway is still often caricatured as a dead soul in a nada-haunted world. Philip Young in the fifties made such statements as: "Hemingway's world is one in which things do not grow, but explode, break, decompose, or are eaten away."[5] Quotations can always be found to back up such statements, which deny the chief vision of the major fiction, a vision which, Young says, "is obsessed with violence."[6] Leslie Fiedler's *Love and Death in the American Novel* established anew in 1960 the idea of a loveless Hemingway, a tradition begun much earlier by Wyndham Lewis; and, in spite of a minority dissent, the wasteland view of Hemingway continues today.

Hemingway's deepest artistic roots are, in spite of the waste-land critics, in the tradition of affirmation. Hemingway was an international writer who drew sustenance from a yea-saying vision he found in Conrad, Joyce, and Gabriele D'Annunzio, the Italian poet who worked in the yea-saying tradition of Nietzsche. Yet the American roots of Hemingway's art probably are deeper than any others. Although he was influenced by fiction writers of his own time, particularly Sherwood Anderson, it was really his debt to Mark Twain that was most important. Young tries to make the reader see this debt in terms of Huck's traumatic soul, in a dubious interpretation of *Huckleberry Finn* that sees the hero setting out on his river journey because of a traumatic experience. For one thing, Huck goes down to the river because there he is happy and free. Huck and Hemingway's chief protagonists all leave home to go on a journey with no determined destination, and along the way they find, among other things, good comrades to be happy with. In one sense they go looking, like all of America's pioneers, for a happiness they cannot find at home. The pursuit of happiness—and what ideal is more essentially American?—is depicted by Mark Twain in *Huckleberry Finn* and by Hemingway in much of his best work. It is this pursuit of happiness in Hemingway that readers and critics have too often neglected. A serious novelist often embraces many traditions. There is undoubtedly some truth in Young's classification that puts Hemingway in a tradition of American violence, but there is another tradition that Hemingway and Mark Twain, and for that matter many other American writers, are a part of—the tradition of the search for happiness and new experience on the open road.

In terms of the American vision, the poet Hemingway resembles most is Walt Whitman, the mastersinger of the open road. In quoting Ecclesiastes in the second epigraph of *The Sun Also Rises*, to the effect that the earth abides forever, Hemingway affirms Whitman's idea of nature as the sustaining mother of man. Furthermore, Whitman's poem "Song of the Open Road" celebrates, among others, two important Hemingway ideas: that happiness is to be found in the open air itself and, what is possibly the most important idea in the poem, that great joy is to be found in the company of comrades met on the open road. First, let us consider the atmosphere of happiness suffusing the open road, which is described in the following lines of the poem:

> The efflux of the soul is happiness, here is happiness,
> I think it pervades the open air, waiting at all times,
> Now it flows unto us, we are rightly charged. . . .[7]

Despite highly diverse styles, both Whitman and Hemingway are one in believing that many of the best Americans, those with a deep zest for life, should and do set out on the open road to find happiness. When Hemingway and his protagonists go to Europe, they are not simply running away from a land they despise; instead they are proving how truly American they are by setting out on Whitman's "long brown path before me leading wherever I choose" (p. 172). Europe—France, Italy, and Spain, in particular— is the open road that Hemingway takes. In *The Sun Also Rises*— the novel many mistakenly consider Hemingway's most pessimistic—Jake Barnes and Bill Gorton, both of whom have left their native shores, are often happy in Paris and in other cities they visit. Robert Cohn and others like him, people whom the author clearly dislikes, have little capacity for happiness; they cannot enjoy Paris or really anything else. A rising young American novelist "with some sort of an English accent" asks Jake if he finds Paris amusing, and gets this answer: "For God's sake. . . . Yes, don't you?"[8] For Jake happiness is in the air: "I was hot and I felt happy" (p. 119). Bill Gorton, a man of the open road who finds New York, Paris, Vienna, and Budapest all "wonderful," clearly enjoys himself everywhere: "He was very cheerful and said the States were wonderful. New York was wonderful. . . . Bill was very happy" (p. 69). Those who cannot enjoy Paris and other cities of the open road often borrow their opinions from others because, having no real love of living, they do not know what they like. Jake thinks, "I wondered where Cohn got that incapacity to enjoy Paris. Possibly from Mencken. So many young men get their likes and dislikes from Mencken" (p. 42). Thus, the contrast is sharply drawn in this book between those Americans who have the capacity to be happy on the open road that Europe offers and the artificial people who have to be told what to like.

Hemingway's chief characters can be happy in the cities of the world, but they come into their own when they are outdoors. Nature, or "country," as the author sometimes calls it, always beckons. Whitman too believed in the efficacy of open spaces:

Now I see the secret of the making of the best persons,
It is to grow in the open air and to eat and sleep with the
   earth. (p. 152)

Jake and Bill Gorton love Paris, but the place where they are the
happiest is in the Spanish forest. At Burguete, Bill looks around
him, and instead of Whitman's generalization we have simply,
"This is country" (p. 117). A few pages later, Bill, full of joy and
laughter, says: "Let no man be ashamed to kneel here in the great
out-of-doors. Remember the woods were God's first temples. Let
us kneel and say: 'Don't eat that, Lady—that's Mencken'" (p. 122).
Nick Adams in "Big Two-Hearted River," part 1, knows a similar
happiness in the woods: "His muscles ached and the day was hot,
but Nick felt happy."[9] Once in the woods, the exciting experience
itself—which is made possible by the same acute sensitivity that
has caused Nick to be both fascinated and repelled by violence—
is all that matters. The word *happy* then is undoubtedly one of the
significant words in Hemingway's work.

Many kinds of happiness are pursued by Hemingway's protagonists on the open road, but the greatest happiness of all, except for the supreme ecstasy found in the arms of the beloved,
comes from comradeship. Whitman's call to comrades ends "Song
of the Open Road," and its importance in the poem cannot be
stressed too much:

Camerado, I give you my hand!
I give you my love more precious than money,
I give you myself before preaching or law;
Will you give me yourself? will you come travel with me?
Shall we stick by each other as long as we live? (p. 159)

Here is an American ideal that Hemingway affirms, one that calls
for exploration. In his own way he agrees with Whitman's celebra-
tion of the "great Companions":

Allons! after the great Companions, and to belong to them!
They too are on the road—they are the swift and majestic
   men—they are the greatest women. (p. 155)

The good comrades in both Whitman and Hemingway are above all else lovers of life and, as such, are capable of great happiness.

The comrades whom Hemingway loves—those who are properly initiated—are easily distinguished from those who do not belong among the comrades—the Robert Cohns, the Pablos, the Miss Van Campens. Hemingway's attitude toward the masses of people—those masses Walt Whitman sought to embrace—is clearly stated in *Green Hills of Africa*: "I had loved country all my life; the country was always better than the people. I could only care about people a very few at a time."[10] A few can be accepted, and these few are rewarded with the love Hemingway always has for his true comrades. Looking for a dominant theme in the author's work, one might not be far wrong to say that it is the search for close personal relationships. Many readers do not realize just how close the relationships between comrades are because of Hemingway's characteristic understatement. Occasionally he tells the reader how much comrades mean to his heroes, as, for example, in *For Whom the Bell Tolls* when Robert Jordan thinks: "I have been all my life in these hills since I have been here. Anselmo is my oldest friend. . . . Agustín . . . is my brother, and I never had a brother."[11] He goes on, "I hate to leave a thing that is so good." Thus the hardbitten Hemingway of popular imagination reveals a tenderness not often found in modern literature.

An examination of the four novels which form the core of Hemingway's work—*The Sun Also Rises, A Farewell to Arms, For Whom the Bell Tolls, Across the River and into the Trees*—will reveal the pattern of personal relationships. In each of the four novels the three basic characters are the hero (through whom the story is presented), the loved one, and the trusted comrade. Along with the third member of this group there are usually several other comrades. Because of Jake's wound, on one hand, and Lady Brett's defects as a woman, on the other, the hero of *The Sun Also Rises* never knows the brief but perfect union with the loved one, as do Frederic Henry, Robert Jordan, and Colonel Cantwell. Nothing, however, prevents Jake from enjoying himself magnificently with his best comrade, Bill Gorton. Once on the open road going to Spain, they are released from the ties of troublesome acquaintances and time-wasting institutions. They are in a word happy, which, next to the ecstasy of love, is the best feeling Hemingway's people can know. In the relationship between Jake and Bill a pattern that will be repeated in later novels becomes apparent: the hero is tight-lipped in expressing his regard for the comrade, while the latter at times opens his heart to show his love for his friend. A tone of badinage preserves from sentimentality speeches that at first glance seem effusive. Consider the following exchange between Bill and Jake on the subject of Henry James:

"I think he's a good writer, too," Bill said. "And you're a hell of a good guy. Anybody ever tell you you were a good guy?"

"I'm not a good guy."

"Listen. You're a hell of a good guy, and I'm fonder of you than anybody on earth." (p. 116)

To understand the contrast between the neurotic expatriates, who are running away from something, and the true comrades, who seek not escape but intense and joyful experience, one must come to grips with a key word—*pity*. Robert Cohn, wallowing in self-pity, is often "sad," as Hemingway sometimes puts it; others of the same ilk follow him in later novels. In *Across the River and into the Trees* Hemingway makes a fundamental distinction between the major characters who suffer but are never "sad" and certain doleful minor characters. Jackson, the colonel's driver, is "sad," but the old man himself, facing death, is never this way: "He did not know, among other things, that the girl loved him because he had never been sad one waking morning of his life; attack or no attack. He had experienced anguish and sorrow. But he had never been sad in the morning."[12] The comrades know anguish, but they have no truck with the loss of nerve that keeps Cohn, Jackson, and the expatriates from living with zest. The morose characters can actually be dangerous, as Robert Jordon makes clear in *For Whom the Bell Tolls*. Pablo, one of the "sad" ones, is no good for the cause, and Jordan tells himself that one must be "gay" to do his job properly. People who are "gay" have the capacity for happiness and the zest for life that distinguishes the good comrades on the open road: "All the best ones, when you thought it over, were gay. It was much better to be gay and it was a sign of something too. It was like having immortality while you were still alive. That was a complicated one. There were not many of them left though. No, there were not many of the gay ones left" (p. 148). Only a few are gay, which is another way of saying that there are not many of the good comrades on the open road.

Two other characters in *The Sun Also Rises*, both of whom are capable of intense happiness, make good comrades. Harris, the Englishman Jake and Bill briefly know at Burguete, is one of the initiated who loves life in the outdoors but who speaks sparingly of his joy. Thus it is only after a bottle of wine that he tells his new-found friends of his happiness:

> Harris was a little tight.
> "I say. Really you don't know how much it means. I've not had much fun since the war."
> "We'll fish together again, some time. Don't you forget it, Harris."
> "We must. We *have* had such a jolly good time." (p. 129)

Another comrade is Brett herself, who is both Jake's lover and his friend. She lacks the emotional health Hemingway's protagonists possess, but her past life is partly to blame for this, as her fiancé, Mike, explains: "She hasn't had an absolutely happy life, Brett. Damned shame, too. She enjoys things so" (p. 138). Like all good comrades, Brett is able, at least for a time, to live joyfully. Even as her personality disintegrates, she can be gay: "Brett was radiant. She was happy. The sun was out and the day was bright."

Hemingway never again in his novels captured the almost pastoral quality of the Burguete section of *The Sun Also Rises*. The relationship between the hero and the comrade in his next novel, *A Farewell to Arms*, is not as joyful as the friendship between Jake and Bill, but it is possibly more intense. Although this novel deals almost exclusively with a love affair, the Rinaldi–Frederic Henry friendship plays an important role in the novel. The pairs of comrades in both novels are often playful, and Rinaldi, like his counterpart, Bill Gorton, is more demonstrative than the hero. The chief difference between the two novels is that in *The Sun Also Rises* the open road leads, for the most part, to joyous experience, while in *A Farewell to Arms* the comrades are led through war-shattered country. The Hemingway protagonist, for reasons Whitman probably would not have understood, must take the open road to look for violence and death in order to find himself. Regardless of where this road leads him, though, the protagonist knows the fierce relationship that exists between true comrades. Rinaldi, like Bill Gorton, reminds his friend just how close they are: "Underneath we are the same. We are war brothers," and, "You are really an Italian. All fire and smoke and nothing inside. You only pretend to be American. We are brothers and we love each other."[13] To this outpouring of feeling Frederic Henry replies, as Jake would have, with characteristic understatement. When Rinaldi says, "Kiss me good-by," Frederic provides an understatement that counterbalances this Latin display of feeling: "You're sloppy" (p. 143). The two friends are finally separated, but next to Catherine, Rinaldi means the most to Frederic Henry.

In *A Farewell to Arms*, as in other novels, the hero briefly meets many comrades, who are immediately recognized and who are hailed in passing. There is Count Greffi at Stresa, whose wisdom and dignity Frederic Henry admires. Also at Stresa is the barman, Emilio, whose generous aid enables Henry to escape with Catherine to Switzerland. Henry is also drawn to the priest, whose home in the Abruzzi he would like to visit. In a short and poignant sentence Henry expresses his love for one of these briefly known comrades: "I had liked him as well as any one I ever knew," he says of Aymo, the soldier killed in the rain (p. 173). Count Greffi's counterpart in *The Sun Also Rises* is Count Mippipopolous, an old man of great knowledge and dignity who understands Jake and Lady Brett. He is simply "one of us," as Brett says. These two wise old noblemen help to provide the hero with the knowledge of the world that he seeks on the open road. Thus the hero seeks and finds not only the joy of comradeship but also the knowledge and experience of life and death, as well as a way to meet the suffering that inevitably comes to this twentieth-century American pioneer.

In *For Whom the Bell Tolls* the familiar situation of star-crossed lovers is present again, and again the hero, now somewhat changed, extends his hand to the comrades he finds in the hills of Spain. It is not clear why Frederic Henry took the open road to war—was it to prove himself?—but Robert Jordan has a mature reason, the desire to fight the forces of evil. The very intensity of this struggle does not allow time for the easy comradeship of *The Sun Also Rises*. There is war, there is Maria, there is little time. Jordan is like Jake and Frederic in his need to learn all he can about life on the war-torn road. He also has comrades. In fact the people he knows in this brief space—those last few days when life must be squeezed into a ball—are the best comrades he has ever had. They are more than friends; they are his real brothers and sisters, as he makes clear in a passage that has already been quoted in part:

> I have been all my life in these hills since I have been here. Anselmo is my oldest friend. I know him better than I know Charles, than I know Chub, than I know Guy, than I know Mike, and I know them well. Agustín, with his vile mouth, is my brother, and I never had a brother. Maria is my true love and my wife. I never had a true love. I never had a wife. She is also my sister, and I never had a sister, and my daughter, and I never will have a daughter. I hate to leave a thing that is so good. (p. 381)

Paradoxically Robert has the best time of his life amid the anguish of war.

Anselmo lacks the high spirits of Bill Gorton and Rinaldi, but he is nevertheless a trusted comrade, and, as Robert says to him, "If I ever get gloomy, when I see you it cheers me up" (p. 199). Although he is never as close to Jordan as Bill is to Jake, he bears a silent love for Robert: "As they went up the hill in the dark, the wind at their backs, the storm blowing past them as they climbed, Anselmo did not feel lonely. He had not been lonely since the *Inglés* had clapped him on the shoulder. The *Inglés* was pleased and happy and they joked together. The *Inglés* said it all went well and he was not worried" (p. 200). It is neither the time nor place for the expansive fellow-feeling of earlier days, but Robert can put his hand on Agustín when he tells him how much he cares for Maria; they feel an unspoken kinship.

Like Jake and Frederic, Robert can drink deeply at joy's fountain; he hates to leave so good a life. He has all the qualities that Whitman demands of those who travel with him on the open road:

> He traveling with me needs the best blood, thews, endurance,
> None may come to the trial till he or she bring courage and
>   health,
> Come not here if you have already spent the best of yourself.
>   (p. 155)

Robert is a man whose "courage and health" enable him to face life with joy and strength. Edmund Wilson has said that Robert Jordan dies with "little to sustain him but the memory of his grandfather's record as a soldier in the American Civil War."[14] He dies with the same intense belief in life that both Jake and Frederic have, a belief based on the certainty that a man can know much happiness during his brief span. He says as he dies: "I have fought for what I believed in for a year now. If we win here we will win everywhere. The world is a fine place and worth the fighting for and I hate very much to leave it. . . . You've had as good a life as any one because of these last days. You do not want to complain when you have been so lucky" (p. 467). Hemingway is a tragic artist who understands suffering and loss because he has known what life can be when it is lived with zest and courage.

In *Across the River and into the Trees* Hemingway portrays a hero who loves life, but who, like Jordan, lacks the youthful high spirits of Jake and Frederic. Possibly Colonel Cantwell is sober, indeed even bitter, because he has known much suffering. Unquestionably, between *The Sun Also Rises* and *A Farewell to Arms* on one hand and the two later novels on the other, Hemingway has attained a greater understanding of human suffering. In *Across the River and into the Trees* the comrades recognize each other by the wounds they see. Although the emphasis on suffering is much greater than before, this is not entirely new in Hemingway. In *The Sun Also Rises*, Jake and Brett admire Count Mippipopolous because, among other things, he bears on his body real arrow wounds. The count has both suffered and loved, and by thus living a full life, as he explains, one gets to know the "values."

Cantwell is like the count in that he has been wounded, by gunpowder and by the loss of loved ones; and, despite all this, he retains a real love for his true comrades. He is far from being as likable as Jake, Frederic, or Robert. But he has a knowledge of life and an understanding of suffering that these three men spend their lives acquiring. The colonel is a man of the open road. He particularly loves three countries—Spain, France, and Italy—and above all cities he loves Venice. He has known much of the world and now that he is about to leave it, he wants to enjoy again some of its pleasures in his favorite city. Like all the Hemingway heroes, he is passionately devoted to life's many pleasures.

The comrade in *Across the River and into the Trees* who is the counterpart of Anselmo, Rinaldi, and Bill Gorton is the *Gran Maestro*, who with Cantwell has formed a club for the initiated, those who have both suffered and known happiness. In this novel Hemingway states the meaning of comradeship, especially that which exists between those who love the open road:

> He advanced smiling, lovingly, and yet conspiratorially, since they both shared many secrets, and he extended his hand, which was a big, long, strong, spatular fingered hand; well kept as was becoming, as well as necessary, to his position, and the Colonel extended his own hand, which had been shot through twice, and was slightly misshapen. Thus contact was made between two old inhabitants of the Veneto, both men, and brothers in their membership in the human race, the only club that either one paid dues to, and brothers, too, in their love of an old country, much fought over, and always triumphant in defeat, which they had both defended in their youth. (p. 55)

Between the colonel and the Gran Maestro there is a radiant feeling which is presumably something like the attachment that exists between Jake and Bill. Although Hemingway does not make as much of the hero-comrade relationship as he does in his earlier novels, he tells us that there is a spell between the two. It is a spell that is easily broken, however, because the colonel lacks much of the old Hemingway zest. In *The Sun Also Rises* the true comrades were drawn to each other for several reasons, but because of their *joie de vivre* as much as anything; in *Across the River and into the Trees* the hero is drawn to the comrade who above all else has suffered: "He only loved people, he thought, who had fought or been mutilated. Other people were fine and you liked them and were good friends; but you only felt true tenderness and love for those who had been there and had received the castigation that everyone receives who goes there long enough" (p. 71). Thus Cantwell and the Gran Maestro have suffered together in war, and, like Count Mippipopolous, they know the "values."

On Hemingway's postwar open road those who have come through the fires of suffering greet each other. In *The Old Man and the Sea*, a long short story (or short novel) that lacks the scope of Hemingway's four great novels, Santiago is able to affirm life even in the agony of his struggle with the great fish. Like Nick and Jake,

Santiago knows the joy of close contact with nature, but, like Jordan—and unlike Jake and Frederic—his experience of intense joy is deepened by the knowledge that suffering brings. In *The Old Man and the Sea* the familiar pattern of the hero and the comrade is repeated. The relationship between Santiago and Manolin, the boy who "keeps me alive," lacks some of the liveliness of earlier friendships in Hemingway, but there is about it a tenderness that is as fine as nearly anything in the earlier novels. There is also something like the playfulness that exists between the hero and the comrade of earlier work, in the discussion the two friends have about baseball. Santiago and Manolin are thus banded together against a world that ignores them both.

This last work again emphasizes a side of Hemingway that is often neglected: the need of the lonely man on the open road, cut off from the usual ties of society, for the love and friendship of others like himself. Americans have always been people searching the empty spaces of a continent with boundless zest and a fierce love for fellow adventurers met in uncharted regions. They also have been lonely people seeking contact with others. Surely Whitman is our greatest singer of the outgoing spirit of the open road, and just as surely Hemingway's work is a spiritual history of the twentieth-century American who still has much of Whitman's love of the outdoors and for good comrades, but who knows the fleeting nature of friendship. Because he is living in a shattered world Whitman never knew, Hemingway also depicts the brevity of comradeship, and he imparts to his reader the meaning of suffering which comes to every man on the open road today.

It must be always kept in mind that, for Hemingway, suffering, as Martin Luther King, Jr., said many times, is redemptive. No Hemingway character better sums up the relationship between love and suffering than does Count Mippipopolous in *The Sun Also Rises*. The count tells Jake that he can enjoy everything because "I have lived very much," an understatement for having suffered much. Thus he can go on to say, "I am always in love" (p. 61). Hemingway links the mythic life of the journey with the suffering inevitably encountered on the journey. Both suffering and the fact of death are accepted by the hero and are overcome at best with courage, even when the suffering eventually brings about the death of the hero. Death is always present as a possibility and an actuality in Hemingway's work, but more often than not it is overcome the way Conrad's Jim at last overcomes death in *Lord Jim*, through adherence to duty and suffering. Hemingway was not death-haunted, as Young and others made out, but a lover of life who knew that love could continue only by facing suffering and death with honor. No statement better sums up the ultimate influence of Conrad on Hemingway than Hemingway's own words: "Survival with honor, that outmoded and all important word."[15]

What is missing in Conrad is also missing in Hemingway: a larger view of man and cosmos. It is something found in only the greatest modern writers, but at least two who worked in the twenties had it. One of them Hemingway knew and greatly admired—James Joyce. Two others were Thomas Mann and Hermann Hesse, but Hemingway seems not to have been influenced by them. Hemingway always knew that Joyce had something more than he had, something more than talent. It was the kind of spiritual and intellectual background that Joyce had earned with great effort and that he used, together with his enormous literary talents, to create a new vision of the triumph of man. Joyce also continued to grow as an artist, and Hemingway after the early thirties lost something during the furious living of his personal life. *For Whom the Bell Tolls*, *Across the River and Into the Trees*, and *The Old Man and the Sea* are as affirmative as the work of the twenties, but they lack the early power. Unlike Joyce, Hesse, and Mann and like Woolf, Fitzgerald, and Forster, Hemingway did not continue to grow as an artist after a certain age, though he never lost his vision of the possibility of a life beyond tragedy. This is the tragedy of Hemingway the man, but it does not diminish the values of the early work.

The Reintegration of Modern Man:
The Transforming Visions of
James Joyce and Hermann Hesse

Anguish and pain pervade most modern writing. Although this fact has caused a great deal of concern among those who would prefer a happier outlook in literature, writers who would be true to their visions must reflect the pain and suffering of their times. A serious writer will always grapple with one or more of the chief problems of his time, and men of letters in our time have generally agreed that this century is a time of the decay of civilized society and of the soul of civilized man. But if a man of letters concerns himself with nothing but the theme of decay, he will write primarily about the failures of people caught up in the collapse of old social structures. He is likely to write, as William Faulkner put it in his Nobel Prize speech, "as though he stood alone and watched the end of man."

So many writers of this century have written about decay and so many critics have discussed these writers and their vision of decline and death that now, as the century wears out, the modern literary scene is suffused with a pessimism that tends to hide what optimism there is in modern letters. The long-standing pessimism in modern literature springs traditionally from the pessimism of the French symbolists, but those literary artists who went beyond this early modern pessimism, particularly in modernism's most creative period between the two great wars, ought to be reexamined in order to understand their hope for a new day beyond modern tragedy and for their indications of paths in our own time that lead beyond tragedy. In fact, the young often demand this reexamination because, along with the many reasons for pessimism in the social dislocation of the modern world, there is a longing for visions of new life. The young find it easy to sink into pessimism, but the very need to find a place for themselves in the world forces them to consider the possibility of life renewal and its optimistic consequences.

The pessimism of our time, with its vision of almost endless tragedy, causes many to weep away their lives over the loss of a once beautiful civilization. To quest for new life, however, one must affirm life, at least some of the time, or else one loses heart and eventually gives up the quest. The two most popular writers on college campuses for the past few years are said to be Kurt Vonnegut and J. R. R. Tolkien; both, despite their faults, do not reveal a loss of heart but rather a facing of destruction with the belief that the good life can be found again. Today readers both old and young are also rediscovering two master novelists whose primary appeal is to our sense of quest—if they are read, that is, at their deepest levels. These novelists are James Joyce and Hermann Hesse.

Both Joyce and Hesse have for too long been seen by older critics as artists who present visions of the modern fragmentation of life. *Ulysses* and *Steppenwolf* do indeed present profound visions of the breakup of modern life, of the gradual fragmenting of all social forms, and of the dissolution of the soul. However, the fragmented world, if seen correctly in their work, is but the *scene*, the wasteland setting, for the journey of a quester who seeks a new life and who, because of his quest, is shown moving toward new life. Joyce and Hesse create quester characters who are on a mythic journey that leads beyond the tragedy of modern anguish. These characters are not shown achieving the good life; but, as questers who continue the mythic journey, they are shown by Joyce and Hesse as people who *affirm* the good in life and receive visions of the reintegration of modern man. These visions release new and creative energies that give the questers new heart to push on into the wasteland, which is everywhere. It is the vision of the reintegration of modern man that I propose to examine. Joyce and Hesse, above all others at work between the wars—Mann, Eliot, Yeats, Gide, Proust—give us visions of new and creative life.

It is still too early for anyone to give a full account of the meaning of the novels of Joyce and Hesse. We can agree with William York Tindall that the symbolist novel is "the outstanding literary development of our time" and still be uncertain at times how to find our way through Baudelaire's forest of symbols that a book like *Ulysses* presents to us.[1] By comparing the complexities of Joyce with the more compact imagery of Hesse, we can possibly understand better the nature of two profound visions of the reintegration of man, two visions whose details are often different but whose essential truths are the same.

Critics have long been aware of the mythmaking powers of both Joyce and Hesse; but because they did not understand the reintegrating force of myth, they concentrated their efforts on analyses of details rather than on basic truths. There is, however, the notable exception of *A Skeleton Key to Finnegans Wake*, in which Joseph Campbell and Henry Morton Robinson show how Joyce moves from the mythic vision of man's death to a great new vision of his rebirth. Their essential statement of Joyce's vision of the renewal of man in *A Skeleton Key* is based on a knowledge of the integrating power of myth and a sensitivity to Joyce's vision of the rebirth of the hero.

Joyce and Hesse encountered the pain of the fragmented modern world, and in their work they show the overcoming of pain through vision. The pain is not physical but is rather a psychic pain of despair, which Kierkegaard called the sickness unto death. This despair is the offspring of a fixation on fragmentation, but in their visions—which contain symbols of an underlying harmony and of the reappearance of a hero who is moving on a mythic journey that will take him past the tragic suffering of our modern fragmented scene—there is a renewal of hope.

There is a remarkable similarity, not only in the essential visions of Hesse and Joyce, but also in their lives. They both had strong religious backgrounds, one Protestant and the other Catholic. They both grew up with a deep awareness of the riches of Western culture. They both devoted themselves to profound study of not one but many civilizations.

Hesse and Joyce grew up amidst strong nationalistic fervor.

The nationalism of Ireland, of course, was fierce at the time Joyce was maturing; and Hesse's Germany in the late nineteenth century was seething with nationalism. Both walked out on the yearnings of the masses caught in the drug of nationalistic fervor, and yet both remained thoroughly imbued with many of the traits for which their nations have been best known.

Hesse was a noted pacifist, and finally in 1912 he could no longer tolerate the militancy of the German nation and withdrew to Switzerland, where he lived the rest of his life. He was an exile, though living in a nearby country of similar culture. He was in fact not nearly so much an exile as Joyce, who felt that he was Irish through and through all of his life, though he lived most of it in various continental cities.

Their profoundest similarities have to do with the fact that Hesse and Joyce both sloughed off their boyhood religious beliefs and yet remained loyal to much of the spirit of Christianity and to many of the ideas connected with their early religious training. They left behind their early religious beliefs in order to become artists and intellectuals, thus denying the complacency of orthodox ideas in order to search for a new way of life. Their search also led them into both a personal and an intellectual involvement with depth psychology. Hesse had a nervous breakdown during World War I and was psychoanalyzed by a Jungian analyst in Switzerland. Joyce, though never psychoanalyzed, was intensely interested in the work of both Freud and Jung. Joyce was particularly close to Jung in his thinking, and in fact when *Ulysses* appeared in 1922, Jung immediately recognized it as a great work and wrote to Joyce praising the book. Joyce himself considered Jung's note one of his most valuable letters and was jubilant that *Ulysses* had been recognized by a man he admired so much.

A study of the life and work of Joyce and Hesse also reveals an intense interest in the new symbology that was being discussed early in this century by modern depth psychologists. It is necessary here to call attention to the use of the image, or symbol, that Jung calls the archetype of the cosmic man. What Jung means by the term *archetype* is often debated. Without joining this debate, I will use as my guidepost one of Jung's own statements, made at the end of his life and recorded in Richard I. Evans' *Conversations with Carl Jung and Reactions from Ernest Jones*. Jung says that archetypes "are instinctual images that are not intellectually invented."[2] In this statement Jung also says that archetypes are "dynamic" and are the origin of mythology.[3] While one must admit that Hesse and Joyce are influenced by Jung, it is also evident that modern writers in general and Joyce in particular influenced Jung. It is clear that Hesse, Joyce, and other symbolists sought and found the image of the cosmic man, that image that I will call the hero hereafter in this chapter. This hero image they found embedded in the psyches of modern people, waiting to emerge in the lives of those questers who would seek the image and its power.

The key to understanding the vision of the reintegration of man, as we see it in Hesse and Joyce, is to understand the meaning of that journey taken by the quester figures in their fiction. The journey is mythic and is a search for the hero image and for the power of the hero, which dwells within everyone and which awaits discovery in order to be activated in a fragmented world. It is the activation of this power, Hesse and Joyce believed, that will bring about the reintegration of man. Hesse and Joyce turned away from the easy acceptance of the dogmas of the church and state because they believed that this acceptance without an accompanying quest would only contribute to the growing fragmentation of man and to the paralysis of man's vital powers that Joyce in particular felt existed everywhere in our urbanized environment.

At the heart of Hesse's major period of creativity between the two world wars stand four novels dealing with the quester and his search for the power of the hero. These are *Demian, Steppenwolf, Siddhartha*, and *The Journey to the East*. Thomas Mann suggested that in the development of the modern novel *Steppenwolf*, published in 1929, is as important in its way as *Ulysses*.[4] Thus Mann, often regarded as the preeminent novelist of modern Germany, officially recognized Hesse as an important figure in the history of the modern novel. A large number of European readers had already seen Hesse as a major novelist, after his publication of *Demian* in 1919. With this book the German author, who had been a successful novelist as early as 1910, became one of the major figures of European fiction.

Demian seized the imagination of many young people in Germany shortly after World War I because it spoke of rebirth, of resurrection, and of a new life that would in time emerge. Demian, the chief character, is a portrait of the hero as a spiritual leader.

He has sought and found the cosmic man within himself; thus he reflects both the image and its accompanying powers in all of his activities. One of his activities consists of guiding the destinies of a group of questers. These questers will form the basis of a new life, which will come with the disintegration of Western civilization. Great visions and dreams come to Demian and reveal to him the nature of man's destiny in the twentieth century. Of these dreams he says: "But for several years I have dreamed dreams which make me feel that the collapse of an old world is imminent. At first these were vague, remote presentiments but they have become increasingly strong and unambiguous. I still know nothing more except that something is going to happen on a vast scale, something terrible in which I personally shall be involved."[5]

Thus Demian speaks to Sinclair, a quester whose life exists in the foreground of the book. Demian also affirms the rebirth of man: "Sinclair, we shall survive whatever this thing is that we have discussed so often. The world will be renewed. There's a smell of death in the air. Nothing new arises without death. But it is more terrible than I supposed" (p. 173). Demian's words are spoken shortly before 1914. When the war erupts, Demian himself is called immediately into service and presumably is killed. Like Christ, Demian is crucified, but his image appears again in the souls of the people who had followed him.

Sinclair himself goes off to war and is badly wounded, and has in the process a great vision of Demian. Finally, as he is being taken care of, Sinclair thinks: "The dressing was a painful business. So was everything else that happened to me afterwards. But when on the many such occasions I find the key and look deep down into myself where the images of destiny lie slumbering in the dark mirror, I only need to bend my head over the back mirror to see my own image which now wholly resembles him, my friend and leader" (p. 184).

Thus ends the book. The images of destiny I take to be those images that Jung called *archetypes*. We can call them anything we like, but they are images, or mythic symbols, that guide us on our journey toward reintegration. Jung said that the chief of these symbols is the mandala, which stands for the unifying power working through all creative beings. Of even more importance, I believe, is the image of integrated man, or cosmic man. Demian is the bearer of this image of the hero, and those who relate to him find the image appearing in their own minds when they look into their own souls. Through this image comes a new leadership and a new friendship along with the kind of guidance Demian gave when he lived. Thus, the cosmic man that shone brightly within Demian continued to appear in the souls of his friends and followers.

Hesse continued to write about the cosmic man in three other novels, published between 1919 and 1931. In *Siddhartha*, Hesse deals with a spiritual quester who lived in India during the lifetime of the Buddha. He is not, as his name might suggest, the Buddha himself. Siddhartha enunciates the meaning of the quest, as well as the meaning of spiritual enlightenment, which is the goal of the quest. He tells a friend who is still seeking the good life: "Seeking means: to have a goal; but finding means: to be free, to be receptive, to have no goal."[6]

Siddhartha lives in the vision of unity and can see the unity of all being, both good and bad, and thus can bless life and love it. He had to become a quester, he says, to find enlightenment, and he had to experience much suffering: "I learned through my body and soul that it was necessary for me to sin, that I needed lust, that I had to strive for property and experience nausea and the depths of despair in order to learn not to resist them, in order to learn to love the world, and no longer compare it with some kind of imaginary world . . . " (pp. 145–46). Siddhartha then tells his friend how he passed through the hell of suffering to learn to accept and love all existence.

Hesse's third novel of the spiritual quest is *Steppenwolf*. Its central figure is Harry Haller, who lives in Europe shortly after World War I. Haller is a man separated from the mainstream of life. He has separated himself in order to search for spiritual unity, but *Steppenwolf*, unlike *Siddhartha*, does not show the quester finding spiritual unity. Yet Haller does learn the meaning of the quest, and in visionary moments he glimpses the archetype of the cosmic man. Siddhartha's journey leads to a final goal of enlightenment, but Harry Haller's journey leads rather to a meeting with archetypal figures springing out of his own unconscious mind. Two of these figures, for instance, are Mozart and Goethe. Through these images that appear to him, he learns to find the meaning of joy and acceptance of all of life. After much suffering, Haller sees that he will have to traverse, as he says, "not once more, but often the hell of my inner being."[7] With the truth of his own quest established in his life, he knows that he will in time, as he says, "be a better hand at the game" (p. 218). He knows that if he continues his quest, he will one day learn to laugh, and that Mozart and other images of cosmic man will be waiting for him. He knows that he will continue to make identification with these archetypal figures that appear regularly to the quester on his journey toward enlightenment.

After *Steppenwolf* Hesse published, in 1931, a great fable entitled *The Journey to the East*. In this book the author presents Leo, who is at the same time the master and the servant of a group called the League. The League's purpose is to make a journey to the East, a journey symbolic of man's communal quest for enlightenment and wholeness. In the novel Leo, who is a Christ figure and therefore is reminiscent of Demian, is sought and found by an archetypal quester, in this case Harry Haller, the protagonist of *Steppenwolf*. Haller has withdrawn not only from the mainstream of society but also from the League, to which he once belonged. Driven by his despair, he seeks Leo; through interacting with Leo, he begins to see that the cosmic man is at once master and servant. Seeking to join the League again, Haller is told that he must accept two tasks: he must burn the archives of the League, and he must tame a wild dog. The former test is a symbol of giving up a reliance on the record of past accomplishments, and the latter is a sign of the first great task of the enlightened man, which is to heal the insane instincts. In his weakness, the quester shrinks from the tasks, but he is reminded that he cannot be a member of the League unless he accepts the trials of those who take the journey to the East. At last, Harry Haller sees that renewing his quest means that he must grow smaller as Leo, who is the symbol of Christ, grows larger in his soul.

From his first novel, *Peter Camenzind* (1904), to his last great work of fiction, *Magister Ludi* (1943), Hesse dealt with themes that were dear to the great Europeans of the twentieth century. In the four novels between 1919 and 1931 he presented what many of his serious readers today believe is his chief theme, the search of a quester for the life of the hero—also considered by James Joyce to be the great theme of his own works. The chief difference between Joyce and Hesse was that after his first work of fiction, *Dubliners*, Joyce concentrated all of his literary efforts on the quester's search for heroism.

Beginning with the gropings of Dedalus in *A Portrait of the Artist as a Young Man* and continuing through the search for a father in *Ulysses* to the presentation of Earwicker achieving heroism in *Finnegans Wake*, Joyce never took his creative eye off the search of man for a new heroism. And for Joyce, Finnegan was the great image of the hero, or cosmic man, who would appear again in the life of the world. What Hesse offers in his four novels is a relatively simple poetic statement of both the quester's life and the life of the hero as we see it in the characters of Demian, Siddhartha, and Leo. What Joyce gives us is a great labyrinth into which he plunges not only his quester but also the reader. From the first, sensitive readers of modern literature were aware of the greatness of Joyce's accomplishment, but now that Hesse and other quester novelists are being understood with a new depth, it is possible for the reader to walk with greater understanding through James Joyce's literary labyrinth.

Hermann Hesse never left many of the ideas of his pietistic background. In *The Journey to the East* he reflects the concern of his father (who was a missionary in India) for the unification of East and West in one great spiritual kingdom, which for Hesse was the kingdom of God as declared by Christ. Thus I would interpret the allegory of *The Journey to the East* as a story in which Leo is Christ and the League is the kingdom of God on earth that will eventually reign triumphant but is now an unrecognized polity.

For Joyce the Catholicism of Dante and of the Ireland of his early years was at the center of his deepest creative visions. From first to last, from *Dubliners* to *Finnegans Wake*, he never left Dublin. He would begin with the wasteland of the city, that center of the modern paralysis; but even in *Dubliners*, which he said was written in the style of naturalism, he thought of himself as creating epiphanies, brief revelations of spirit amidst the horror of modern life. By the time he approached the end of *Finnegans Wake*, he presented as archetypal heroes Saint Patrick and Saint Kevin. And he ended the *Wake* with the old women waiting for Finn, that mythic hero of Ireland who is also the one hero working through the saints who created the Christian civilization of Ireland.

The fictional beginning of Joyce's search for heroism is *A Portrait of the Artist as a Young Man*. Joyce in this book prepared his readers for *Ulysses*, as he in fact prepared himself for the mythic journey that he as an artist seeking a new life would take. Joyce originally saw himself as Stephen Hero, but he changed his fictional name to Stephen Dedalus. Stephen, of course, suggests Saint Stephen, the first Christian martyr, and Dedalus is the Greek craftsman who built the Labyrinth and who later escaped imprisonment in the Labyrinth by making wings and flying out of it. Joyce changed his name from Hero to Dedalus because he saw that his search for heroism was like that of the Greek Dedalus, which was to construct the Labyrinth and then to find a way to escape from it. In a real sense his two masterpieces, *Ulysses* and *Finnegans Wake*, are at once labyrinths and the means, if properly understood, of escaping the labyrinth that is the modern urban jungle. The two works, along with *A Portrait of the Artist as a Young Man*, express Joyce's act of freeing himself from that land ruled by the tyrant Minos in order to go to another land where he would accomplish works of art in which he would freely express his own soul. Thus Dedalus tells a friend in *A Portrait of the Artist as a Young Man*: "When the soul of a man is born in this country, there are nets flung at it to hold it back from flight."[8] It is only by the flight of the soul, Joyce believed, that one could achieve a higher vision and a deeper unity whereby man could be renewed to build a new society. Joyce saw that man would have to have a new society to express himself more fully and that the church, the home, and the nation as we know them in our present society are in fact binding man rather than helping him to achieve spiritual release; therefore, as Dedalus tells us in *A Portrait*, he would use "silence," "exile," and "cunning" to accomplish his ends in his quest to create works of artistic power.

At the end of *A Portrait*, Joyce says that he goes forth to "encounter for the millionth time the reality of experience and to forge in the smithy of my soul the uncreated conscience of my race" (p. 253). I think his statement concerning the conscience has to do with man's unconscious mind, which is "uncreated" because it is no longer understood. The conscience for Joyce is also the knowledge within the unconscious that medieval man called simply "inwit." This inwit, or inner knowledge, is in fact a complex of symbols, or archetypes, dwelling within the individual soul. Archetypes, as Jung suggests, are accompanied by powers, and these powers produce a strange pain which Joyce, borrowing from medieval man, called "Agenbite of Inwit," meaning remorse of conscience. To escape this painful remorse, man must first understand his prison, or labyrinth, and then like Dedalus he must learn to fly to a new land of the spirit, as Joyce would do in leaving Ireland to seek to "discover the mode of life of art whereby your spirit could express itself in unfettered freedom" (p. 246).

In *Ulysses* Joyce shows the continuation of the journey of Stephen Dedalus. He shows us the search for meaningful human relationships in a world in which man is fixated on the forms and facts of existence, on history and on institutions. When Mr. Deasy speaks of history, young Dedalus answers: "History is a nightmare from which I am trying to awake."[9] This nightmare is created by the fixation of man on the forms of time. The escape from the nightmare can come only for one like Dedalus who searches for freedom. On the quest for freedom one knows epiphanies, which are moments of vision in which one briefly apprehends the archetypes and comes to know, if only momentarily, their power to set free and to unify in loving harmony with other questers. Dedalus and Leopold Bloom, the Ulysses of Joyce's novel, both are seeking a new life of freedom and love. After passing through the hell of Bella Cohen's brothel, they both know a time together of unity encountered by man on the spiritual quest. *Ulysses* is a book full of irony, but irony is not the dominant tone, because Joyce accepts man in his blindness and shows us love and humor dwelling in the midst of a modern labyrinth. However, though love is known for brief periods, modern man is beset by much longer periods of psychic anguish.

During those brief moments of unity there emerges the archetype of the hero, and it is thus possible to see the relationship between Bloom as anti-hero, the role he plays most of the time, and that Bloom in whom the hero emerges in brief, poignant moments. Like all of us, Bloom is at once hero and anti-hero. The same is true of his wife, Molly. She is all women, but she is also a single woman fixated on the forms of existence. She is possessed by a powerful lust for maleness, but the hero at the center of her soul— that hero who is a perfect union of male and female—can affirm all existence, can say yes to both good and bad, beauty and ugliness.

It is in *Finnegans Wake* that Joyce shows us the full emergence of the hero, or cosmic man, as Jung often calls him, the man whose power can overcome the disintegration of the modern wasteland. *Finnegans Wake* is essentially about the dying of the old man and the birth of that new man who is in fact heroic man. The old man is Finnegan, an Irish hod carrier, the archetype of the common man of our time, whose wake is described in the prelude of the book. Those who have come to pay their last respects to the dead Finnegan splash whiskey on the corpse, and suddenly he arises ready to begin life again as Finn. Thus, the title *Finnegans Wake* is also Finn Again Wakes. Just as Leopold Bloom is at once the anti-hero of the modern world and the hero Ulysses of another day, so Finnegan is at once the common man immersed in the tedium of our time and the great Irish hero Finn MacCool. Seen in one age, man is anti-hero; seen in the light of a succeeding age, he is the hero. Hero and anti-hero are one.

In his view of the ages of man, it is well known that Joyce follows Giambattista Vico, the great Italian philosopher of history. Vico tells us that man passes from the theocratic age to the aristocratic age to the democratic age and finally into the fourth age of chaos. With his visions of the modern urbanized existence of the twentieth century as a state of paralysis, Joyce obviously believed that we are now in the age of chaos. His vision of chaos is not essentially one of despair because he knows that one age prepares the way for another. In fact, one of Joyce's initial statements in *Finnegans Wake* is that of the thunderclap which summons man back to the age of theocracy, when the image of God will once again be seen shining through all created being. Eliot uses this same thunderclap to announce in *The Waste Land* the coming of the healing rain that restores old societies exhausted from the ceaseless jangling of clashing egos. To one schooled to see with the inner eye, there is always the vision of a new heroism growing within the chaos of a dying period of history.

Finnegans Wake moves on beyond the announcement of Finn Again Wakes to the actual statement of the process of man awakening to the new heroism. Another way of looking at the title of the book, of course, is End Again Wake; but awakening is a difficult process. It is, in fact, the purgatorial process of being freed from the guilt that is incurred from a fixation on the forms of time. H. C. Earwicker, the central figure of the work, goes through this purgatorial process and achieves at last a reunion with his wife, Anna Livia Plurabelle. He witnesses as well the union of the warring brothers Shem and Shaun, who are also the Biblical Cain and Abel. Thus Joyce describes the mythic process, set in elaborate detail in Dublin, as the setting forth of a quester who accepts the tests of the mythic journey by encountering the shadow side of himself in the form of his own guilt and who finally achieves heroism through union with the anima, the female side of himself.

The union of opposites in terms of man and woman is an important statement of the reintegration that accompanies the emergence of the hero archetype in the life of man. Thus, man moves in a great circle from where he began as God-centered heroic man in a theocratic age through forgetfulness to a new theocratic age of heroism. As Shelley's Prometheus is united at last with his feminine opposite, Asia, in *Prometheus Unbound,* so Joyce's HCE is united with Anna Livia Plurabelle. To save the soul means to integrate oneself with the dark and estranged side represented as a woman in the case of men and as a man in the case of women. The union of those basic opposites, male and female, is a statement of the dynamic interplay of polar energies that bind the world together.

H. C. Earwicker, whose initials mean Here Comes Everybody, is the medieval Everyman who sets out to achieve the salvation of the soul, a worn-out term meaning in our sense reintegration of the personality, or in another sense the achieving of wholeness of conscious and unconscious minds. Joyce shows salvation to be the unleashing of powerful creative energies through the dynamic union of the previously warring parts of HCE's personality. These energies are the powers that accompany the archetype of the hero in the life of man.

Writing what is probably the greatest of all the novels in the symbolist tradition, Joyce moves easily from past to present to future and back again with the sense of one who acts on the assumption that all three are aspects of one continuum, just as hero and anti-hero, man and woman, Cain and Abel, are in fact one. It is fitting that Joyce, as an Irishman, should evoke the presence of Saint Patrick as one of the great heroes of the past by showing him overcoming the Druids to make way for a new age of heroism in the life of Ireland, the age of Christian Ireland. And as a clairvoyant of heroism, Joyce foresees a new city of Is, when past, present, and future are obliterated to make way for the vision of the divine in all created being. This city for Joyce is a kind of new Atlantis, come again at last.

To one who knows *Finnegans Wake* well, it is clear that Joyce fulfills the dictum of symbolists like Rimbaud and Mallarmé that the poet of the modern age must be a seer. It was Mallarmé who thought that the symbolist poets were called to write a sacred book, which if anything must mean a book about the triumph of the hero and a new heroic age. Thus Eliot and Yeats were fascinated with the stories of heroes they found in Frazer and in the writing of past mythic ages of both the East and the West. Mann would turn at last to writing about Joseph, the dream interpreter, and Lawrence would concern himself with both Christ and Quetzalcoatl, and Faulkner would write of the death and resurrection of Jesus in our time in the allegory he called *A Fable*. It is time we cease to look at Joyce as some sort of grand but eccentric genius writing about the modern wasteland in acid words, and begin to see him as one of the major figures of the great tradition of literature in the West from the time of the romantic poets to the present, an age that has in much of its greatest work the striving for liberation of the Promethean hero within Western man from the guilt and chaos of a time of anti-heroism.

No modern novelist represents the culmination of the creative side of the symbolist tradition as do James Joyce and Hermann Hesse. Much of this tradition represents a withdrawal from life in order to worship the beauty of art or the imagined brilliance of the individual ego. As a tradition in modern literature, symbolism first begins in poetry. As Edmund Wilson traces it in *Axel's Castle*, it begins with Poe and then is found in great French poets like Baudelaire and Mallarmé and those of other countries who would follow these two. We can see the emergence of the spirit of symbolism in fiction in the late nineteenth century in the work of Huysmans and Wilde. The attitude of these men and others like them is one of withdrawal from the ugliness of the modern world into the realm of art and knowledge. In the twentieth century we find a handful of poets and novelists who work in the symbolist tradition but whose withdrawal is for the purpose of achieving a new integration of the individual psyche. Thus, Joyce and Hesse wrote about a quester who withdraws but who also plunges into a chaotic world in order to seek a new heroism both in himself and in others.

Joseph Mileck has described Hesse's withdrawal and spiritual quest in this way: "In Montagnola escape became quest, and in quest Hesse's inner problems resolved themselves into the basic 'malaise humain,' into the tension between the spiritual and the physical (*Geist und Natur*). For years he was to oscillate between these poles, acclaiming first one, then the other, then neither."[10] Hesse's struggle with the warring parts of himself is but a symbolic statement of the schism found in all the activities of modern man, a schism defined in detail in two of his later masterpieces, *Narcissus and Goldmund* and *Magister Ludi*. Unlike those symbolists who seek to overcome the chaos of our time by embracing that chaos, or those who seek to escape chaos through a contemplation of beauty and knowledge, Hesse and Joyce show man moving through chaos in order to find moments of new unity, to experience briefly, that is, the life of the reunified man. And in both novelists' work the quest is rewarded by visionary glimpses of the archetype of the hero, that goal of man's search for the good life.

That the creative union of opposites is basic to Joyce's idea of heroism can be seen at the end of *Finnegans Wake* in the reunification of H. C. Earwicker and Anna Livia Plurabelle, a scene symbolic not only of man and woman being united in a new creativity, but of the reunion of all the male and female elements in the individual psyche and in social and cosmic relationships. That Joyce intended to symbolize the coming of a new heroic man and a new heroic age is also seen in the merging of the two brothers Shem and Shaun, who have been at war with each other in the modern labyrinth but who at last will work in harmony in a new age of heroism. From Stephen's search for a way to express himself to the great vision of the reunification of man in *Finnegans Wake*, there is in Joyce's work a concern for the coming of a new unification of man.

These visions of heroism in the work of Joyce and Hesse are essentially the same as the vision of the great psychologist to whom both authors were so deeply indebted—C. G. Jung. Jung summarizes his own position on the subject of psychic energy by saying: "I see in all happening the play of opposites, and derive from this conception my idea of psychic energy."[11] The integrated man seen in the visions of renewal of great writers like Joyce and Hesse is in fact the archetype of the hero, who is seen as a figure of great power for good because of the harmonious and dynamic fusion of all the opposite powers of his personality.

The story of the quester who seeks the hero in himself and in the world may properly be called myth. Myth, as Jung tells us, is in fact the life of the archetypes. Of the great archetype of harmony called the mandala, which guides the quester on his journey, appears in times of chaos to remind man of the heroic self buried deep in his psyche, and must be evoked so that the spread of chaos can once again be checked, Jung speaks in conversations recorded by Richard I. Evans in 1957, only four years before the death of the psychologist. Some of the pertinent statements concerning the mandala are these:

> It is what is called "ultimo exquadra circulae," the square in the circle, or the circle in the square. It is an age-old symbol that goes right back to the pre-history of man. It is all over the earth and it either expresses the Deity or the self; and these two terms are psychologically very much related, which doesn't mean that I believe that God is the self or that the self is God.

> It expresses the fact that there is a center and a periphery, and it tries to embrace the whole. It is the symbol of wholeness.

> As a matter of fact, however, it is highly important and highly autonomous, a symbol that appears in dreams, etc., and in folklore. It is, we should say, the main archetype.[12]

I have quoted Jung at length concerning the mandala because there is still a debate among Jungians as to what the meaning of the mandala is and in fact as to what Jung meant by the term *archetypes*. That there should be such a debate is an excellent sign of the times because out of debate will at last come clarity. Meanwhile, anything we can do to clarify terms is to the point. In this chapter I have tried to state clearly some of the ideas found in a writer like Joyce, whom Jung himself admired greatly, and to put beside these ideas some of Jung's own basic statements.

Clearly Jung and writers like Joyce and Hesse were striving to tell man certain things he needed to know about himself in this century. Neither Jung nor Joyce nor Hesse achieved the status of heroism, nor did they ever pose as heroes. They lived in a century when most people strongly felt the need of great human figures who could guide the destinies of people in a time of personal and social chaos. But Jung, Joyce, and Hesse discouraged that fixation on individual figures, which has so characterized our age and has led to the hailing of numerous false messiahs. Instead, they pointed to the individual quester like themselves, who would seek the hero and, through glimpses of the archetype of the hero in imaginative encounters, would achieve a renewal of psychic powers. The rewards of their personal quests led them to believe with certainty that the powers of the hero would appear at last in full force to form the basis of the reintegration of man in a new age of creativity. I think their certainty was based on their own patient reading of stories and legends of many cultures, stories that always speak of the interplay of quester and chaos and the reward of this interplay: the dynamic harmony of the hero, who after long absence appears in the lives of many people to tame the chaos monster of myth, always emerging and always put back in its hole. Thus, the hero at the center of man's soul is represented by a symbol—or archetype, if one likes—because this hero is not an individual or a "thing" but is rather a power which includes within itself a dynamic interplay of opposite powers. It is this power of heroism that will once again make possible the reunification both of individuals and of the societies and cultures that individuals erect. It is a tribute to the visionary powers of Jung, Hesse, and Joyce that they foresaw the coming again of this reintegrating power of heroism.

Man's Divine Rootedness
in the Earth:
Romain Gary's Major Fiction

After World War II, Paris for a time became once again the central
city of the modernist spirit. Figures like Sartre and Camus made
the French capital the focus of journalistic attention as the leader
of the Western intellect. However, by 1950 the spirit of modernism
had finally become so widespread that no one city could contain
the whole movement, and since that time the movement has been
truly international. In fact, if we study Sartre and Camus closely
we will see the shadow of Hemingway standing behind both of
them. Hemingway, in some ways a deeply American writer, turned
himself into an international literary figure whose influence, both
stylistically and philosophically, could be felt all over the world.
The directness of Camus' style and the sense of nothingness found
in Sartre's drama and fiction are all in Hemingway. In fact, one
may well wonder if the awareness of modern tragedy is anywhere
else as deep in this century as it is in the Hemingway short story
"A Clean Well-Lighted Place." Yet there is one writer of the Paris
renaissance that began in 1945 who did go beyond Hemingway in
his major fiction, which consists probably in only one large novel,
The Roots of Heaven. Romain Gary is as deeply French as Heming-

126

way is deeply American, and yet he is fully as international as Hemingway, if not more so. As a thinker and a visionary, Gary certainly goes beyond Hemingway.

In one sense Hemingway was as much a literary beginning place for Gary as he was for Camus and Sartre, but stylistically Gary moves beyond Hemingway's simplicity of style to a complexity of style and structure that sometimes reminds one of Hemingway's chief master, Conrad. Gary also has a visionary sweep that allows him to show how romantic idealism plays a role in modern life. Gary projects man into a new age that lies beyond modern tragedy; at the same time, *The Roots of Heaven* evokes the hell of the Hitlerian domination of Europe and contains one of the deepest contemporary views of the sufferings of man in modern times. Strangely, though, his answer to man's problems is similar to Hemingway's and is even shown revealing itself in a place Hemingway greatly admired, the continent of Africa. Hemingway in his second epigraph to *The Sun Also Rises* answers his first epigraph, Gertrude Stein's statement about the lost generation, by quoting from the Bible to the effect that the earth abides forever. This is Gary's vision in *The Roots of Heaven*, yet he has a far deeper philosophical sense of man's psychic roots being embedded in the earth than Hemingway ever demonstrates. Gary's ontology is based on the idealism of both romanticism and neoromanticism, and it is bolstered by a strong sense of the freedom of the will. The idea, so strong in *The Roots of Heaven*, of man's being able to achieve his freedom by exercising free choice can be attributed in part to the existentialism of Sartre and Camus. Yet Gary has also found this idea in the mainstream of modern fiction, which includes writers like Conrad and Hemingway, whom he often resembles. Also he must have found it in the literature that sprang from the Nazi concentration camps, which he so often invokes—especially Viktor Frankl's *Man's Search for Meaning*, also entitled *From Death Camp to Existentialism*. Frankl, like Gary, exalts man's ability to "make a decision, a decision which determined whether you would or would not submit to those powers which threatened to rob you of your very self, your inner freedom. . . ."[1]

The Roots of Heaven stands at the end of the modern tradition and points toward the beginning of another. It contains visionary insights found in only a few books of this century. These insights

and their relationship to modernism as well as to romanticism
and to those vague stirrings of some new movement form the basis
of a great novel.

The story in *The Roots of Heaven* is about a Frenchman named
Morel who loves elephants and who believes that they should be
preserved because man today needs all the friends he can get. Because of their size, Morel feels, elephants make better friends than
smaller animals, especially dogs, who are now too small to bear
the burden of human friendship. While imprisoned in a German
concentration camp during World War II, Morel learns to bear suffering by imagining herds of elephants charging across African
plains. After his release he goes to Africa to be near the great animals, and soon he finds himself working to protect them from
slaughter. At first he circulates petitions, but then he begins to take
physical sanctions against hunters who kill elephants. Around him
gathers a small group, among whom are a German prostitute, a
Danish naturalist, an African revolutionary leader, and an outcast
American Air Force Officer. French authorities try to capture Morel but fail. Finally, the Negro revolutionary leader breaks with
him and attacks a large herd of elephants. Morel escapes the
leader's attempt to kill him, and at the end of the book is still free
somewhere in Africa. This is a story that is interesting in itself; at
the same time it is a work of extreme technical subtlety, reminiscent of Joseph Conrad's novels. The philosophy of the book, however, makes it far more than a well-told story.

Morel bears the chief burden of Gary's ideas. He is a new kind
of idealist whose appeal to certain characters in the book is best
explained by the prostitute, Minna: "Here's a man who believes in
you . . . who appeals to you to try and save something. . . . He believes in some beauty in life . . . that everything is not irremedia-
bly doomed to ugliness."[2] Morel's idealism is in some ways like
that of humanists and humanitarians who bear the vague title of
"liberal." Like Morel, these people have strong feelings about certain injustices, but they differ from him in that they have political
and social aims. Morel, on the other hand, believes that as a new
kind of idealist he must work to give meaning to new *symbols*: for
without the symbols which man has lost, his social and political
action is meaningless. But the idea behind the phrase "roots of
heaven" is more than just a matter of symbols in the usual sense.
The flora and fauna of nature can actually place a person in a re-

lationship with a power whose source must be called heaven. Morel is advocating a return to a feeling for the tree of life, a motif central to mythology and religion. One of Morel's followers, Peer Qvist, explains it thus: "Islam calls that 'the roots of heaven,' and to the Mexican Indians it is the 'tree of life'—the thing that makes both of them fall on their knees and raise their eyes and beat their tormented breasts." Also among these "roots" are "our needs—for justice, for freedom and dignity" (p. 172). Humanists in the past, Qvist suggests, talked too much of these matters as abstract ideas (a habit Europeans got from the Greeks). Morel and his followers propose to bring man back to the basic roots of life. This return, they proclaim, will renew man's feeling for justice, freedom, and other abstract values. The flora and fauna of nature will be seen then to contain some of heaven's energy. Also they are seen to serve as true symbols which stir the soul (that root of heaven in ourselves) so that renewed power and a renewed vision of the ideal can come to man.

Morel in one sense takes up where the older humanitarians leave off, but in another sense he proposes a new beginning. Humanitarianism is after all only a part of romanticism, a movement much broader in scope than most people imagine. In the broadest sense its dates, if we include neoromanticism, are roughly 1750 to 1950, and it consists of two 100-year periods, the second one being our own modern period. That the old humanitarianism, the old liberalism, has died along with romanticism can be seen in the abstractness of what is left of the movement; once there was motive force also, now there is abstraction without feeling. With the last upsurge of liberal political action in the 1930s, and the last romantic art that could truly be called art, romanticism came to an end; and the cynicism, materialism, and general sense of hopelessness that were rampant even in Goethe's day finally reigned in the West. But the fact that Ghandi and Schweitzer captured many imaginations during the forties and fifties shows a deep longing for a new idealism. These two men, who are sometimes invoked in the novel, are really at the end of the old romanticism, although it is possible to call them transitional figures. Morel, however, is a novelist's image of what the new idealist will be.

The ways in which he is not like the old idealists, even a Ghandi or a Schweitzer, are made quite clear by Gary. For one thing, he has to fight practically alone against great forces of cynicism and materialism, as any new idealist would have to do. His very words appear strange to most people. For another thing, Morel concentrates his efforts on building a spiritual kingdom of a few followers who believe in the roots of heaven; he cares nothing for the political kingdom with its social and economic ideals. Morel leaves behind much of the Western past, but he keeps certain essentials; for instance, he always remembers that he is a Frenchman. Like any true spiritual revolutionary, he does not disown the past but takes what he needs from it in order to accomplish a mission for the good of the future. His personality is that of a new man. His energies are concentrated, but he is not a fanatic. He is sincere, earnest, angry in that he "refused to cooperate"; he is firm, even obstinate. He is simple and often blunt. A character says of Morel: "I had come to meet him expecting to find a man worthy of his legend, and I had been disappointed by his simplicity, his small stature, his rather rough appearance. But that simplicity was the very sort possessed by all the heroes of popular tales whose victories and naiveté will never cease to be told and retold" (p. 99). Morel's most striking characteristic is his enormous self-confidence, and with this goes a "gleam of gaiety," which is always present in his eyes.

What has driven Morel to seek intimate knowledge of, as well as protection for, the roots of heaven (specifically, the elephants), is a suffering so extreme that only an unworn image could save him. In a Nazi concentration camp, where a systematic attempt to destroy the spirit was made, Morel knew an attack on the soul that no idealist like Ghandi or Schweitzer ever encountered. The way he survived was to keep in his mind the picture of wide-ranging elephants as an image of freedom. This ordeal was the beginning of his career as a new idealist. His real work from then on would be to bring himself and others into an emotional·as well as a mental relationship with an image, and at the same time to establish once again a vital contact with nature. To do this work, he had to shed completely the materialistic philosophy of the West. Morel is Western man, voluntarily dispossessed, beginning a new religious life on the frontier of the world; Schweitzer, on the other hand, is simply the old humanitarian who brings modern medicine to primitives. Morel finds a way for himself and other dispossessed Westerners to get into contact with the power and beauty of heaven. Like religious leaders before him—the Buddha and Lao

Tzu, for instance—he is not concerned with theological questions but only with a *way* to know something about heaven. Unlike the Buddha and Lao Tzu after their enlightenment, he is only at the beginning of a religious career.

The break with Western materialism is underlined by Gary in the contrast he draws between Morel's idealism and the political idealism of the revolutionary leader Waïtari. Revolutionary doctrine will only bring Western totalitarianism to Africa; everything that Morel suffered in Germany will be repeated on the last great frontier of the world. The search for the political kingdom is shown as leading to inhumanity; thus the spiritual kingdom, it is suggested, will become man's chief hope. The journey to the new kingdom is filled with great pain, and only a few can begin to take it. Gary makes much of this, as he also makes much of the necessity of beginning with one particular symbol. Elephants will seem to most people to be a strange, even absurd, symbol, or root, of heaven; but the complexities of Morel's life suggest that in times of total spiritual collapse man must accept what he can receive. To put it another way, strange visions come in time of great suffering. Gary makes it clear that his hero is making a beginning. Indeed, he shows Morel progressing toward a profounder vision of heaven. Before discussing this progress, which is chiefly what the novel is about, it is necessary to examine further the book's relationship to romanticism and neoromanticism.

The movement we call "romantic" is only a continuation of the period that in a sense is the crisis of medieval culture, the Renaissance. José Ortega y Gasset in *Man and Crisis* shows how the Renaissance was an attempt by European man to strip away some of the complexity of a life weighed down with civilized institutions. Too many institutions stand between man and his true self. The back-to-nature movement, Ortega explains, is only one attempt to live a freer life:

> Thanks to culture, man has gotten away from himself, separated himself from himself; culture intervenes between the real world and his real person. So he has no course other than to rise up against that culture, to shake himself free of it, to rid himself of it, to retreat from it, so that he may once more face the universe in the live flesh and return to living in very truth. Hence those periods of a "return to nature," that is to say, to what is natural in man, in contrast to what is culti-

vated or cultured in him. For example, the Renaissance; Rousseau and romanticism; and our entire period.[3]

Those powerful currents of the Renaissance that we call the Reformation and the Counter-Reformation sought to give new force to old symbols or, in some cases, to do away with symbols altogether. By 1750 the spirit of the Renaissance had died, and a new spiritual movement had already begun. Again there was an attempt to give new meaning to Christianity; but for the most part the only result was lower-class pietism, like Methodism, and up-per-class medievalism, like the Oxford Movement. The main-stream of Western civilization marched toward a worldwide in-dustrial organization; and in their spare time people of the West experimented with extravagant idealisms, many of them political, which would free man from the trammels of all organization. So, for 200 years we have had philosophies that glorify both total or-ganization and total freedom.

Of the currents of romanticism, one of the chief has been hu-manitarianism in its many socialistic and democratic forms, al-ways preaching freedom for man. We should never forget our debt to this movement, for had it not existed the Industrial Revolution would likely have become by today nothing more than one great satanic mill. Yet many of the greatest spirits of the period saw that humanitarianism was not enough to sustain the West; but their attempt to refurbish Christianity, or to create a substitute for it, which we see in such representative figures as Wordsworth, Goethé, Chateaubriand, Nietzsche, Tolstoy, and Emerson, was a failure. The time was not ripe, and these visionary leaders were not prepared to make the sweeping beginning that was necessary. The romantics were too close to the old civilization; they were, in fact, too soft. The best they could achieve was a personal philoso-phy like transcendentalism. Gary's viewpoint in *The Roots of Heaven* has in it some of the old humanitarianism, but his concern with new symbols as a way to combat the pain of modern life, and his understanding that man must make a decisive break with the past, place him among that small group of people in this century who are feeling their way into a new period of cultural history that will follow the two-century age of romanticism and modernism that we have only recently left behind us.

The great thrust of energy and idealism in the nineteenth century is followed in the twentieth century by a feeling of despair and negation—a view summed up in literature and art by the image of a wasteland. Gary begins *The Roots of Heaven* with a general presentation of the modern wasteland situation. We are told that Western civilization is now in "the age of impotence, the age of taboos, of slavery, inhibitions, and almost physiological submission, when man is triumphing over his most ancient truths and renouncing his deepest needs" (p. 114). Gary depicts a suffering so great that it creates in a few people a renewed awe of the mystery of an image. Romantic suffering is one great lament, with death as its end. In Gary we have a suffering which, for the few people who can survive it, leads to renewed creative spiritual energy. Gary takes one step beyond the romantics, just as they took one step beyond the Renaissance. None of the romantics believed in a few images so intensely that they could devote their whole lives to a true contemplation of them. The old romanticism, from Rousseau, Goethe, and Wordsworth down to D. H. Lawrence and William Faulkner, was an attempt to get back to religious beginnings, and indeed back to the roots of heaven; but the romantics were too soft, too civilized, too complex, and often too neurotic to believe as intensely as Morel does. Their beginning carried Western man that much closer to nature and to a new experience, and so a little further from the old center of European civilization. So too does Morel's beginning carry the Westerner further still—to a new geographical area, to a new simplicity of character, and, most important, to a new intensity of vision. Yet Gary makes it clear that Morel still has far to go. The book is a record of the progress Morel makes, and at the end of it we see vast new possiblities; we feel that there will be new images, new visions, and finally a new way of life.

The climax of the book brings with it Morel's leap into the future. After he has been betrayed by Waïtari, the African political leader, Morel sets out on a desert march with his little band of followers. Among these is Youssef, a man assigned by Waïtari to kill Morel. When it comes time to execute these orders, Youssef cannot pull the trigger because the Frenchman faces him with love and courage, offering his life as a sacrifice. Thus, Youssef is converted to Morel's cause, becoming his first real African follower. The last we see of Morel, he has plunged deep into Africa, accompanied by Youssef; instead of killing Morel, the African tells him:

"I think we can still go a long way together" (p. 370). Morel sends Minna back with Abe Fields, an American cameraman, to whom he entrusts his briefcase filled with tracts, manifestos, and petitions. He tells Fields to go on with that work, and that he will some day return to ask Fields what he has done.

With Youssef, Morel demonstrates the proper relationship between the spiritual man, that is, one who has the calling to deal with matters of the spirit, and the man of nature, who has become infected with the disease of modern materialism. Youssef is himself a spiritual man in the making, but his relationship to Morel is largely that of student to teacher, of primitive man to civilized man. Youssef can be won to the cause of heaven only by an act of courage and love. The climax, when Morel is confronted with death, shows him to be in living possession of one of religion's deepest and most difficult truths—to resist not evil. The spiritual man of romanticism was never completely at ease with the man of nature, no matter how much he might admire him nor how much he might plead his cause. This is particularly true of the man of nature who was potentially a spiritual leader. Morel, with the help of his symbol of heaven, has established a religious relationship with a member of the primitive community. Again love flows between man and man, and the basis for a true kingdom is established with spiritual man and the man of nature playing roles they believe in, both subservient to, and in a loving relationship with, some of the roots of heaven. And although he does not take Minna with him, the woman he loves, Morel has reestablished the true man-woman relationship, which cannot exist unless both members are related to heaven through its symbols. The romantics talked endlessly of brotherly love, and we still live under the aegis of "brotherhood." Still, brotherhood in all its forms from friendship to marriage must fail if heaven is not worshipped. Minna, the prostitute, is contrasted to modern women, some of whom even hunt elephants. Knowing Morel, she renounces her old ways and learns again the role of true service to heaven through helping to preserve heaven's roots.

Finally, Gary makes it clear that Morel is only part of a new worldwide awakening. We find Morel himself thinking:

From Moscow to Madrid and from Peking to the Chad, the hidden springtime of humanity living its subterranean life in darkness would burst into the open with all the irresistible power of its millions of weak and groping shoots. . . . A slowly rising murmur, hard to detect, but the roots were strong and deep in the heart of man and the shoots were breaking their slow way into the open, and his ear was keen and as he lay there on his back he could almost hear them and his laughing eyes could almost see, in the deepest recesses of the earth, the slow thrust of that ancient and difficult spring. (p. 312)

This idea of a new beginning is underlined at the end of the novel. Even Father Fargue, a priest who had refused to sign Morel's elephant petition, says of him:

Of course he's a man of pride and a blasphemer, someone who ought to go down on his knees and pray instead of showing his fists. But it isn't entirely his fault. His heart's so full that he couldn't take a long enough run, it's too heavy. So he stopped short, he stopped at the elephants. But perhaps a good kick in the ass will give him just the run he needs. Meanwhile I don't want him to get himself killed half-way, where he got stuck, like a mad dog, without having had time to understand and to address himself and his petitions to the Right Quarter. (pp. 351–52)

The book ends with a statement by a Jesuit paleontologist, a minor character who appears from time to time. He is probably a portrait of Père Teilhard de Chardin, a priest of this century who believed that Christianity and evolution are in some way related and man may yet evolve into a higher species. The reader is told, concerning the priest, that "for a long time the tree had been his favorite sign on earth, before even the sign of the cross" (p. 372). So the central idea of the book is restated: the flowering of nature is a fitting root, sign, and symbol of heaven. It is where man must begin in order to rediscover his lost self and his lost feeling for the power and glory of heaven. This time there must be a life-commitment to the roots of nature and not just a flirtation, as in the days of the romantics.

   Morel's career illustrates one solution to a problem that has harassed thinkers and artists since the early days of romanticism: how to maintain idealism in the face of civilization's decay. In Morel's vision, true optimism and a complete acceptance of modern corruption are held in tension. This vision is only possible to one who believes in new creation and a new spiritual beginning. If this book can be written in the fifties, one can imagine new religious beginnings in the latter part of the twentieth century. Gary's contribution to a worldwide awakening is a clear, existential statement of several of the most important truths of a new beginning: that symbols must be found; that they must be believed in fervently; that true belief must come slowly, and it must develop by being tested in the fires of hardship and suffering; and, finally, that new beginnings are often made in remote places, sometimes on the very edge of civilization. These truths are stated as a part of a myth of our time, the essence of which is: the rejection of materialism by a new spiritual man, the search for new images of heaven, the reunion with the people of nature—provincial woman and man—and after that the continuing search for a greater understanding of heaven through closer union with its roots. This myth is a part of the larger myth of the hero, which Joseph Campbell calls in *The Hero with a Thousand Faces* the one great myth of man.

Campbell writes of the one great world myth of the hero who is tested and finally achieves the boon of creative power, with which he revives the dying world. Ever since the beginning of romanticism, the West has been moving toward the recovery of the ancient truths contained in the myth of the hero, which were lost sometime before or during that crisis of our civilization called the Renaissance. A study of the myth that Campbell describes and of the myth in Gary's novel, on the one hand, and the new beginnings in romanticism, on the other, might begin with three important English poems whose meanings today are either neglected or misunderstood: Blake's *The Mental Traveller*, Coleridge's *The Ancient Mariner*, and Shelley's *Prometheus Unbound*. These poems contain elements of the world myth, and at the same time they are symbolic representations of the deepest currents of the past 200 years. They speak variously of the spiritual leader's crime against nature and the people of nature, of the tyranny of an evil king and queen who replace the spiritual man, and of the leader's banishment to a desert where he must do penance for his sins. Blake's poem, which contains the widest vision of the three, tells how the spiritual man, after he has been cast out of his kingdom, seeks a new woman (a symbol of nature and her people). After finding each other, the spiritual man and his woman wander in terror and dismay through the desert, surrounded on all sides by beasts. The spiritual man grows younger until he becomes a Babe, the symbol of the birth of a new religion. By then the woman has become a hag and she begins to persecute him, and so begins again the cycle which Blake describes at the beginning of the poem.

The romantic period was the beginning of spiritual man's awareness of his crime against nature; with this awareness came his alienation from a society that no longer had any real use for him. The new period, which is even now beginning, should, if the myth is fulfilled, see the spiritual leader's reconciliation with nature and her people, an event which will be accompanied by a new awareness of his vocation. With this awareness will come a series of tests which he must survive in order to rule nature and to encounter the divine in man and nature. He will then know the creative energy of the cosmos, which will recreate the world. Thus Gary's book is a visionary statement pointing toward the next step in history.

Gary is more like Hermann Hesse in his display of continental idealism than he is like the French authors after 1945; and Hesse himself, as I have earlier suggested, recorded in his work a vision of the reintegration of man not found in most of the new writers after 1945. In Hesse, Gary, and the later Joyce there is a persistent attempt to overcome man's "dissociation of sensibility," to use T. S. Eliot's term for the disintegrated personality. Both Hesse and Gary write about the achieving of personal unity through a relationship with nature. In Hesse's *Siddhartha* we learn about a man who becomes holy because he contemplates a river: ". . . he knew more than you and I, without teachers, without books, just because he believed in the river."[4] Both Gary and Hesse also show man sloughing off the superfluous aspects of civilization to find what is essential for unity in both nature and human culture.

Above all, Gary's chief novel deals in the new energies and thus illustrates in its own way Campbell's statement concerning the chief function of myth:

It would not be too much to say that myth is the secret opening through which the inexhaustible energies of the cosmos pour into human cultural manifestation. Religions, philosophies, arts, the social forms of primitive and historic man, prime discoveries in science and technology, the very dreams that blister sleep, boil up from the basic, magic ring of myth.[5]

Today, at the end of modernism, our art and institutions have become stale because we are out of touch with the "inexhaustible energies of the cosmos." A novel like *The Roots of Heaven* is one sign, however, that men are once again seeking to realize in their lives the ancient truths of myth and religion. At its deepest, *The Roots of Heaven* is about the return of modern man to basic human doctrines of the freedom of the will and the ontological basis of creation.

Beyond Diabolism:
Flannery O'Connor's
Religious Existentialism

On the journey though the despairing wasteland the mythic quester must encounter, before he achieves the boon of epic power, the
forces of destruction traditionally called diabolical. He encounters
them not once but many times, until he learns that they are but
shadows of the one reality he seeks, shadows that in effect serve to
ward off the unwary and the unfit who would approach the shrine
which contains the boon. The influence of the shadow figures
causes, knowingly and unknowingly, both the tragic actions and
the numbing despair of the wasteland. No novelist in this century
successfully shows the release of the epic power for the good reason that it has not yet occurred, and only a few successfully show
human questers on the path leading beyond the tragic wasteland.
Of these few, fewer still are aware of the nature of diabolism. Flannery O'Connor is one of them.

Walker Percy credits Flannery O'Connor with being one of two
southern writers—Faulkner being the other—to transcend what
he calls the "Southern Obsession."[1] She did it because she was a
great artist who mastered the tradition of modern symbolism
through a patient study of two important masters of the symbolist
novel, Bernanos and Mauriac, and because she based her work

firmly on philosophical and theological traditions. She was also fully conversant with the currents of existential thought, particularly as it is found in the writing of modern religious existentialists from Kierkegaard to Buber. She is one of the few fiction writers in American literature who had a first-rate intellect, and she used it well. But intellect without imagination is not enough, and O'Connor had imagination in abundance. She used her intellect and imagination to create some of the most powerful literary symbols in contemporary literature.

Stanley Edgar Hyman, affirming the symbolic power of O'Connor's fiction, says that it is a "powerful example of what Kenneth Burke calls 'symbolic action.'"[2] Her strongest literary ability lies in her evocation of both the diabolical and the power of grace that transcends the diabolical, a grace depicted in "The Artificial Nigger" and "Revelation." Her power to evoke evil is sometimes so great that the very feeling of the twisted nature of destructiveness in her fiction has brought forth some of the angriest criticism against her. Hyman in this matter is one of her best defenders when he reminds us that "All art, to the extent that it is new and serious, is shocking and disturbing. . . ."[3] Part of the problem is that what she is doing is not often found in American fiction. She herself turned for inspiration to the continent, although Poe and Hawthorne are also influences on her work. To understand her fiction in terms of modernism, we must examine her work in relationship to the tradition of both symbolism and existentialism as we see it in Baudelaire and Dostoevski. These two giants of modern literature, together with lesser figures like Oscar Wilde and Charles Williams, invoke in their work the powers of evil without leaving us with the impression, as, for instance, William Golding's *Lord of the Flies* does, that evil reigns supreme in the world and will never be overthrown.

Only very recently has O'Connor been seen as a major figure in the mainstream of modern letters. There are many reasons for this, but probably the most notable is that she had very few themes. Robert Drake successfully defends her against this charge: "Her range was narrow, and perhaps she had only one story to tell. (But then didn't Hemingway?) But each time she told it, she told it with renewed imagination and cogency."[4] Actually, close examination of her total work will reveal that she had more than one story to tell, but she did have only a few themes; and they are chiefly about the failures or the successes (much rarer than the failures) of individuals in overcoming diabolic influences. Some of her characters put aside, for a time at least, diabolic influence; others are overcome by this influence; and still others recognize its influence in their lives and show signs that in the future they might well overcome it, might move beyond it because they know it for what it is and they know what to do about it. One of her last works deals with an individual in this third category.

The Lame Shall Enter First, a novella published in 1962 in the summer issue of *The Sewanee Review*, ties together most of Miss O'Connor's major themes, many of which were announced in her first novel, *Wise Blood*, published in 1952. *The Lame Shall Enter First* also sums up the major themes of *The Violent Bear It Away*, her second and last novel, published in 1960. Comparison of the two is very much to the point. In both she shows a teenage boy caught between two opposed viewpoints—one that of a fanatical backwoods preacher who sees people as either damned by themselves (in the case of old Tarwater) or saved by God, and the other that of a secular humanitarian who believes man can shape his own destiny. The boy has been reared, and mistreated in the process, by the preacher, and is forced against his will to live with the humanitarian. He clings to the ideas of the preacher and even tries to convert a child who is in the care of the humanitarian. Although the basic situation is the same, the working out of the two plots is different in that the boy Tarwater in *The Violent Bear It Away* murders a child and falls into the hands of the Devil, only to reject him and go to the city to become a prophet; whereas Rufus Johnson in *The Lame Shall Enter First* admits that the Devil already possesses him, then finally convinces the humanitarian, Sheppard, that he too is in the power of the Devil. In *The Violent Bear It Away* the humanitarian remains unchanged in his viewpoint, but in the novella Sheppard, in a final confrontation with evil as he finds it in the boy, sees that he has denied his own child love. In this moment of understanding he vows to change his ways; he rushes to the child's room, only to find that the child has committed suicide. Even this brief account of similarities and differences should indicate that Miss O'Connor developed in the novella certain ideas implicit in *The Violent Bear It Away*. In fact, in the novella, one of the last works of her life, she presented a vision that summed up her deepest insights into the God-man relationship.

Flannery O'Connor began with a protagonist in *Wise Blood* who preached a religion without Jesus; she writes in this book of a man naturally religious who is called to preach but who has to admit that he cannot believe in the Saviour. In her best-known short story, "A Good Man Is Hard to Find," we see a protagonist who passionately desires the certainty of belief in Jesus; not finding it, he turns to murder and other evil as his only consolation, stating in effect one of the basic ideas in O'Connor's work: whether one is a criminal or a respectable citizen, without Jesus he can only commit evil. In Tarwater the author presents the same passionate desire to believe without the certainty that leads to acceptance of Jesus as Saviour. The result is that Tarwater falls into the hands of the Devil, yet he escapes to flee to the "dark city, where the children of God lay sleeping."[5] With these final words of the novel, O'Connor states her belief that man, in spite of his inevitable sin, is still in God's keeping. Rufus Johnson in *The Lame Shall Enter First* is still fleeing, stopping from time to time to commit acts of senseless destruction. He is different from the others, however, in knowing why he is like he is: he is possessed by the Devil, who is not, as in *The Violent Bear It Away*, personified, but who nevertheless exists as a force within the breast of Johnson.

He also differs from the others in seeing the possibility that one day he will give himself to Jesus. In fact, he believes that it is people like himself—the lame, those with the deepest soul sickness—who will be saved first. After ten years of working with the violent protagonist—one great symbol of modern man, who has come to love destruction for its own sake—O'Connor has pointed the way toward the eventual acceptance of Christ as Saviour, which for the Christian writer like O'Connor is man's only hope.

Those who do not accept the theological viewpoint in O'Connor's work often consider her to be "just another Southern writer" dealing with regional decay, that is to say, someone like Carson McCullers. Others, who have accepted her viewpoint, wonder why she deals with violent and grotesque people.[6] Those who see that it is necessary for the modern writer to deal with the decay of our times often do not understand that what gives Flannery O'Connor's work a depth not found in many writers who deal with the same sort of material is her view of the modern world from the standpoint of philosophy and theology, and her ability to create powerful symbols out of her struggle with the raw material of human destructiveness and the theological vision which explores the human heart at war with itself and with others.

The reply to those who accept her theology but dislike the violence of her stories is that any basic truth to have meaning in literature must be seen in relationship to the essence of life in a particular time; by now, nearly everyone has accepted the fact that Western man has in his soul a powerful destructive element, which often makes him behave in a violent and grotesque manner. Religious thinking has become pale and peripheral during the past hundred years precisely because it has left out of its main consideration the existential struggle with the principle of destruction traditionally called the Devil. Writers of fiction have played a large role in the great task of showing to modern man the conflict that exists between humanity and this principle of destruction.

Through her character, Rufus Johnson, Flannery O'Connor is writing about a basic figure in modern existential literature—the criminal who is seeking God. Rufus is like Raskolnikov in *Crime and Punishment*. Although he may lack the depth and subtlety of Raskolnikov, his struggle with evil is more sharply etched. Rufus must struggle not only with the Devil in himself but with two other diabolical forces: a decaying humanitarianism, which, as he says in effect, does good for people but is not based on truth, and with a religious fanaticism that holds to truth but does no good. Rufus begins his life struggling with his grandfather's fanaticism, which directed toward the boy is converted into the diabolism of constant beatings. The story makes clear that humanitarianism consists of deeds without belief in God and that fanaticism is belief without deeds, the result of not truly accepting God. Fanatics quite often hold to basic truths, but truths are themselves only a signpost to reality. The task of the best of modern existential literature and philosophy has been to show the necessity of testing ideas by living them. But Rufus Johnson in inheriting his grandfather's diabolism is aware that the ideas of an evil man can be true. Although he is often confused in his attitude toward the world, he is sure that his grandfather held the only ideas possible for the good life and that he might even live these ideas sometime in the future, something his grandfather could never do.

O'Connor's final and most basic point, suggested by the title of her novella, is that the criminal who longs for God will make the necessary submission first. The work has in a sense summed

up where we stand in the rhythm of history. Societies begin with
true religions truly lived. After a time many believers fall into fanaticism, heresy, and hypocrisy; and secular philosophies like hu-
manitariansim, which emphasize good deeds, spring up. Since
these philosophies have no real metaphysical viewpoint, they soon
fall into decay. Then when evil, or the Devil, is rampant, people
gifted with the ability to understand theological truths rescue religion from the fanatics and hypocrites by living the truths. Thus
O'Connor shows that the world will have to be saved by those who,
like Rufus Johnson, have the keenness of mind to perceive theological truth amidst evil and who have suffered long at the hands of
the Devil, even aiding the destructive principle in its work. What
is required is the acceptance of the reality that the truth points
toward.

Yet when we first see Rufus in the novella, he has no desire to
be free from the Devil. Instead, he revels in the hatred for the
world that has been his grandfather's legacy. At last his struggle
with humanitarianism, the dominant philosophy of the urban
world he has entered, forces him to define his own position in relationship both to it and to the old fanaticism, which he has clung
to as a protection against the new ideas he encounters. His response to the city is a series of destructive acts. In the reformatory
to which he is sent he meets Sheppard, psychologist and humanitarian, who takes him home on parole to try to indoctrinate him
in the modern viewpoint. Sheppard's wife is dead and he lives
with his small child, whom he is busily educating in the ideas of
humanitarianism. These ideas can be summed up in this way:
man can perfect himself by education and good deeds. Education
for Sheppard means mastering scientific knowledge. The resulting
accomplishment, which more than any other will prove the efficacy of the modern philosophy of secular humanitarianism, will
be man's conquest of space. Sheppard gets a telescope for the further indoctrination of Rufus and his son. But from the beginning
the theology of Rufus's grandfather is too strong for Sheppard, and
soon the child is more interested in Jesus than he is in space ships.
Rufus sums up his attack on humanitarianism in this way: "Those
space ships ain't going to do you any good unless you believe in
Jesus."[7] The chief weakness in Sheppard's philosophy—that it puts
man in God's place—is quickly detected by Rufus: ". . . he [Shep-
pard] thinks he's God. I'd rather be in the reformatory than in his

house, I'd rather be in the pen! The Devil has him in his power. He don't know his left hand from his right, he don't have as much sense as his crazy kid" (p. 377).

Once Rufus recognizes the Achilles heel of the humanitarian philosophy, it is only a matter of time before Sheppard has to admit failure. The more he tries to help Rufus, the more destructive the teen-ager becomes until finally Sheppard has to give up and let the police take him back to the reformatory. The result of the struggle is that both are forced to define exactly where they stand. They both see quite clearly what it means to be in the hands of the Devil. In the deepest sense, that person is influenced by the Devil who lives for himself instead of for God. The source of Rufus' criminality is not so much his bad background or his lame foot, as the humanitarian thinks, but his desire to prove that he is of value in his attempt to live for himself. He tells Sheppard: "I lie and steal because I'm good at it! My foot don't have a thing to do with it" (p. 377). The way of life that Sheppard believes in is ultimately just as diabolical as aimless destruction, because it is based on egotism. What finally makes Sheppard see this is that he hates Rufus when he finds that his efforts to save the boy are a failure. The Devil within Rufus has called forth the diabolical within Sheppard, which he has been hiding behind a screen of good deeds. He has lived to do good; and in the process of relying on his philosophy to prove his existence, he has come to hate and hurt the very people he has sought to help. In a flash he realizes that he has thus denied love to his own child: "His heart constricted with a repulsion for himself so clear and intense that he gasped for breath. He had stuffed his own emptiness with good works like a glutton. He had ignored his own child to feed his vision of himself. He saw the clear-eyed Devil, the sounder of hearts, leering at him from the eyes of Johnson" (p. 379). This moment of insight creates in Sheppard's heart a spontaneous flow of love for his child, but it is too late: the boy has committed suicide. It is the juvenile delinquent, the boy criminal who has believed in God but has not accepted Him, who has the final say: "The lame shall enter first! The halt'll be gathered together. When I get ready to be saved, Jesus'll save me . . . " (p. 377).

With *The Lame Shall Enter First* O'Connor rounded out her view of life. With boldness and economy she sums up the modern scene with three basic characters: the man of social respectability who proves his existence with good deeds, the juvenile delinquent of motiveless malignancy who holds to the old theological truths, and the helpless child caught between them and destroyed. These three characters appear in various forms in her short stories and novels, but it was not until *The Lame Shall Enter First* that she pointed the way toward the salvation of modern man in a manner that is unmistakable. Although the child is lost, the father sees that his own philosophy has stood in the way of love, which alone could have kept his child alive. Deeds without the acceptance of God avail nothing and in fact only increase egotism. The juvenile delinquent at last sees that he can be saved only by accepting the reality of God's love and grace as they are revealed in Christ.

It is not enough simply to know the truth; only the leap of faith, or the act of letting go and receiving and acting on the Word, can bring back the love that will banish destructiveness and make the life of true childhood possible again. Any other approach to religion, O'Connor demonstrates, only creates fanaticism or hypocrisy. Here with her dramatization of the "leap of faith" she sums up in her work the essential doctrine of the man who is credited with founding existentialism, Sören Kierkegaard. Like Kierkegaard, O'Connor believed that the world will be renewed by those who, as world destructiveness grows, accept the leap of faith, man's only true hope. Her hope is rare among modern artists and thinkers; it is the hope of paradox and prophecy, which is still hard for many to accept who have not known intimately the kind of paradox that is at the basis of all true religious thought.

The prophecy that through the motiveless criminal shall come a new man free of the Devil is itself the sort of miracle that the secular mind trained in probabilities and statistics finds it hard to accept. Yet it is this same kind of prophecy that has been central to the work of the greatest storytellers of the century, including Mauriac and Bernanos, both of whom served as fictional guides to O'Connor. The two Frenchmen are themselves part of the large tradition of the symbolist novel, but like O'Connor they based their symbolist fiction on certain propositions that are basic to Christianity, and, in fact, to all the world's major religions. I think the power of her work is greater than that found in her two mentors'. It is this power that makes her the most important fiction writer working in the Christian tradition in the contemporary period, if not indeed in the entire century. Not only does her work have imaginative power but it has a kind of intellectual incisiveness found in some of the greatest Christian thinkers. William Barrett has said that Kierkegaard "stated the question of Christianity so nakedly, made it turn so decisively about the individual and his quest for his own eternal happiness, that all religious writers after him seem by comparison to be symbolical, institutional, or metaphorical—in a word gnostic."[8] The same might also be said of O'Connor, and yet I think she goes even beyond Kierkegaard in that her vision of God's love of man is greater, just as her vision of diabolism is deeper. Kierkegaard is not, as Barrett seems to say, the end of something but is the beginning of a literary, theological, and philosophical school that combines some of the best insights and deepest visions of both existentialism and symbolism.

Walker Percy
and the Archetypes

Walker Percy belongs among a small group of writers in our time who have done something for modern American literature that many people thought would never be done. He and novelists like Saul Bellow, Flannery O'Connor, and J. F. Powers—to name people from three different regions—have given to contemporary American fiction an intellectual and even a philosophical tone lacking in classic modern writers like Hemingway and Fitzgerald. Percy and writers like him have become intellectually involved with European thinkers and novelists and have used insights gained from this involvement without losing their own native genius for writing fiction. They have not cut themselves off from their ethnic and regional traditions but rather have followed these traditions back to their sources in the Old World. They have derived benefits from being Jewish or Catholic or even Episcopalian that other and perhaps greater writers of the American past often did not know. Thus Percy cannot be pigeonholed as, say, a Catholic novelist. Instead, Percy is a novelist of profound intellectual curiosity and sensitivity. He feels himself more closely aligned with the continental novelists, for "the European novels are more philosophical, more novels of ideas"[1] than English and American novels are.

148

The ideas in Percy's novels are basically Kierkegaardian, but the novels are not simply a framework for presenting the Danish philosopher's ideas. Instead, Kierkegaard is, for Percy, as Emerson was for Whitman, a kind of flame that brought the author to a boiling point. When one writer influences another the way Kierkegaard influenced Percy, it is not because one gives and the other takes certain ideas. It is because the older author brings the younger author face to face with one or more of the archetypes. It is Kierkegaard's encounter with the archetypal mythic quester, his "knight of faith," that helped to shake Percy out of his mental fixation on the general laws of science. Ideas usually inspire men and women to generate more ideas, but archetypes set flowing a stream of images in the psyches of artists who are receiving a torch from their masters.

Neither the work of Percy nor of Kierkegaard reveals an understanding of the theory of the archetypes. One of the subtlest of literary and philosophical psychologists, Kierkegaard arrived too early on the modern scene to encounter archetypal psychology. And Percy's serious knowledge of depth psychology does not go very far beyond Freud. He greatly respects Freud, having once elevated him, in his own words, "far beyond the point that even [Freud] would place himself."[2] But an understanding of the relationship between modern depth psychology and the visionary experiences of certain modern artists who have been influenced by it is missing in Percy. Perhaps, though, it is best that the artist-thinker not have a clear picture of what he is doing while he is doing it. At the Oracle of Delphi a priestess spoke the message of the gods but others translated it.

What is important is that Percy and Kierkegaard reveal that they have encountered the power of the archetypes. Both began their serious literary work as thinkers who were not content to settle for a view of life from the angle of general laws, but who insisted on preserving, along with general laws, a sense of the mystery of individual life. They came up early in their careers against that problem suggested by T. S. Eliot's now well-known term *dissociation of sensibility*. Both Kierkegaard and Percy show in their work that if man clings to reason alone and the systems that reason inevitably spins out, then he will stifle imagination and the sense of individual mystery and, in time, will destroy reason too. They also know that if one holds imagination higher than reason, as some romantics did, he may well become lost without a guide in a world of visions without meanings. For Kierkegaard the answer was to set out on a quest for God with belief that he would be successfully guided through the modern desert of empty thought systems. Thus he could indict Hegelian idealism and nineteenth-century institutional Christianity as systems that sought to imprison the mind and the soul. Because he refused to surrender his reason, he saw clearly when other nineteenth-century philosophers reacted with repressed, tangled emotions.

But Kierkegaard had problems that relate to his own time as well as to our time. He encountered the realm of archetypes, and it is this encounter that gives his writing that peculiar and haunting force missing in the dead language of so much prose prophecy of the last century. Kierkegaard's chief problem was that he was seized, or possessed, by several of the archetypes; and it is this seizure that accounts for the fanaticism, the hypersensitivity, and the murkiness that inform some of his best writing. Walker Percy has intuitively grasped this seizure, and the protagonists of his novels, who in a sense begin their quests as twentieth-century Kierkegaards, are aware of their own seizures. A quester goes into the realm of the archetypes to experience their power and to know deeper levels of human awareness thereby. But if he is seized and held by one or more archetypes, he is in danger of losing the very power he sought to gain or even of losing his powers of reason and imagination. And what is particularly important for Percy's fictional protagonists is that their quest for archetypal powers is an effort to overcome an inherited partial possession by archetypes that hold everyone in the protagonists' society.

Before examining the quest for archetypal power and the danger of archetypal possession in Kierkegaard and Percy, a definition of archetypes must be reviewed. The theory of archetypes is as old or older than Plato and as new as C. G. Jung. As one who formulated a theory of the archetypes for our century, Jung seeks simplification by occasionally calling archetypes "primordial images." At other times he speaks of "instinctual images," which are not intellectually invented but which are always present in the conscious and unconscious thought patterns of people in all historical periods and in all regions of the earth. In the book Jung began work on at the end of his life, *Man and His Symbols*, he particularly emphasizes the importance of the anima and the animus, the wise

old man or woman, the shadow, and the Self. Above all he emphasizes the mandala. Jung points to the many different forms that
individual archetypes take in different cultures, but his main emphasis is always on the power of archetypes to release the energies
of the individual psyche.

As for possession by an archetype, Jung is continually giving
in his work the example of the conventional middle-aged man who
suddenly throws up everything and runs off with a beautiful young
girl, his mind and soul possessed by her image. The archetypal
interpretation of this story is that the personality of an individual
is caught up, sometimes totally and sometimes partially, in a fixation on the image of the "eternal feminine," an image Jung calls
the archetypal image of the anima. Archetypal encounter is a different matter. The individual on this quest or pilgrimage encounters anima, animus, wise old man or woman, hero, shadow, and
other such patternings and is not possessed or bewitched and held
up on his journey. Instead this individual moves past the dangers
of destruction inherent in archetype possession. This quest toward
archetypal encounter is the movement that is the basis of the universal story called *myth*. There are dangers, suffering, even the
agony of personality dissolution, but there is the encounter with
ever deepening psychic powers until there is a breakthrough to a
new personality with expanded consciousness and deepened creative energies. Thus Mircea Eliade defines the "initiatory schema"
of myth and ritual as "comprising suffering, death, and resurrection (= rebirth)."[3]

When we find a novelist like Percy who, guided by Kierkegaard and Dostoevski, writes of mythic protagonists on pilgrim-
ages in contemporary America, we must turn to Jung and to the
solid work of people in various fields for a deeper understanding
of Percy's meanings. There is, besides Jung, the Eranos Round
Table in Switzerland, which for many years brought together men
and women in many different disciplines to discuss psychology,
mythology, religion, and related subjects. In America, during recent years, Mircea Eliade, Joseph Campbell, and others have in-
corporated in their work both the old and the new materials of
psychology, mythology, and religion. Even the laboratory work of
controlled experiments with LSD, done by psychologists in California, indicates that Freudian, Jungian, and other interpretations
of experience exist in the unconscious mind. Finally, British psy-

chiatrist R. D. Laing gives full credit to Jung for his work: "Jung broke the ground here but few have followed."⁴ Laing also discusses the theory of archetypes and of the mythic journey in terms of the schizophrenia of the 1960s, the decade in which Jung died and Percy published his first novel.

In *The Politics of Experience* Laing speaks of the archetypes and of the basic mythic theme of death and rebirth: "True sanity entails in one way or another the dissolution of the normal ego, the false self completely adjusted to our alienated social reality; the emergence of the 'inner' archetypal mediators of divine power, and through this death a rebirth, and the eventual re-establishment of a new kind of ego-functioning, the ego now being the servant of the divine, no longer its betrayer."⁵ Binx Bolling in *The Moviegoer* is almost an exact fictional statement of Laing's insight. As the novel opens we see him fairly well adjusted to what everyone around him calls "the good life of contemporary America"; but Laing would call it "our alienated social reality"—because we are alienated from what he also calls "'inner' archetypal mediators of divine power." For Laing, archetypes are symbols that, when they emerge, bring with them a kind of creative power traditionally called divine. When these symbols are missing in one's life, the kind of despair we today call angst—which Kierkegaard, as one of the first modern psychologists, analyzed so well—becomes so deeply embedded in the individual's life that it is not even noticed. Jung too saw the encounter with archetypes as an encounter with creative energies that lift the human being out of everyday boredom and apathy, those casual symptoms of genuine despair, and set him on a path moving toward personality integration.

Binx Bolling learns to face his own despair and begin what he regards as a search for God: "What do you seek—God? you ask with a smile," Bolling writes in his notebook. He goes on to answer himself by writing that Americans have already "settled the matter for themselves" because "polls report that 98% of Americans believe in God and the remaining 2% are atheists and agnostics—which leaves not a single percentage point for a seeker."⁶ But simple belief, Bolling sees, would not change anything for him. "The only possible starting point: the strange fact of one's own invincible apathy—that if the proofs were proved and God presented himself, nothing would be changed. Here is the strangest fact of all" (p. 146). Only some kind of affirmation or commitment will do, Bolling sees. And because he sees and affirms God, he becomes in a contemporary sense a quester seeking the creative powers of the universe that are mediated through the archetypes. It is true that Bolling only makes a beginning; certainly both he and Percy reveal a metaphysical diffidence not found in either Kierkegaard or Dostoevski. But any seeker who questions the attitudes and the values of the society he lives in, and who begins a search for the living power of what has been called the divine, does encounter within himself the archetypal quester and is aided by the power of this symbol. Thus, as he searches, Bolling encounters this archetype and is aided by it.

Bolling moves at the beginning of the novel from his static position at Kierkegaard's esthetic level, cultivating pleasurable sensations in business, reading, and casual love-making. His life of sensations is summed up by his pleasurable contemplation of the images on the moving-picture screen. At the end of the novel Bolling would seem not to have changed much, but his whole life in fact is turned in a new direction because he has encountered not only the archetype of the quester but also the archetype of the anima, that symbolic manifestation of the eternal feminine. The change in Bolling is revealed in a passage near the end of the novel when he observes a young man from the North going to New Orleans, his head filled with images of sexual pleasure. He is Bolling's double, as it were, one who has set out on a search for an archetypal female beauty in New Orleans even as Bolling has sought the ultimate pleasure in a great movie palace of Chicago. But Bolling is different from his double in that he is now in the process of being dispossessed of the anima archetype. All of his conscious pleasures and particularly his movie-going are but projections of this one entanglement with the feminine.

Part of Percy's genius as a novelist and much of his value as a philosopher of the contemporary mythic quest are that he can depict the struggles of a protagonist partially possessed but gradually being freed from archetypal possession. Bolling's movement beyond possession is feeble, but then so is contemporary man's. To write any other way would be to fabricate myth, which is a common enough fad in our times, or to write religious propaganda, which has never had any appeal except to the dullest of readers.

Bolling's movement from anima possession to anima encounter is seen in his relationship with the one woman in his life who is not totally connected with those fantasies of endless pleasure that always surround the anima-possessed psyche. He flees to Chicago to lose himself in the movie palace that he calls a great Urwomb, symbol of his desire for total immersion in the feminine, which is the goal of the journey of the anima-possessed; but he is at the same time taking a journey of encounter with the woman that he will marry.

The movement toward a deepened encounter with the feminine is a journey out of anima possession, and it means struggle and pain mixed with joy, whereas the journey into anima possession is a continual grasping at sensations that lead the bewitched psyche to a final surrendering of all ties with the world around him. Anima encounter, or animus encounter if the quester is a woman, leads to an enriching of all of one's experiences in this world because one is continually discovering the complementary "other" of oneself that is hidden in the psyche and symbolized by an image of the opposite sex. Benign anima and animus figures appear in the dreams, fantasies, and actual experiences of men and women moving on the journey of individuation. But those moving toward deeper anima or animus possession are giving up more and more of both the powers in their own souls and the good that is in the world around them in order to become more deeply involved in the life of sensations related to the anima or the animus. "All for love," or "the world well lost," to use the words of Dryden's other title of his play about anima possession, is the eternal rallying cry of the anima-possessed individual; or, when the anima image is projected onto other images associated with the pleasures of the remembered womb, the cry may then become, as in Bolling's case, "all for movies and the rest of the world be damned." When the world has been thrown over for the sensations of the archetype of anima or animus, these figures in dreams, fantasies, and actual experiences become threatening and destructive. Then the anima figures become witches that devour the soul.

Percy loves the world too much to abandon it to the dim memories of the womb, but he will not surrender the anima archetype either. His protagonists therefore must encounter the anima and not be possessed by it or by a substitute for it (e.g., the movies). Literature since the romantic movement has produced two extreme types of artists: one who clings to one or more of the archetypes and sinks into isolation and madness and the other who

thinks he has escaped madness by denying the archetypes altogether and clings to what he takes to be the "real" world; but the
dullness of his "realistic" art can also cause madness or at least
disguise madness. The greatest artists since 1750, however, have
let go neither the archetypes nor the world but have struggled to
keep both. Nobody sums up the problem better than Goethe, who
has his Faust exclaim: "Zwei Seelen wohnen, ach, in meiner
Brust," which is to say, "Two souls, alas, dwell in my breast." One
soul clings to the earth with a lover's lust, Faust says, and the other
flies up to heaven, abode of the divine powers. Not to surrender
either soul is the mark of an artist's greatness, but what strategy
is needed to hold the two together? Faust made a deal with the
archetype of the shadow, symbol of the destructive powers of the
universe. He encountered the power of the shadow in hopes of using it for his own benefit, but found that he became destructive to
those he should have served. Faust is unable, like a classic mythic
hero such as Orestes, to placate the powers of destruction so that
they find their proper sphere without becoming dominant in the
community. In his first three novels, Percy did not pit his archetypal quester against the shadow. In the fourth the hero is possessed first by the anima and then by the shadow. I will suggest
toward the end of this essay that if Percy is to continue his journey
into the realm of archetypes, he must deal with encounter, not possession. But before Percy can successfully depict the encounter
with the shadow, an achievement that might make him a major
world novelist, he must on a deeper level invoke the powers inherent in that archetype Jung calls the main archetype—that is, the
mandala, or Self.

Archetypally speaking, Percy's first two novels are one, or one
might say *The Moviegoer* lays the foundation for *The Last Gentleman*. In this second novel the protagonist, Williston Barrett, has
already made the choice to seek God that Bolling makes at the
beginning of *The Moviegoer*. Of Barrett, Percy says at the beginning
of the novel: "Thereafter he came to see that he was not destined
to do everything but only one or two things. Lucky is the man who
does not secretly believe that every possibility is open to him."[7]
Both Bolling and Barrett begin their pilgrimage with a quest for
God, which sets powers loose within their souls that begin to free
them from possession by the archetypes. But Barrett's involvement with the centrality of inner guidance is much deeper than

Bolling's, and thus his working out of the details of his journey is a much more complex matter.

As his journey proceeds, Barrett becomes more deeply involved with the truth of the chief archetype, the mandala, which Jung has thus characterized, as we have seen in chapter 7:

> It is what is called "ultimo exquadra circulae," the square in the circle, or the circle in the square. It is an age-old symbol that goes right back to the prehistory of man. It is all over the earth and it either expresses the Deity or the self; and these two terms are psychologically very much related. . . . It expresses the fact that there is a center and a periphery, and it tries to embrace the whole. It is the symbol of wholeness.[8]

Anyone familiar with archetypal symbolism will be immediately aware of the poverty of this type of emblem in Percy's work. Yet the truth of the mandala resides in the actions of both Bolling and Barrett. They center their minds on the guidance of the inner creative power and thus are led to encounter the archetypal powers that are held in balance by the center, symbolized in the mandala by the center point. Without overt mandala symbolism, that psychic center nevertheless suggests the controlling or master power holding together those powers symbolized in the mandala by four or multiples of four.

Symbols that have imaginative impact arise spontaneously out of voyages into individual psyches, and Percy knows that in our time we must begin these voyages slowly and with great care because of our psychic poverty. Archetypal encounter, if it is real, must be limited. If Percy were "rich in symbols" at this point in history (when other novelists readily paste myths and symbols onto threadbare plots), it would be a sign that no true journey had been attempted. To plunge deeply into the "forest of symbols," to use Baudelaire's phrase, is too dangerous for the limited voyager of today. Like Percy's protagonists, the journeyer who walks into the forest proceeds haltingly.

That Percy was fully aware of the contrast between his voyager and the mythic journeys of earlier times is seen in Barrett's contrasting himself with an Apache youth at the beginning of *The Last Gentleman*: "When he was a youth he had lived his life in a state of the liveliest expectation, thinking to himself: what a fine thing it will be to become a man and to know what to do—like an Apache youth who at the right time goes out into the plains alone, dreams dreams, sees visions, returns and knows he is a man. But no such time had come and he still didn't know how to live" (p. 11). In an age like ours, when knowledge is more prevalent than imaginative experience, we think too highly of ourselves in the areas of science and technology, and yet we long for visionary experience. We are mesmerized by the images of earlier archetypal encounters. Thus among "born again" Christians, chanting devotees of Krishna, and believing astrologers, archetypal possession is everywhere. Why journey into the soul when one can easily slip into the apparel of a holy man?

Barrett thinks only briefly of the Apache youth and sets forth on a quest for visions of his own. Yet how characteristically modern that he should think of himself as somehow inferior to the Apache. He does not have any clear-cut idea of what he should do, but as his journey continues he is given directions concerning tasks he must perform. Instead of being like the Apache who knows what to do once he has had visionary experiences, he is more like Parsifal, who must continually admit to a failure of knowledge. Percy's Barrett is in many ways like a medieval knight beginning a quest. Percy calls him the last gentleman because he is the last of a long line of gentle knights helping ladies in distress. But he is also a beginning. He is Kierkegaard's knight of faith, and he is a modern shaman in the making.

Barrett suffers from amnesia caused in part, we might say if we viewed him through psychoanalytical eyes, by the repressed pain of his life. His illness also includes epilepsy, and of his health Percy has said: "The reader is free to see him as a sick man among healthy business men or as a sane pilgrim in a mad world."[9] How fitting that the year this remark was published (1967) was also the year of the publication of Laing's *The Politics of Experience*. For Laing the sign of the voyager is his seeming "insanity," and he reminds the reader that our sanity (that of average "sane" people) is not "true sanity." He goes on to say:

Their madness is not true madness. The madness of our patients is an artifact of the destruction wreaked on them by us and by them on themselves. Let no one suppose that we meet "true" madness any more than that we are truly sane. The madness that we encounter in "patients" is a gross travesty, a mockery, a grotesque caricature of what the natural healing of that estranged integration we call sanity might be.[10]

Laing ends his work on the same note:

> In this particular type of journey, the direction we have to take is *back* and *in*, because it was way back that we started to go down and out. They will say we are regressed and withdrawn and out of contact with them. True enough, we have a long, long way to go back to contact the reality we have all long lost contact with. And because they are humane, and concerned, and even love us, and are very frightened, they will try to cure us. They may succeed. But there is still the hope that they will fail.[11]

In Laing's view, then, many are called to the voyage leading to the archetypal powers we associate with the shaman, who undergoes the transformation of his psyche through a visionary relationship with archetypal images. That Laing is speaking in the tradition of shamanistic experience going back to the most primitive peoples can be seen in a study of any one of many scholars in the field of shamanism. Two quotations from Mircea Eliade's *Myths, Dreams, and Mysteries* illustrate both Laing and Percy on the subject of the archetypal voyage: "The future shaman marks himself off progressively by some strange behavior: he seeks solitude, becomes a dreamer, loves to wander in woods or desert places, has visions, signs in his sleep, etc. Sometimes this period of incubation is characterized by rather grave symptoms." Concerning the supposed insanity of the future shaman, Eliade says:

> In the first place, it is not correct to say that shamans are, or must *always* be, neuropaths: on the contrary, a great many of them are perfectly sound in mind. Moreover, those who had previously been ill have *become shamans just because they succeeded in getting well*. Very often, when the vocation reveals itself in the course of an illness or an attack of epilepsy, the initiation is also a cure. The acquisition of the shamanic gifts indeed presupposes the resolution of the psychic crisis brought on by the first signs of this vocation. The initiation is

manifested by—among other things—a new psychic integration.[12]

In relationship to Percy I must emphasize the statement concerning epilepsy, one of Barrett's problems. Seen in the light of shamanistic experience, Barrett's journey into the South can be seen as part of his "getting well," a process that brings with it certain powers that are archetypal, or shamanistic, and that makes him "saner" than those around him because he is slowly achieving a measure of "psychic integration" while others are disintegrating. He can, for instance, turn away from his intensive ego-centeredness to take an active role in aiding those like Kitty and Sutter Vaught who are floundering in their psychic fragmentation.

An understanding of the making of the shaman in many different cultures is helpful for an understanding of the archetypal experience of any writer, but the development of that experience—if it is true and not fabricated experience—must take place in the framework of one's own culture. An Apache youth and a young Indian prince like Gautama Siddhartha, who became the light of Asia, must achieve archetypal experience through their own traditions; similarly modern man, as C. G. Jung many times observed, cannot go deep within himself by dressing up in the clothes of foreign mythologies. Wisely, Percy chooses Kierkegaard as shaman, or a fictional starting point for portraying archetypal experience, because Kierkegaard himself encountered the first archetype of our culture. This archetype of the quester—the one who rejects easy solutions to human problems in a society that has denied its people the lived experience of its religion—is necessary to begin the voyage.

Both Percy and Kierkegaard satirize an easy Christianity and the new idealistic systems that have tried to replace religion in decline, systems that promise easy and painless solutions to problems that are simply repressed and forgotten by those who accept them. In Kierkegaard's day it was Hegelian idealism that offered a system of rational spirituality one could accept without the pain of archetypal encounter or the need to make an either/or choice, which the quester must make in order to progress through a psychic wasteland. For Kierkegaard the real movement into archetypal territory comes with acceptance of the experience of the quester and with making the either/or choice of obeying God—the leap of faith. Kierkegaard published in 1843, at age thirty-two, his most basic works, *Either/Or* and *Fear and Trembling*, the first dealing with the necessary choice of the quest and the second with painting pictures of the knight of faith.

The picture Kierkegaard paints of the knight of faith in *Fear and Trembling* is of a man who can live comfortably with all of the feminine aspects of life because he has successfully encountered the anima archetype. Yet Kierkegaard says in *Fear and Trembling* that he must "admit that in my practice I have not found any reliable example of the knight of faith."[13] Kierkegaard himself was not the knight of faith because, when he set out on his own journey, he did not go anywhere. Although he preached faith, he could not himself find the faith to overcome archetypal possession. When he encountered the power of the anima archetype, he reacted in a way typical of many nineteenth-century poets and philosophers: he rejected the eternal feminine, an action which is as much an indication of anima possession as is abandoning oneself to the life of the feminine, as many twentieth-century poets do. On October 11, 1841, Kierkegaard made his final break with his fiancée, Regina Olsen, and thereafter developed his doctrine of the single one. "In order to come to love," he said of his renunciation of Regina, "I had to remove the object." Martin Buber in his essay on Kierkegaard, "The Question to the Single One," gives this quotation and adds his own comment: "Creation is not a hurdle on the road to God, it is the road itself."[14] Yet no more beautiful picture of one who accepts creation exists in nineteenth-century literature than Kierkegaard's of his knight of faith: "He takes delight in everything, and whenever one sees him taking part in a particular pleasure, he does it with the persistence that marks the earthly man whose soul is absorbed in such things. He tends to his work." Then: "On his way he reflects that his wife has surely a special little warm dish prepared for him, e.g., a calf's head roasted, garnished with vegetables."[15] I quote at length this picture of the knight of faith because Kierkegaard's vision is a perfect statement of Barrett's encounter with the anima on his journey into the South in *The Last Gentleman*.

That Barrett is himself a knight of faith is seen in the fact that he, unlike Kierkegaard, who has only glimpses of the archetypes, can perform certain acts of service on his way to a fuller realiza-

tion of the archetype of the hero, or cosmic man, as Jung sometimes calls this archetype of creative power. Barrett's first important task, after encountering the anima in the form of Kitty
Vaught, is accomplished in the guise of the anti-hero archetype,
which is how others see him. He is called to save Jamie Vaught
from dying outside the Church. As he is dying, Jamie can nod assent to the basic truths of religion because of his belief in Barrett
and Barrett's own tacit acceptance of these truths. Barrett's "saving" of Jamie has not been overt, or "heroic," but indirect. Barrett
performs an act of spiritual aid by bearing Jamie's burden of loneliness and allowing Jamie to communicate without words his own
belief. Father Boomer's explanation of the "truths of religion" that
Jamie accepts are a Christian statement of the truth of the mandala: "Do you accept the truth that God exists and that He made
you and loves you and that He made the world so that you might
enjoy its beauty and that He himself is your final end and happiness, that He loved you so much that He sent His only Son to die
for you and to found His Holy Catholic Church so that you may
enter heaven and there see God face to face and be happy with
Him forever" (p. 403).

Barrett must also struggle against the death wish of Sutter
Vaught, who is suffering from mythic identification. Mythic identification happens readily to those who become involved with the
heroic stories of man, as did Don Quixote, and who do not see that
one cannot choose on his own to act out the role of any of the
archetypes. If one hopes not to lose his mental balance through
mythic identification—either in a delightful way, like Don Quixote, or in a dangerous way, like Faust—all he can do is to seek an
ever closer identification with the divine center, or the Self, as
Jung calls it. The Hindus teach that the lotus (the chief form the
mandala takes in the Far East) is the sun within—that is, the basic
cosmic energy at the center of the individual and the cosmos. But
those who approach the archetype from the outside, without concentrating their minds on the center—whose power upholds and
unites the two, the four, and the multiples thereof—will tend to
identify, as Sutter does, with the archetype of the hero. In other
words, they see myth from the outside.

Myth seen from the inside is the quest for personality, or
psychic integration; that quest entails encountering along the way
the power of the archetypes, which themselves perform service to

others as their energies are released within the soul. The sign that heroic actions are the result of archetypal encounter is the fact that the true hero is never separated from love, the unifying power that always protects the sanity of the true quester. By trying to set himself up as a hero instead of seeking that integration that activates the hero archetype within himself, Sutter is condemned to isolation and cynicism; thus he seeks to "redeem" his seeming failure by suicide. Sutter is like his nineteenth-century forebears, Kierkegaard and Nietzsche, who also were idealists possessed by the hero archetype. Kierkegaard became in his own eyes the great exposer of a phony "Christendom" and Nietzsche became Zarathustra, a prophet of power and a denier of anti-power. They both set out on journeys like Percy's Sutter, but theirs ended in bitterness, destructiveness, and madness. Sutter's journey too would have ended so, were it not for Barrett's love, alloyed though that love is with a desperate need for friendship. Thus when Sutter encounters the depth of Barrett's concern for his life, he is checked in that destructive madness that so often accompanies archetypal possession.

Love in the Ruins continues Percy's epic of man freeing himself from archetypal possession. Dr. Thomas More is caught up in the web of both the anima and the hero archetypes. He is in certain ways both Sutter Vaught and Binx Bolling, and the novel is in part the story of his freeing himself in order to encounter the power of the archetypes. But *Love in the Ruins*, unlike *The Last Gentleman*, is not primarily a book about archetypal pilgrimage. To analyze it as such would be to miss much of the wit of Percy's comedy of manners. It is as if the author were taking a kind of holiday from the more serious occupations of his life, in writing this satire about such matters as the sexual revolution and the cult of psychiatry, about white suburbs and black revolutionaries. Yet *Love in the Ruins*, with its apocalyptic theme, also contains a suggestion of Percy's next serious fictional encounter with the archetype.

In Percy's fourth novel, *Lancelot*, there is movement toward shadow possession. The protagonist in his insanity reveals the influences of a shadow destructiveness. Lancelot, who was first possessed by the anima with its womblike, mother-haunted vision of a past southern community of glory and pleasure, moves into possession by an archetype of the hero. As his name suggests, he is as archetypally possessed as his namesake. He will, like Don Quixote, take up his lance and create again the good of the remembered past by destroying the enemies who are decimating the old order. But the good society cannot be created by an act of the will, and to try to do so is to be at best pathetically humorous to those who look on. In setting Lancelot in contrast to the character Percival, who listens to his ravings, Percy has performed another remarkable service for modern man. He has outlined the two approaches possible for the person who sees the emptiness of our pseudo-culture. One is Lance's attempt to reform by destruction and the other is Percival's way, which is to do simple parish work and to "forgive the sins of Buick dealers."[16] Like Parsifal, Percival is with those in Percy's earlier novels who see that they must begin in the simplest ways to take upon themselves the burdens of the Christian cult, which stands at the center of what is left of our old Western culture.

It is extremely important that the priest will *forgive*, because one cannot forgive who does not love. And love cannot be an act of the conscious will but instead is a gift given to those who follow the path of pilgrimage, which leads again and again to the shadow powers. Those who overcome these destructive powers, not once but many times, receive the love and creative power necessary for the re-creation of culture, thus becoming culture heroes in that they allow the hero archetype to work through them. And as Percy suggests, the two ways into the future are that of the one who allows the archetypes to seize and carry off his personality and his humanity, and that of the one who through pilgrimage grows into that state of individuation, as Jung called it, in which one becomes human, individual, creative, and loving.

I have already suggested that Percy must bring his fictional characters of the future into a profounder relationship with the shadow than he has already done if he is to continue his exploration of archetypal territory. The shadow has been appearing with greater frequency in modern literature since 1945. Mann, Golding, Powers, O'Connor, Gary, and Cheever are only a few of the novelists who have invoked the shadow in fiction of the postwar era. In the life and literature of our time there is a fascination with images of destruction, so much so that one might suspect that possession by the shadow is becoming widespread, an event our civilization has not witnessed since the late Middle Ages, though we have seen something of it in the religious madness of the sixteenth and the seventeenth centuries and in the political madness of the Nazis. Certainly Lancelot is possessed by the shadow. But today more than ever we need pilgrims who will face and overcome the power of the shadow archetype. This pilgrim is the shaman who can encounter archetypes without being possessed by any one of them. Perhaps Percy is now ready to write about him.

The rise to power in our time of the archetype of destruction poses the question of what form art itself will take. Possibly the novel really is dead, as some critics have been saying for several decades. Or possibly what is dead is a certain kind of novel—the novel, I would suggest, of the tragic ego. Whether it was *Moby Dick* or *The Golden Bowl, The Sun Also Rises* or *The Sound and the Fury*, the novel that held the attention of the good reader for a hundred years was the novel of the tragic ego. The tragic egos of contemporary literature lack the ability to struggle against archetypal powers, even as Goethe's tragic Faust struggled to maintain his own personality while being used by the shadow. The result in much literature today, including, finally, *Lancelot*, is that archetypes like the anima and the shadow often overcome human personality. Without a vision of personality, works of literature cannot serve the deepest needs of man, and they eventually become relegated to the level of artifacts in a museum.

The renewal of literature begins when individual works deal with protagonists who, through encountering the archetypes, undergo a deepening of personality. The subject of myth essentially is the growth and development of personality through encounters with suprahuman powers. Today the ego is so swamped by archetypal images that it cannot cope with them; therefore the forms of tragic art have broken down. Percy and novelists like him are not tragic artists. They write comedies, in the Dantesque sense of the word, stories with happy endings. We are used to such stories being fabricated for our daydreams, pseudo-myths of no archetypal significance. But the stories of Percy and others do have archetypal power, and because they do there is hope that we might with the help of new-found shamans be moving out of the tragic phase of our civilization. The furies of the apocalypse must still do their work, but the comic artist must look beyond the end of the world, and with the shaman he must take those steps that lead beyond tragedy to a new, lasting comedy. Walker Percy without doubt is one of those who travels on the journey of man that goes beyond tragedy.

The Search for Unity in Modern Times

Harold Bloom has written that "poets from the Greek Orphics to our contemporaries live in guilt cultures" and that the critic is a "solipsist."[1] Modern literature contains much about guilt and even more about the solipsism of modern man. But where there is guilt and solipsism, there is often a search for the washing away of guilt and for the removal of the barriers of solipsism—the two in fact, guilt and solipsism, being aspects of each other. If the world's societies had not been capable in the past of freeing themselves from guilt and solipsism, man would have ceased to exist. Those societies who cannot, for a time at least, move into a period of a partially successful overcoming of guilt have no link with the present, because all societies we have drawn from have given us something of their wisdom about the release from guilt. The record of this release is found in their myths and rituals.

Bloom says that the guilt societies we live in cannot accept a theory of the origin of poetry that is found in many studies of shamanism and that he ascribes to the Italian historian and philosopher Vico, who influenced Joyce greatly. The theory says that poetry came into being as "a system of ceremonial magic," and those figures who invented this poetry of magic "are the anthropological equivalents of wizards, medicine men, shamans, whose vocation is survival and teaching others to survive."[2] This poetry of survival is exactly what I find at the heart of the best work of many of the most advanced artists of modernism, a kind of incipient shamanism that must find its completion at a later time if man is to go on living. The shaman is both a singer who renews language and a prophet who looks before and after, as Eliot tells us in "Little Gidding." To achieve these powers necessary for survival, the shaman-to-be must move on a journey in which he suffers and continually risks his life. Thus, he overcomes his own guilt by finding unity both within himself and within the world.

The search for unity is not as unusual an event as we might imagine in the twentieth century. We find it not only in the arts but also in the sciences. In a world in which the subjective and the objective, realism and idealism, head and heart, analysis and vision are often separated, we see, if we look, those who move momentarily beyond the opposites to achieve glimpses of unity. For instance, Jacob Bronowski, a philosopher of science and a student of the visionary poet Blake, speaks mythically when he says: "Rationalism is the exploration of the world as human adventure. . . ."[3] And of science he says: "For science is not a book, either of facts or of rules; it is the creation of concepts which give unity and meaning to nature."[4] I would disagree with him at only one point, when he says that these concepts are "created by the human mind for the human mind."[5] Instead, I would agree with Einstein when he speaks of Leibnitz's idea of a "pre-established harmony" and goes on to say, about his colleague Max Planck, ". . . the longing to behold this pre-established harmony is the source of the inexhaustible patience and endurance with which Planck has devoted himself, as we see, to the most general problems of our science. . . ."[6] To search for pre-established harmony is to seek the power associated with the archetype of the mandala, images of which appear in every society known to man, the archetype serving as the basic symbol of that which is sought, found, and lost countless times— so much so that Alan Watts can even define myth as a game of hide and seek. Those who have encountered the pre-established harmony receive that shock of recognition of the genius of all others who have discovered the harmony, as Einstein, on Planck's sixtieth birthday, announced his own recognition of his fellow genius.

While Planck and Einstein were moving on a path leading to the beholding of the inner unity of the cosmos, certain poets were on the same path. I have selected three to discuss—Mann, Joyce, and Eliot, the three who have probably received the most international recognition. They began their work in that period before 1912, when guilt and solipsism prevailed among the advanced thinkers and artists of the day, and moved into the next two periods of modernism to achieve glimpses of unity. All three began under the influence of French symbolism, and in time all became stylistically eclectic. They fully encountered the sense of death recorded by the symbolists, and recorded what they found; then they moved on to a larger vision of unity. To review briefly their journey is to remind ourselves of what their careers meant in terms of a general search for a pre-established harmony.

In the first symbolist-influenced phase of the careers of Mann, Joyce, and Eliot, symbols of death, sterility, paralysis, and of a kind of life-in-death predominate. Anna Balakian in *The Symbolist Movement* has said that the chief symbols of the movement called symbolism are related to death and hopelessness: "Death is always there, hidden in the shadows. . . ."[7] Mann's major work of this period, which lasts roughly until World War I, is *Buddenbrooks* (1900–1901), a novel dealing with the decay and death of an old family in North Germany. His major piece of short fiction in the period, *Death in Venice* (1913), is about the psychic decay and final death of a man who closely resembles the composer Gustav Mahler (1860–1911). Venice, where the story takes place, becomes in Mann's vision a major symbol of a disease-haunted city where death permeates everything.

The most important work completed by Joyce before World War I is "The Dead," the chief piece of short fiction in *Dubliners* (1914). In this work the characters are all caught up in a kind of living death, or paralysis of the heart, which frustrates all attempts to be creative. Snow is one of the chief symbols of the work, and Joyce uses it to evoke the coming of an age of human isolation, and of the mental and the emotional paralysis accompanying such an age.

T. S. Eliot wrote little before World War I, but the few poems he did write had a stunning effect on the development of modern poetry, though not immediately. The most important of these poems is "The Love Song of J. Alfred Prufrock" (1910–11). In it Eliot paints one of the important wasteland scenes of the century. Images of castration and psychic paralysis fill the poem; an atmosphere of life-in-death pervades the work. Prufrock's final gesture is to walk by the seashore and to invoke, unsuccessfully, the life-giving, ever-renewing powers of the sea. When the attempt fails, his final vision is of death by drowning: " . . . human voices wake us, and we drown."[8]

The final line of "Prufrock" is still thought by many to be a summing up of the voice of serious modern literature, because symbolism is still believed to be the chief school of modern poetry. In fact, however, the line can be viewed as a prologue to the second and by far the greatest phase of the work of Mann, Joyce, and Eliot. Before discussing that phase, however, it is necessary to mention certain important currents in the early development of modern literature.

The opening years of modernism in the fourth quarter of the nineteenth century saw the establishment of two groups that had been gathering strength in Western society for more than a hundred years. They can be identified by their beliefs about man and society, and they replaced, almost completely, the conflicting forces of religion that had once occupied the central stage of European life. The first group, overwhelming in its numbers, believed that through the use of science and technology man could improve his environment and make for himself a good life. The other group, much smaller but including some influential figures, reacted against this dominant group and pointed to the facts of mental, emotional, and psychic decay, suggesting that here were the important facts of modern life.

The first group expressed itself in the arts in a set of formularized image patterns which always pointed toward the triumph of man over his problems through the use of machines and machine-like organization. The other group expressed itself primarily in the styles of literary naturalism and symbolism. Naturalism presented modern life as a kind of jungle in which people tore each other to pieces for money, power, and sexual pleasure. Symbolism, on the other hand, painted a picture of a few superior individuals withdrawing from the human jungle into a world of their own making where they might encounter death, sterility, isolation, and motivational paralysis while always seeking to encounter beauty and rationality.

Naturalism, which came into its own with Emile Zola after 1870, emerged as the dominant literary style for most second-rate works of serious fiction. The morbidity and decadence of symbolism became dominant in the work of the majority of serious European poets. Yet the great modern literary artists moved beyond both naturalism and symbolism in the second great period of modernism, which extends roughly from 1912 to 1945. They adopted several styles, and their dominant images in this, the most creative period we have known in the twentieth century, transcended the symbols of death and paralysis that earlier had dominated symbolist poetry.

Balakian has written at length to demonstrate that Mallarmé is a symbolist poet and so is Verlaine, but that Rimbaud is not.[9] Rimbaud, she says, is a force, and the sense of death is absent from his work. Her statements concerning Rimbaud make a basic point concerning the change that occurred in modern literature after 1912. Rimbaud himself was but a precursor of that new drive of major figures to break through the dominating cloud of death symbols that hung over Europe between 1870 and 1914. It is true that those great precursors of symbolism, Poe and Baudelaire, reveal in their work an energy and an awareness of the quest needed to take an artist beyond the wasteland of death and paralysis; but in their work, as in that of the symbolists, the images of the wasteland are in the foreground. For that matter, these same symbols seem to dominate the literary landscape after 1914, so much so that the twenties are thought by many to be a period of disillusionment for the arts. Yet major figures like Joyce, Mann, and Eliot use the wasteland as a backdrop for the movement of the quester figure, who seeks the kind of illuminating visions and symbols of transformation that Rimbaud himself cultivated.

In one sense Rimbaud's brief career resembles the longer careers of Mann, Joyce, and Eliot in that he faced the wasteland of his own day and found the energy to seek and find illuminations of a unity that lies behind the broken surfaces of the modern period. In *Illuminations* (1886) he evokes the image of the poet as a seer striding the wintry blast of world convulsion that first appeared in the Franco-Prussian War. But the three great international figures seasoned themselves in the ways of the wasteland over a period of years and went on to find, not only the knowledge of, but also the vision of the quester and the seer. For this reason their symbols have a world-resounding quality not found in Rimbaud's. It is as if the three writers prepared themselves for the fullness of convulsion that came in 1914, and then found the new energy that would enable them to bring forth major modern images of both the quester and the seer.

Harry Levin describes the new burst of energy that came to Joyce in the very year of the guns of August: "The tenth year of exile was, as Joyce had prophesied, his *annus mirabilis*. In 1914 *Dubliners* was finally published, the *Portrait of the Artist* completed, *Exiles* composed, and *Ulysses* begun."[10] For Mann and Eliot the new burst of energy would come shortly after World War I. Before the war Mann had already written fiction that had stamped him as one of the century's leading realists, but the new vision and the new symbols that appeared in his creative life after the war enabled him to write *The Magic Mountain* (1924), one of the most influential books of our time. Eliot in 1920 published a collection of poems containing works like "Gerontion" that were still in the tradition of sterility and despair, but in 1921 he had the emotional breakdown that led to his writing the most influential poem of the twenties, *The Waste Land* (1922). The three men, together with W. B. Yeats, who also found new symbols, with their new-found creative powers changed the avant-garde tradition of modern letters. And at the heart of their work was a new set of symbols, largely unrecognized at the time because those schooled in avant-garde literature could see only the symbols of despair, which in fact were in the foreground of *Ulysses*, *The Magic Mountain*, and *The Waste Land*.

Wasteland symbols were in the foreground of the new masterworks, but it was as if the three men were deliberately hiding their new symbols. And what were these new symbols? The most important was that of the mythic quester, who had appeared earlier in poets like Poe and Baudelaire but who had made little or no progress on the mythic path. Even in the work of the twenties the quester appears only in illuminating glimpses. Stephen Dedalus in *Ulysses*, Hans Castorp in *The Magic Mountain*, and "I," the speaker in *The Waste Land*, all move toward a deeper awareness of the cosmic forces within themselves and the universe, but their movement is seen in fleeting glimpses. Even more fleeting is the illumination of the cosmic forces the quester encounters, forces of creativity and destruction that we can understand only through the symbolic forms they take in an individual's life.

In our time we tend to erect intellectual structures to explain the meanings of symbols, and too often the structures interfere with a living encounter with symbols. Yet the theories of C. G. Jung must be invoked for anyone seeking to isolate major symbols in Mann, Joyce, and Eliot. Mann and Joyce were directly influenced by Jung's theory of archetypes, and Eliot's major symbols so closely resemble Jung's archetypes that no modern figure can better help us understand Eliot than the late Swiss psychologist. Thus, when we examine the symbols of the powers of creation and destruction that emerge in the three authors' major works of the twenties, we must consider at least three archetypes: the shadow, the anima or animus, and the mandala. The shadow and the anima-animus are the two important archetypes of twenties, and the mandala is the important archetype of the thirties and beyond.

Examples of shadow symbolism appearing in sometimes terrifying illuminations are found in the encounter with the Circe image in Bella Cohen's brothel in *Ulysses*, in Castorp's vision of the dark powers of ancient Greece hidden behind the sunny images of classicism, and in the realization of the "I" in *The Waste Land* that modern London has become Dante's Inferno. The fructifying powers associated with the anima archetype also appear. The recurring "yes" of Molly Bloom in *Ulysses*, the hyacinth girl in *The Waste Land*, and several figures in the sanitorium in *The Magic Mountain* all reflect powers associated with the anima image. Anima figures, in fact, dominate the best poems of Eliot in the late twenties, works like "Marina" and *Ash-Wednesday*. Working as they do in the tradition of Poe, Baudelaire, and Rimbaud, the three men put far more emphasis on the anima images of creativity than do their predecessors, who were absorbed more with the powers of the shadow image than with any others in their best-known works.

The anima, however, only points the quester on the way to his destiny and is not the goal of his journey. The eternal feminine leads us upward, Goethe's Faust says of this archetype. The goal of the mythic journey is contained in the meaning and the experience of the symbol Jung called the most important archetype: the mandala. Looked at in terms of human growth, the mandala is the symbol of that unified personality the quest for which leads Hans Castorp out of the death-oriented sanitorium into the reality of his own vocation. The same quest leads Stephen Dedalus out of his literal and figurative tower into a search for that true father who will initiate him into the mysteries of manhood. The mandala is, among other things, the symbol of the unified personality we all carry within us—called by Jung the cosmic man, who "is not only the beginning but also the final goal of all life—of the whole of creation."[11] The role of the poet as quester and seer is to experience the underlying unity of the individual and of the universe symbolized by the seemingly endless forms that the square-circle combination called the mandala takes throughout the world. This underlying unity is created by a central creative principle within the individual, which Jung called the Self. And the mandala, or symbol of totality, is a symbolic statement of the Self: "The whole inner psychic reality of each individual is ultimately oriented toward this archetypal symbol of the Self."[12]

Rimbaud in *Illuminations* sought to render the visionary world of the poet who has been lifted to the level of seer, or *voyant*. He felt that the poet could achieve this level by a planned disordering of the senses. For Mann, Joyce, and Eliot no planned disordering was necessary; instead, they throw their questers into the modern wasteland to encounter the chaos-making, sense-disordering powers of the shadow. Here they also find the healing powers associated with the archetype of the anima. Their work is in one sense an extension of Rimbaud's *Illuminations*; but in their later visions of the power of the mandala they complete what he had barely begun, revealing in their work that the seer in any area of life comes into being when he encounters the cosmic man within himself.

In his tetralogy *Joseph and his Brothers* (1933–44), Mann centers his attention on Joseph the seer and on his leadership both in the world of dreams and in the world of human affairs. Goethe, in many ways the father of modern literature, wrote in his Wilhelm Meister novels the story of the development of a man who is the master of his own soul and of the world around him. Deeply influenced by Goethe, Mann creates a Joseph who, through the use of the gifts of prophetic dreams and dream interpretation, becomes a master of a society destined for spiritual leadership in all ages of history. Mann also projects in his work a vision of a "Third Humanism" in which man will work in harmony with the invisible God and will thereby reorder his life on earth.

No modern writer delves more deeply into man's need to reorder his inner and his outer life than does James Joyce. Always writing under the influence of Freud and Jung, Joyce in his final work,

Finnegans Wake, begun in 1922, after *Ulysses*, and published in 1939, presents a vision of man's psychological and social reunification (examined in detail in chapter 7). Among other meanings, the mandala represents the union or reconciliation of opposites. Joyce has created a character who, having died as Finnegan, the common man who dominates our century and who is the archetype of the anti-hero, awakes in his coffin as Finn, the cosmic man. After showing the emergence of Finn, Joyce then presents another character who represents Everyman, H. C. Earwicker. He is finally united with his wife Anna Livia (Everywoman), and they are reunited with their two sons, Shem and Shaun, who in turn are reunited with each other—the one representing the life of the seer and the other, the life of practicality. As the family is reunited by the end of the book, so is the life of man on earth, symbolized by the rejuvenation of Joyce's native Ireland and the restoration of man's relationships to the creative cosmic powers.

Joyce's *Finnegans Wake* was at first rejected by many serious readers because of its difficulty, but it is now finding its own audience because of its poetry and its vision of world renewal. Eliot's *Quartets*, completed in 1943, met with a similar opposition, and some critics still feel that this work represents a falling off from the poetry of the twenties. Yet in *The Four Quartets* Eliot brings to completion, with his recurring symbol of the child, the poetic quest from Rimbaud forward for the visionary powers of the seer. The four poems record the growth of the visionary powers of one who seeks expanded consciousness and renewed creative powers. Beginning in a rose garden, the quest leads past the modern wasteland into a perception of the waters and the fires of destruction and of creation, and ends with a renewed vision of the rose, which Joseph Campbell reminds us is the most prevalent form the mandala takes in the West. Eliot's final vision in "Little Gidding" is one of the reconciliation of opposites in which "the tongues of Flame" are infolded.

> Into the crowned knot of fire
> And the fire and the rose are one.[13]

Early in the last section of "Little Gidding," Eliot repeats the line "Quick now, here, now, always," which are the words of "children in the apple-tree" describing the eternal visionary moment of the seer. Before this passage he speaks of the coming of the dove of the Spirit, bringing once again new life and new language.

The visions of reconciliation set down by Mann, Joyce, and Eliot in the period between 1921 and 1943 present some of the important symbols of the renewal of modern man and of the ultimate reconciliation of all of his warring elements. But man cannot simply reach out and make the power of the symbol of totality his own; he must earn this power. It is this earning process that is the chief subject of the third period of modernism, which begins sometime in the thirties and continues even to the present day, though the seventies must be the seed time of a new period of creative endeavor. The earning process consists in the quester's facing the power of the shadow, symbol of the forces of destruction and chaos that always challenge man's forward movement. The period since 1945 has seen the depiction of both diabolic and apocalyptic themes, and literary works dealing with the shadow have grown in number in the decades since World War II. Yet the greatest novel about diabolism of this century was written by the dean of modern fiction, Thomas Mann.

It is difficult for some to comprehend that Mann at twenty-six could publish *Buddenbrooks*, one of the great novels of human decay, and then at the end of his career could publish *Dr. Faustus* (1948), the great modern novel dealing with the shadow. Joyce, who died in 1941, had only the two periods of modernism, but Mann made important contributions in all three. Mann's Faustus is a prototype of the modern artist-philosopher who would with his visions liberate man, but who fails because he cannot overcome the power of the shadow—the nemesis that pursues anyone who would seize the creative fire. The novel is also a statement about the seizing of Germany by the powers of diabolism. In Mann's novel he who would save man is himself destroyed because he cannot invoke the powers associated with the mandala. Vision fails him, and he mistakes destruction for creation.

Mann and Eliot both record the journey of those who encounter the shadow in their search for expanded consciousness and accompanying creative powers. The popular view today concerning the renewal of vision, or the achieving of expanded consciousness, is that the new vision can be had through so many meditation sessions. Yet in all societies the records of the journey show that pain and danger are inevitable and that failure is sometimes the result. Today we speak of the coming of new shamans, or culture heroes, who will restore society; but the word *shaman* is related to the Sanscrit word *'sram*, meaning "to exhaust or fatigue." Mann in *Dr. Faustus* records a painful journey which ends in the quester's possession by the archetype of the shadow. Eliot, on the other hand, wrote three plays, beginning with *Murder in the Cathedral* (1935), that deal with relatively successful encounters with the threatening powers of destruction. *Murder in the Cathedral*, set in the Middle Ages, is artistically the most successful, but *The Family Reunion* and *The Cocktail Party* are more interesting to many because of what they suggest about the future of the quester in literature. Eliot is saying in *The Family Reunion* that demonic forces can be, if rightly approached, "bright angels" (Eliot's term), which lead the quester on his journey. In *The Cocktail Party* he deals with the movement of the quester beyond everyday urban existence into the mysteries of personal sacrifice. Unlike *Dr. Faustus*, Eliot's plays after *Murder in the Cathedral* are but shadows of the poet's former triumphs, yet it well may be that these later works will form bridges to the new period we are undoubtedly entering.

In the new period even more terrifying symbols of apocalyptic terror and dismay will probably emerge. Yet the work of Mann, Joyce, and Eliot points man toward new symbols of totality and toward concepts of the renewal of man through contact with the power associated with images of the cosmic man. The three men in their work indicate that Western civilization and the Judeo-Christian tradition are by no means finished, as so many think, but that we have been passing through a tragic phase and may again experience renewal. Their combined efforts in modern literature also indicate that man may yet avoid the pitfall of seizure by the powers attendant upon the images of the shadow, the anima or the animus, and the cosmic man. Seizure results when the image becomes foremost in the mind of the quester, instead of the creative center, or Self, symbolized by the mandala. It is this involvement with the Self that leads the quester into a creative relationship with the other archetypes and on to the integration of his personality. But the Self is approached only by the way of the archetypes.

A theory of the archetypes was formulated by Plato and others; the microcosm-macrocosm theory of the Renaissance and earlier periods deals with much the same material as Jung gives us.

Mann, Joyce, and Eliot—and the learned men like Frazer, Freud, and Jung who influenced them—give us new knowledge, as well as new symbolic visions of the growth of the personality. The work of these men and a few others demonstrates that the development of all human potentialities is possible in a period of personal and social decay. And it may well be that the great artistic symbols of modernism will one day not be seen as the images of the shadow that seem now to be in the foreground, but rather as mandala images that appear almost unnoticed in some of the great art-speech of our cultural period. In a century when scientists have made the world aware of their visions of the harmony to be found in the material universe, it is only fitting that in time artists and philosophers will help people see the harmony within man that can be achieved by that quester who encounters his self through the images of totality living in the myths of man and in the human soul. These artists and philosophers, in bringing humanity back to a vision of harmony, will be acting in a mythic manner and bringing to birth the new myths needed to carry us all past that "dissociation of sensibility," to use again Eliot's famous term, which has been the curse of modern times.

Notes

NOTES TO CHAPTER 1

1. Walter Kaufmann, *Existentialism from Dostoevsky to Sartre* (New York: Meridian Books, 1956), p. 11.

2. Leo Marx, *The Machine in the Garden* (New York: Oxford University Press, 1964), p. 364.

3. Ibid., p. 365.

4. Joseph Campbell, *The Hero With a Thousand Faces* (New York: Meridian Books, 1956), p. 391.

5. Leslie Fiedler, "No! In Thunder," in *Twentieth Century American Writing*, ed. William T. Stafford (New York: The Odyssey Press, 1965), p. 564.

6. Norman N. Holland, *The Dynamics of Literary Response* (New York: W. W. Norton & Co., 1975), p. 31.

7. Ibid., p. 261.

8. Harold Bloom, *The Influence of Anxiety* (New York: Oxford University Press, 1973), p. 96.

9. Ibid., p. 94.

10. Holland, p. 7.

11. Joseph K. Davis et al., eds., *Literature* (Glenview, Ill.: Scott, Foresman, and Co., 1977), p. 540.

12. The translation of Aristotle's *Poetics* used in this study is that of S. H. Butcher (London: Macmillan, 1917).

13. Joseph Campbell, Introduction, *The Portable Jung* (New York: Viking Press, 1971), p. xxi.

14. Ibid., p. xxii.

15. Ibid., p. xxi.

16. Mircea Eliade, *Myth and Reality* (New York: Harper and Row, 1963), pp. 14–15.

17. Campbell, *The Portable Jung*, p. xxviii.

18. Eliade, *Myth and Reality*, p. 10.

19. Ibid.

20. Edith Hamilton, *The Greek Way to Civilization* (New York: New American Library, 1948), p. 131.

21. Ibid., p. 132.

22. Morse Peckham, *Beyond the Tragic Vision* (New York: George Braziller, 1962), p. 368.

NOTES TO CHAPTER 2

1. William Dean Howells, *Criticism and Fiction and Other Essays*, ed. Clara Morburg Kirk and Rudolf Kirk (New York: New York University Press, 1959), p. 15.

2. Ibid., p. 62.

3. Virginia Woolf, *The Common Reader* (New York: Harcourt, Brace & Co., 1925), p. 237.

4. Elizabeth Drew, *The Novel* (New York: Dell Publishing Co., 1963), p. 140.

5. Ibid., p. 20.

6. For Jeannette King the essence of tragedy for George Eliot, as well as Henry James and Thomas Hardy, lies in the tension between determinism and free will. See her *Tragedy in the Victorian Novel* (Cambridge: Cambridge University Press, 1978), pp. 16–35.

7. J. Hillis Miller, *The Form of Victorian Fiction* (Notre Dame, Ind.: University of Notre Dame, 1968), p. 123.

8. T. S. Eliot, *The Cocktail Party*, in *The Complete Poems and Plays* (New York: Harcourt, Brace & World, 1952), p. 356.

9. George Eliot, *The Mill on the Floss* (New York: Houghton Mifflin Co., 1961), p. 252. Subsequent page references are to this edition.

10. Gordon S. Haight, *George Eliot and John Chapman* (New Haven: Yale University Press, 1940), p. vii.

11. George Eliot, *Middlemarch* (London: Oxford University Press, 1947), p. xv. Subsequent page references are to this edition.

12. F. R. Leavis, *The Great Tradition* (London: Chatto & Windus, 1950), p. 85.

14. Ibid., p. 125.

15. Viktor E. Frankl, *Man's Search for Meaning*, trans. Ilse Lasch (New York: Pocket Books, 1963), p. 104.

16. Ibid., p. 117.

NOTES TO CHAPTER 3

1. Ernest A. Baker, *The History of the English Novel* (London: H. F. G. Witherby, 1938), pp. ix, 81.

2. Samuel C. Chew, *A Literary History of England*, ed. Albert C. Baugh et al. (New York: Appleton Century Crofts, 1948), p. 1470.

3. Albert J. Guerard, Jr., *Thomas Hardy: The Novels and Stories* (Cambridge: Harvard University Press, 1949), p. 152.

4. Arthur Mizener, "*Jude the Obscure* as a Tragedy," *Southern Review* 6 (Summer, 1940):201: "But because he was unable to place the source of the idealism by which he measured the world and found it wanting outside of time and therefore, *faute de mieux*, came to believe in the gradual ennoblement of man; his attitude is

such as to preclude a formal structure which pits the idealist against the practical man in equal combat. There is no basic, unresolvable tragic tension between the real and ideal in his attitude, and there is as a consequence no tragic tension in the formal structure it invokes as its representation."

5. J. Hillis Miller, *Thomas Hardy: Distance and Desire* (Cambridge: Harvard University Press, 1970), p. 267.

6. Walter Kaufmann, *Existentialism from Dostoevsky to Sartre* (New York: Meridian Books, 1956), p. 11.

7. Jeannette King, *Tragedy in the Victorian Novel* (Cambridge: Cambridge University Press, 1977), p. 103.

8. Michael Millgate, *Thomas Hardy* (New York: Random House, 1971), p. 227.

9. F. L. Lucas, ed., *The Complete Works of John Webster* (London: Chatto & Windus, 1927), 1:40.

10. Edith Hamilton, *The Greek Way to Western Civilization* (New York: New American Library, 1949), p. 183.

11. Lascelles Abercrombie, *Thomas Hardy: A Critical Study* (London: M. Secker, 1912), p. 25.

12. Hamilton, p. 131.

13. Ibid., p. 133.

14. Thomas Hardy, *Tess of the D'Urbervilles* (New York: Harper, 1920), p. 293. Subsequent page references are to this edition.

15. Hamilton, p. 144.

16. Thomas Hardy, *The Mayor of Casterbridge* (New York: Random House, 1951), p. 422. Subsequent page references are to this edition.

17. Thomas Hardy, *Jude the Obscure* (New York: Random House, 1951), p. 414. Subsequent page references are to this edition.

18. Aristotle, *De Poetica*, trans. Ingram Bywater, in *The Works of Aristotle*, ed. W. D. Ross (Oxford: Oxford University Press, 1924), 11. 1452–53.

19. Thomas Hardy, *The Return of the Native* (New York: Random House, 1950), p. 388. Subsequent page references are to this edition.

20. Emily Brontë, *Wuthering Heights* (New York: Macmillan, 1945), p. 87.

21. Holbrook Jackson, *The Eighteen Nineties* (Harmondsworth: Penguin Books, 1950), p. 63.

22. Mizener, "*Jude the Obscure* as a Tragedy," p. 203.

23. Thomas Hardy, *Poems of the Past and Present* (London: Macmillan, 1927), p. 42.

24. Baker, *History of the English Novel*, pp. viii, 5.

NOTES TO CHAPTER 4

1. Anna Balakian, *The Symbolist Movement* (New York: Random House, 1967), p. 115.

2. William York Tindall, *Forces in Modern British Literature* (New York: Vintage Books, 1956), p. 287.

3. Harold Bloom, *The Anxiety of Influence* (London: Oxford University Press, 1978), p. 96.

4. Ibid., pp. 5–6.

5. Walter Pater, *The Renaissance* (London: Macmillan, 1924), p. 251.

6. In an article exploring the idea of a devil's advocate in Wilde's total work, Arthur H. Nethercot seems to suggest that Wilde expresses Pater's views when he says that Wilde's work is "the romantic philosophy of consuming individualism in all that life has to offer." See Arthur H. Nethercot, "Oscar Wilde and the Devil's Advocate," *PMLA* 59 (1944):833–50.

7. Oscar Wilde, *The Picture of Dorian Gray* (London: Keller, 1907), p. 44. Subsequent page references to this edition.

8. Balakian, *Symbolist Movement*, p. 115.

NOTES TO CHAPTER 5

1. E. M. Forster, *Aspects of the Novel* (New York: Harcourt, Brace & World, 1954), p. 125.

2. T. S. Eliot, *The Complete Poems and Plays* (New York: Harcourt, Brace & World, 1962), p. 141.

3. E. K. Brown, *Rhythm in the Novel* (Toronto: University of Toronto Press, 1950), p. 9.

4. Thomas H. McCabe, "Rhythm as Form in Lawrence: 'The Horse-Dealer's Daughter'," *PMLA* 87 (1972):64.

5. Panthea R. Broughton, *William Faulkner* (Baton Rouge: Louisiana State University Press, 1947), p. 28.

6. Horace Gregory, *D. H. Lawrence: Pilgrim of the Apocalypse* (New York: Grove Press, 1957), p. xv.

7. D. H. Lawrence, *Women in Love* (New York: Random House, 1943), pp. 531–32. Subsequent page references are to this edition.

8. D. H. Lawrence, *Sons and Lovers* (New York: Random House, 1943), p. 489. Subsequent page references are to this edition.

9. D. H. Lawrence, *The Rainbow* (New York: Random House, 1943), p. 464. Subsequent page references are to this edition.

10. D. H. Lawrence, *Kangaroo* (London: Penguin Books, 1955), pp. 220, 221. Subsequent page references are to this edition.

11. D. H. Lawrence, *The Plumed Serpent* (New York: Vintage Books, 1959), p. 456. Subsequent page references are to this edition.

12. D. H. Lawrence, *Selected Essays* (Harmondsworth: Penguin Books, 1954), pp. 47–48.

13. D. H. Lawrence, *Studies in Classic American Literature* (New York: Doubleday & Co., 1953), p. 190.

14. William Faulkner, *Absalom, Absalom!* (New York: Random House, 1951), p. 178. Subsequent page references are to this edition.

15. William Faulkner, *The Sound and the Fury* and *As I Lay Dying* (New York: Random House, 1946), p. 306. Subsequent page references are to this edition.

16. William Faulkner, *Light in August* (New York: Random House, 1950), p. 419. Subsequent page references are to this edition.

17. William Faulkner, "Delta Autumn," in *Go Down Moses* (New York: Random House, 1942), pp. 350–51.

18. Miguel de Unamuno, *Tragic Sense of Life*, trans. J. E. Crawford Flitch (New York: Dover Publications, 1954), p. 330.

NOTES TO CHAPTER 6

1. Quoted by Carlos Baker, *Hemingway: The Writer as Artist* (Princeton, N.J.: Princeton University Press, 1956), p. 71.

2. Frederic I. Carpenter, in "Hemingway Achieves the Fifth Dimension," *PMLA* 69 (1954):712, speaks of a "mystical idea of a 'fifth-dimensional experience of the perpetual now'" which Hemingway "first suggested . . . and then practiced . . . consciously in his best fiction." For a discussion of ways in which Hemingway extends basic religious ideas found in the romantic movement, see Ted R. Spivey, "Ecstasy and Suffering

in Hemingway," in *Religious Themes in Two Modern Novelists* (Atlanta: Georgia State College, 1965).

3. Robert Penn Warren, "Hemingway," in *Literary Opinion in America*, ed. Morton Dauwen Zabel (New York: Harper & Bros., 1951), p. 450.

4. Ibid., p. 451.

5. Philip Young, *Ernest Hemingway* (Minneapolis: University of Minnesota Press, 1959), p. 39.

6. Ibid.

7. Walt Whitman, *Leaves of Grass*, ed. Harold W. Blodgett and Scolley Bradley (New York: New York University Press, 1965), p. 153. Subsequent page references are to this edition.

8. Ernest Hemingway, *The Sun Also Rises* (New York: Charles Scribner's Sons, 1954), p. 21. Subsequent page references are to this edition.

9. *The Short Stories of Ernest Hemingway* (New York: Random House, 1938), p. 308.

10. Ernest Hemingway, *The Green Hills of Africa* (New York: Charles Scribner's Sons, 1935), p. 128.

11. Ernest Hemingway, *For Whom the Bell Tolls* (New York: Charles Scribner's Sons, 1940), p. 381. Subsequent page references are to this edition.

12. Ernest Hemingway, *Across the River and Into the Trees* (New York: Charles Scribner's Sons, 1950), p. 289. Subsequent page references are to this edition.

13. Ernest Hemingway, *A Farewell to Arms* (New York: Charles Scribner's Sons, 1949), p. 141. Subsequent references are to this edition.

14. Edmund Wilson, *Eight Essays* (New York: Doubleday & Co., 1954), p. 114.

15. Quoted by Alfred C. Aronwitz and Peter Hamill, *Ernest Hemingway* (New York: Lancer Books, 1961), p. 101.

NOTES TO CHAPTER 7

1. In his survey of modern British literature, *Forces in Modern British Literature* (New York: Vintage Books, 1956), Professor Tindall discusses the nature of the modern symbolist novel. In the chapter entitled "The Forest of Symbols," he examines the development of the symbolist novel, calling it the "outstanding literary development of our time" (p. 287).

2. Richard I. Evans, ed., *Conversations with Carl Jung and Reactions from Ernest Jones* (Princeton, N.J.: D. Van Nostrand Co., 1964), p. 48.

3. Ibid. In the same statement Jung says: "They [the archetypes] are always there and they produce certain processes in the unconscious that one could not but compare with myths. That's the origin of mythology. Mythology is a pronouncing of a series of images that formulate the life of archetypes."

4. See Thomas Mann, "Introduction," in Hermann Hesse, *Demian*, trans. Michael Roloff and Michael Lebeck (New York: Bantam Books, 1968), p. ix. Mann's introduction was written in 1947.

5. Hermann Hesse, *Demian*, trans. W. J. Strachan (London: Peter Owen Limited, 1960), pp. 172–73. Subsequent page references are to this edition.

6. Hermann Hesse, *Siddhartha*, trans. Hilda Rosner (New York: James Laughlin, 1951), p. 141. Subsequent page references are to this edition.

7. Hermann Hesse, *Steppenwolf*, trans. Basil Creighton, rev. Joseph Mileck and Horst Frenz (New York: Holt, Rinehart and Winston, 1963), p. 128.

8. James Joyce, *A Portrait of the Artist as a Young Man* (New York: Viking Press, 1965), p. 203. Subsequent page references are to this edition.

9. James Joyce, *Ulysses* (New York: Vintage Books, 1961), p. 34.

10. Joseph Mileck, "Introduction," in Hesse, *Steppenwolf*, p. xix.

11. C. G. Jung, *Modern Man in Search of a Soul*, trans. W. S. Dell and Cary F. Baynes (New York: Harcourt, Brace and Co., 1954), p. 120.

12. Evans, pp. 62–63.

NOTES TO CHAPTER 8

1. Viktor E. Frankl, *Man's Search for Meaning*, trans. Ilse Lasch (New York: Pocket Books, 1963), p. 104.

2. Romain Gary, *The Roots of Heaven*, trans. Jonathan Griffin (New York: Simon and Schuster, 1958), p. 78. Subsequent page references are to this edition.

3. José Ortega Gasset, *Man and Crisis*, trans. Mildred Adams (New York: W. W. Norton & Co., 1958), p. 101.

4. Hermann Hesse, *Siddhartha*, trans. Hilda Rosner (New York: James Laughlin, 1951), p. 148.

5. Joseph Campbell, *The Hero with a Thousand Faces* (New York: Meridian Books, 1956), p. 3.

NOTES TO CHAPTER 9

1. Walker Percy, "Southern Comfort," *Harper's* 258 (January, 1979): 80.

2. Stanley Edgar Hyman, *Flannery O'Connor* (Minneapolis: University of Minnesota Press, 1966), p. 45.

3. Ibid., p. 44.

4. Robert Drake, *Flannery O'Connor* (Grand Rapids, Mich: William B. Eerdmans: 1966), p. 42.

5. Flannery O'Connor, *The Violent Bear It Away* (New York: Farrar, Straus & Cudahy, 1960), p. 243.

6. Granville Hicks deals with this problem in "A Writer at Home with Her Heritage," *Saturday Review* 45 (May 12, 1962): 23. In his interpretation of what Miss O'Connor has to say about her use of the grotesque, Mr. Hicks writes: "Her argument, I gather, was that in these times the most reliable path to reality, to the kind of reality that seems to her important, is by way of the grotesque. The grotesque, she puts it, is more real than the real, and what many people regard as the real seems to her more grotesque than any of the characters she has created."

7. Flannery O'Connor, *The Lame Shall Enter First*, *The Sewanee Review* 70 (Summer, 1962): 373. Subsequent references are to this edition.

8. William Barrett, *Irrational Man* (New York: Doubleday and Co., 1958), p. 156.

NOTES TO CHAPTER 10

1. Barbara King, "Walker Percy Prevails," *Southern Voices* (May / June, 1974), p. 19.

2. Ibid., p. 22.

3. Mircea Eliade, *The Sacred and the Profane*, trans. Willard R. Trask (New York: Harcourt, Brace & World, 1959), p. 196.

4. R. D. Laing, *The Politics of Experience* (New York: Ballentine, 1967), p. 168.

5. Ibid., pp. 144–45.

6. Walker Percy, *The Moviegoer* (New York: Noonday, 1961), pp. 13–14.

7. Walker Percy, *The Last Gentleman* (New York: Noonday, 1966), p. 4. Subsequent page references are to this edition.

8. Richard I. Evans, ed., *Conversations with Carl Jung and Reactions from Ernest Jones* (Princeton, N.J.: D. Van Nostrand, 1964), pp. 62–63.

9. Ashley Brown, "An Interview with Walker Percy," *Shenandoah* 18 (Spring, 1967):7.

10. Laing, *The Politics of Experience*, p. 144.

11. Ibid., p. 168.

12. Mircea Eliade, *Myths, Dreams, and Mysteries*, trans. Philip Mairet (New York: Harper & Row, 1960), pp. 75, 77.

13. Sören Kierkegaard, *Fear and Trembling and The Sickness Unto Death*, trans. Walter Lowrie (Princeton, N.J.: Princeton University Press), p. 49.

14. Martin Buber, *Between Man and Man*, trans. Ronald G. Smith (London: Routledge & Kegan Paul, 1947), p. 52.

15. Kierkegaard, *Fear and Trembling*, p. 50.

16. Walker Percy, *Lancelot* (New York: Farrar, Straus, and Giroux, 1977), p. 256.

NOTES TO CHAPTER 11

1. Harold Bloom, *The Anxiety of Influence* (London: Oxford University Press, 1973), pp. 60, 96.

2. Ibid., p. 59.

3. Jacob Bronowski, *A Sense of the Future* (Cambridge: M.I.T. Press, 1977), p. 260.

4. Ibid., p. 261.

5. Ibid.

6. Albert Einstein, *Essays in Science*, trans. Alan Harris (New York: Covici-Friede, Inc., 1934), p. 4.

7. Anna Balakian, *The Symbolist Movement* (New York: Random House, 1967), pp. 117–18.

8. T. S. Eliot, *The Complete Poems and Plays* (New York: Harcourt, Brace & World, 1962), p. 7.

9. Ibid., pp. 54–71.

10. Harry Levin, *James Joyce* (Norfolk, Conn: New Directions, 1960), p. 15.

11. C. G. Jung, M. L. von Franz, et al., *Man and His Symbols* (Garden City, N.Y.: Doubleday & Co., 1964), p. 202.

12. Ibid.

13. Eliot, *The Complete Poems and Plays*, p. 145.

Index

Aaron's Rod, 79
Abercrombie, Lascelles, 46
Absalom, Absalom!, 85, 87
Across the River and into the Trees, 100, 101, 105, 106, 108
Adam Bede, 28
Age of the Avant-Garde, The, ix
Anatomy of Criticism, 4
Ancient Mariner, The, 136
"And Did Those Feet," 55
Anderson, Sherwood, 97
Anna Karenina, 20, 23
Anxiety of Influence, The, 6, 58, 59
Apocalypse, 84
Archetypal criticism, 6
A Rebouts, 71
Aristotelian catharsis, 15, 45
Aristotle, 9, 16, 42, 45, 49, 102
Arnold, Matthew, 25, 35, 58, 60
"Artificial Nigger, The," 140
Ash-Wednesday, 171
Aspects of the Novel, 37, 73
Atlantis, 82, 121
Auden, W. H., 60
Axel's Castle, 122

Bailey, J. O., 42
Baker, Carlos, 96
Baker, Ernest, 43, 55
Balakian, Anna, 57, 71, 169
Barrett, William, 147
Baudelaire, Charles, 2, 58, 61, 111, 122, 140, 156, 169–71
Baugh, A. C., 62
Beerbohm, Max, 60
Beethoven, Ludwig van, 8
Being and Time, 61
Bellow, Saul, 148
Bergson, Henri, 61, 74
Bernanos, Georges, 139, 146
Beyond Freedom and Dignity, 3
Beyond the Tragic Vision, 17
"Big Two-Hearted River: Part I," 99
Blake, William, 136, 137, 166
Bloom, Harold, 6, 56, 58–60, 70, 165
Bloomsbury Circle, 96
"Books," 83
Bray, Nat, 29
Bronowski, J., 166
Brontë, Emily, 37, 50, 55, 73

Brontë sisters, 55
Brooks, Van Wyck, vii
Broughton, Panthea, 74
Brown, E. K., 73
Browning, Robert, 34, 42, 70
Buber, Martin, 140, 160
Buddenbrooks, 167, 174
Buddha (Gautama Siddhartha), 115, 130, 159
Burke, Kenneth, 140
Byron, George Gordon, Lord, 50

Cambridge ritualists, 9
Campbell, Joseph, 5, 10–12, 14, 16, 39, 111, 136, 137, 151, 173
Camus, Albert, 95, 96, 126, 127
Carlyle, Thomas, 23, 29, 33
Carnegie, Andrew, 2
Chartreuse de Parme, La, 20
Cheever, John, 163
Chew, Samuel C., 43
"Clean, Well-Lighted Place, A," 96, 126
Cocktail Party, The, 24, 38, 175
Coleridge, Samuel Taylor, 58, 136
Comte, Auguste, 25
Conrad, Joseph, 60, 85, 94, 95, 97, 108, 127, 128
Conversations with Carl Jung and Reactions from Ernest Jones, 112
Counter-Reformation, 10, 132
Courbet, Gustave, 4
Cowley, Malcolm, 96
Cox, Harvey, 18
Creative Evolution, 61
Crime and Punishment, 143
Criticism and Fiction, 21

Daniel Deronda, 33, 34, 72
D'Annunzio, Gabriele, 97
Dante, Alighieri, 117, 171
Darwin, Charles, 2
Davis, Joseph K., 7
Dead, The, 167
Death in Venice, 167
Debussy, Claude, 2
Delphi, 17
Demian, 113

Desperate Remedies, 41
D. H. Lawrence: Pilgrim of the Apocalypse, 75
Dickens, Charles, 21, 42
Dostoevski, Fyodor, ix, 37, 38, 54, 73, 140, 151, 153
Drake, Robert, 140
Dreiser, Theodore, 46
Drew, Elizabeth, 21, 22
Dr. Faustus, 174, 175
Dryden, John, 154
Dubliners, 116, 117, 167, 170
Dynamics of Literary Response, The, 6

Ecclesiastes, 97
Einstein, Albert, 166
Either/Or, 160
Eliade, Mircea, 11, 12, 14, 39, 151, 158
Eliot, George, ix, 20–30, 31–39, 41–43, 52, 56, 66, 72
Eliot, T. S., ix, x, 8, 15, 19, 38, 39, 52, 59, 60, 73, 75, 81, 111, 122, 137, 149, 166–67, 171, 173–76
Emerson, Ralph Waldo, 23, 29, 132, 149
Eranos Round Table, 151
Euripides, 17
Evans, Elizabeth, 29
Evans, Richard I., 112, 124
Exiles, 170
Existentialism, 2, 44, 95, 140, 146, 147
Expressionism, 19

Fable, A, 122
Family Reunion, The, 175
Farewell to Arms, A, 102, 103
Faulkner, William, ix, x, 5, 37, 73–75, 81, 85, 86, 88, 89, 91–93, 95, 122, 133, 139
Faust, 69, 71, 155
Fear and Trembling, 160
Felix Holt, 33, 34
Feuerback, Ludwig Andreas, 23
Fiedler, Leslie, 5, 96

Finnegans Wake, 117–21, 123, 173
Fish, Stanley, 6
Fitzgerald, F. Scott, 95, 108, 148
Flaubert, Gustave, 2, 20, 21, 36
Florence, 29
Flowers of Evil, 2
"For Life I Had Never Cared Greatly," 56
Forms of Victorian Fiction, The, 21, 22
Forster, E. M., 37, 60, 73, 75, 96, 108
For Whom the Bell Tolls, 100, 101, 103, 108
Four Quartets, 173
Frankl, Viktor E., 37, 38, 127
Frazer, James, 3, 9, 10, 12, 74, 122, 176
Freud, Sigmund, 4, 10, 75, 112, 149, 172, 176
Frye, Northrop, 4

Gandhi, Mohandas K., 129, 130
Gary, Romain, ix, x, 126–29, 131–34, 136, 163
George Eliot and John Chapman, 29
"Gerontion," 170
Gide, André, 58, 59, 111
Goethe, Johann Wolfgang von, 23, 24, 29, 50, 61, 69, 71, 115, 129, 132, 133, 155, 171, 172
Golden Bough, The, 9, 236
Golden Bowl, The, 164
Golding, William, 140, 163
"Good Man is Hard to Find, A," 142
Great Tradition, The, 21
Greek Way to Civilization, The, 45, 47
Green Hills of Africa, 100
Gregory, Horace, 75
Guerard, Albert J., 43, 44

Haight, Gordon, 29
Hamilton, Edith, 16, 17, 45, 47
Hardy, Thomas, viii, ix, 5, 23, 25–27, 37, 41–56, 66, 97
Harvard University, 86
Hassan, Ihab Habib, ix

Hawthorne, Nathaniel, 34, 71, 140
Hegel, Georg Wilhelm Friedrich, 16
Heidegger, Martin, 61, 95
Hemingway, Ernest, ix, x, 94–102, 105–8, 126, 127, 148
Hero, The, 9
Hero with a Thousand Faces, The, 11, 136
Hesse, Hermann, ix, 71, 108, 110–113, 115–17, 122–25, 137
Holland, Norman N., 6, 7
Hollywood, 74
Howells, William Dean, 20, 21
Huckleberry Finn, 97
Hugo, Victor, 8
Humanitarianism, 35, 44, 129, 132, 143–45
Huxley, Aldous, 60, 66
Huysmans, Joris-Karl, 58, 71, 122
Hyman, Stanley Edgar, 140

Illuminations, 169, 172
Immanent will, 43, 44
Irish nationalism, 112
Irrational Man, 235

Jackson, Holbrook, 50, 55
James, Henry, 21, 24, 34, 35, 36, 41, 43, 60, 101
Jesus Christ, 84, 92, 114, 116, 122, 142, 146
Joseph and His Brothers, 172
Journey to the East, The, 113, 116, 117
Joyce, James, ix, x, 11, 14, 16, 17, 19, 59, 60, 71, 81, 85, 94, 95, 97, 108, 110–13, 116, 117–25, 137, 165, 167–76
Jude the Obscure, 42, 43, 46, 48, 51–53, 55, 56
Jung, C. G., 5, 10–14, 18, 39, 97, 112–14, 123–25, 150, 151, 159, 161, 163, 171, 172, 175, 176
Jungian archetypes, 5, 10, 11–14, 16–19, 112–14, 123–25, 150, 152–56, 158–64, 166, 171, 172, 175

Kangaroo, 79–81
Kaufman, Walter, 2, 44
Keats, John, 55
Kermode, Frank, 96
Kierkegaard, Sören, 111, 140, 146,
    147, 149–53, 157, 159, 160, 162
King, Jeannette, 22, 44, 45
King, Martin Luther, Jr., 107
King Lear, 16
Kramer, Hilton, ix

Lady Chatterley's Lover, 79, 85
Laing, R. D., 152, 157, 158
Lame Shall Enter First, The,
    140–42, 145, 146
Lancelot, 162, 164
Lao Tzu, 130, 131
Last Gentleman, The, 155, 156, 160,
    162
Lawrence, D. H., ix, x, 27, 37, 55,
    56, 58, 60, 72–86, 89, 92–95, 122,
    133
Leavis, F. R., 21, 24, 34, 35, 36, 41
Leibnitz, Gottfried Wilhelm von,
    166
Levin, Harry, 170
Lewes, George Henry, 29, 31
Lewis, C. S., 60
Lewis, Wyndham, 96
Life magazine, vii
Light in August, 90
Literary History of England, A, 43,
    62
Little Gidding, 73, 166, 173
Lord Jim, 108
Lord of the Flies, 140
*Love and Death in the American
    Novel*, 96
Love in the Ruins, 162
"Love Song of J. Alfred Prufrock,
    The," 167, 168
Lucas, F. L., 45

Macbeth, 69
Machine in the Garden, The, 4
Madame Bovary, 4, 20
Magic Mountain, The, 170, 171
Magister Ludi, 116, 123

Mahler, Gustav, 167
Mallarmé, Stéphane, 4, 61, 73, 122,
    169
Man and Crisis, 131
Man and His Symbols, 150
Mann, Thomas, ix, x, 11, 19, 36, 71,
    108, 111, 122, 163, 168–176
Man's Search for Meaning, 127
Man Who Died, The, 85
"Marina," 171
Marx, Karl, 4
Marx, Leo, 4, 5
Masks of God, The, 11
Mauriac, François, 139, 146
Mayor of Casterbridge,The, 42, 52
McCabe, Thomas H., 73
McCullers, Carson, 142
McHaney, Thomas, 74
Meliorism, 43, 53, 54
Melville, Herman, 37, 50, 73
Memphis, 85
Mencken, Henry L., 98, 99
Mental Traveller, The, 136
Methodism, 132
Middlemarch, 20–24, 28–32, 34, 38,
    39
Mileck, Joseph, 122
Mill, John Stuart, 35
Miller, J. Hillis, 5, 21–23, 43
Millgate, Michael, 44
Mill on the Floss, The, 28, 29
Mississippi Delta, 92
Mizener, Arthur, 43, 44, 53, 54
Moby Dick, 164
Modernism, vii–xi, 1–3, 8, 9, 10,
    22, 23, 42, 72, 94, 110, 126, 128,
    132, 138, 168, 174, 176
Moviegoer, The, 152, 155
Mozart, Wolfgang Amadeus, 115,
    116
Mrs. Dalloway, 95
Murder in the Cathedral, 175
Myth and Reality, 11
Myths, Dreams, and Mysteries, 158

Narcissus and Goldmund, 123
Naturalism, 3, 24, 26, 28, 37, 94,
    168, 169

Neoromanticism, vii, 37, 38, 42, 43, 57, 72, 127, 129
New Criticism, 6
New York, 3, 74, 98
Nietzsche, Friedrich, 16–18, 44, 97, 132, 162

O'Connor, Flannery, ix, x, 139–48, 163, 235
Oedipus complex, 81
Old Man and the Sea, The, 106–8
Olsen, Regina, 229
O'Neill, Eugene, 15
Oracle of Delphi, 149
Oresteian trilogy, 15
Ortega y Gasset, José, 131
Othello, 69
Oxford movement, 132

Paris, 4, 94, 98, 126
Pater, Walter, 58–62, 70, 71, 95
Peckham, Morse, 17, 18
Percy, Walker, ix, x, 139, 148–51, 153–59, 162–64
Peter Camenzind, 116
Phoenix, as D. H. Lawrence's personal symbol, 78
Picasso, Pablo, 8
Picture of Dorian Gray, The, 55, 58–62, 66, 71
Planck, Max, 166
Plato, 150, 175
Plumed Serpent, The, 81, 83, 85, 89
Poe, Edgar Allan, 50, 54, 122, 140, 169–71
Politics of Experience, The, 152, 157
Portrait of a Lady, The, 24, 34
Portrait of the Artist as a Young Man, A, 117, 118, 170
Postmodernism, viii, x, 4, 8, 15, 18, 22, 42
Pound, Ezra, 72, 94
Powers, J. F., 148, 163
Prometheus Unbound, 53, 121, 136
Proust, Marcel, 111

Quetzalcoatl, 122

Raglan, Fitzroy Richard Somerset, Lord, 9
Rainbow, The, 76–78
Realism, 19, 20, 22–25, 36, 38, 41, 94
Reformation, 10, 132
Renaissance, 10, 17, 29, 70, 132, 133, 136
Renaissance, The, 59, 70, 175
Return of the Native, 42
"Revelation," 140
Rhythm in the Novel, 73
Richardson, Samuel, 22
Riesman, David, 19
Rimbaud, Arthur, 3, 122, 169, 171–73
Rite of Spring, 72
Robinson, Henry Morton, 111
Romanticism, viii, 19, 23–26, 35, 38, 42, 45, 50, 55, 57, 58, 72, 127–29, 132–36
"Romantic Nineties," 55
Romola, 28, 29, 32
Roots of Heaven, The, 126–28, 132, 133, 138
Rouge et le Noir, Le, 20
Rousseau, Jean Jacques, 23, 133
Russell, Bertrand, 74

Saint Kevin, 121
Saint Patrick, 121
Saint Theresa of Avila, 30, 39
Salomé, 58, 60
Sanctuary, 85
Sartre, Jean-Paul, 15, 95, 96, 126, 127
Savonarola, 29, 30, 32
Schopenhauer, Arthur, 74
Schweitzer, Albert, 130
Sewanee Review, The, 141
Shakespeare, William, 8, 15, 46, 59
Shaw, George Bernard, 60
Shelley, Percy Bysshe, 23, 25, 29, 50–55, 121, 136
"Shelley's Skylark," 53
Siddhartha, 113, 115, 137
Silas Marner, 22, 28

Skeleton Key to Finnegans Wake, A, 111
Skinner, B. F., 3
"Song of the Open Road," 97, 99, 104
Sons and Lovers, 72, 73, 75–77, 93, 134
Sophocles, 15
Sound and the Fury, The, 5, 87, 88, 164
"Southern Obsession," 139
Southern Review, 43
Spencer, Herbert, 4, 25
Spinoza, Baruch, 38
Stein, Gertrude, 3, 94, 127
Stein, R. A., 14
Stendhal, 20, 36
Steppenwolf, 110, 113, 115, 116
Stevens, Wallace, 73
Stravinsky, Igor, 8, 72
Studies in Classic American Literature, 84
Sun Also Rises, The, 95, 97, 98, 100, 102, 103, 105–7, 127, 164
Swinburne, Algernon Charles, viii, 41, 42, 52, 61, 71
Symbolism, 19, 22, 57, 58, 73, 94, 109, 122, 139, 140, 147, 167, 168, 169, 171
Symbolist Movement, The, 167
Symbolist novel, 58, 72, 73, 94, 95, 109
Symbols of Transformation, 10

Taos, New Mexico, 80
Teilhard de Chardin, Pierre, 135
Tess of the D'Urbervilles, 42, 56
Thackeray, William M., 21, 42, 52
Thoreau, Henry David, 23
Tillich, Paul, 18
Tindall, William York, 58, 111
Tintern Abbey, 31
Tolkien, J. R. R., 110
Tolstoy, Leo, ix, 8, 20, 21, 23, 35, 36, 38, 43, 132
To the Lighthouse, 95

Tragedy in the Victorian Novel, 22
Tragic Sense of Life, 93
Trojan Women, The, 17
Turgenev, Ivan, 36
Twain, Mark, 97

Ulysses, 81, 110–13, 117–19, 170, 171, 173
Unamuno, Miguel de, 93

Venice, 167
Verlaine, Paul, 169
Vico, Giambattista, 120, 165
Victorianism, 1, 2, 19, 22, 25, 66, 71
Violent Bear It Away, The, 141, 142
Vonnegut, Kurt, 110

Warren, Robert Penn, 96
Warwickshire, 23
Waste Land, The, 75, 81, 120, 170, 171
Watts, Alan, 166
Waugh, Evelyn, 66
Webster, John, 45
Westminster Review, 35
White, Morton, 1
Whitman, Walt, 84, 97, 98–100, 102, 104, 107
Wilde, Oscar, ix, 57–64, 66, 67, 69–71, 122, 140
Williams, Charles, 60, 140
Wilson, Edmund, 105, 122
Wise Blood, 141, 142
Women in Love, 76, 77–80
Woolf, Virginia, 21, 22, 95, 96, 108
Wordsworth, William, 23–26, 29–31, 35, 39, 42, 55, 58, 132, 133
Wuthering Heights, 50

Yeats, William Butler, x, 19, 60, 72, 73, 111, 122
Young, Philip, 96, 108

Zola, Emile, 3, 124, 168